Monetary Policy and Financial Stability

Monetary Policy and Financial Stability

A Post-Keynesian Agenda

Edited by

Claude Gnos

Associate Professor, Université de Bourgogne, Dijon, France

and

Louis-Philippe Rochon

Associate Professor, Laurentian University, Sudbury, Canada

NEW DIRECTIONS IN MODERN ECONOMICS

Edward Elgar
Cheltenham, UK • Northampton, MA, USA

Published by
Edward Elgar Publishing Limited
The Lypiatts
15 Lansdown Road
Cheltenham
Glos GL50 2JA
UK

Edward Elgar Publishing, Inc.
William Pratt House
9 Dewey Court
Northampton
Massachusetts 01060
USA

A catalogue record for this book
is available from the British Library

Library of Congress Control Number: 2008932888

ISBN 978 1 84844 069 2

Printed and bound by MPG Books Group, UK

Contents

PART TWO MACROECONOMIC POLICY AND THE GLOBAL ECONOMY

Figures

Tables

Contributors

Jean-Pierre Allegret is Professor of Economics at the University of Lyon. He is the author of many books and studies on international monetary issues such as the implementation of the euro, financial liberalization in emerging economies and the new architecture of the international financial system. He has published in such journals as *Louvain Economic Review*, *Open Economies Review*, *Review of International Organizations*, *Review of International and Political Economy*, *Journal of Economic Integration*, *European Journal of Development Research*, *Revue Economique* and *Revue Française d'Economie*.

Philip Arestis is University Director of Research, Cambridge Centre for Economics and Public Policy, Department of Land Economy, University of Cambridge; Adjunct Professor of Economics, University of Utah; Senior Scholar, Levy Economics Institute, New York; Visiting Professor, University of Leeds; and Visiting Professor, School of Oriental and African Studies (SOAS), University of London. He is currently Vice-Chair of the ESRC-funded Macroeconomics, Money and Finance Research Group, and an elected member of the Executive Board of the Eastern Economic Association (EEA), USA. He is Chief Academic Adviser to the UK Government Economic Service (GES) on Professional Development in Economics. He has published as sole author or editor, as well as co-author and co-editor, a number of books, contributed in the form of invited chapters to numerous books, produced research reports for research institutes, and has published widely in academic journals.

Angel Asensio is lecturer at the University Paris 13, and researcher at the CEPN (Univ. Paris 13-CNRS). He is a member of the ADEK (Association pour le Développement des Etudes Keynésiennes). He has recently published research papers on post-Keynesian theory, monetary and fiscal policies interactions, international interdependences and economic policies coordination.

Eric Berr is Associate Professor at the University of Bordeaux and member of the Groupe de recherche en économie théorique et appliquée (GREThA-CNRS). His fields of research are development economics, sustainable development and post-Keynesian economics. His papers have been published in the *Brazilian Journal of Political Economy*, *Economie Appliquée*, and *Revue Tiers-monde*. He also co-edited *Le développement en question(s)* (Presses universitaires de Bordeaux, 2006).

Luiz Carlos Bresser-Pereira is an economist and social scientist at Getulio Vargas Foundation. He was was born in São Paulo, in 1934. He holds a bachelor's degree in law from the University of São Paulo, an MBA from Michigan State University, and a PhD and Livre Docência in economics from the University of São Paulo. He has edited the *Brazilian Journal of Political Economy* since 1981; offers regularly a one-month course at the École de Hautes Études en Sciences Sociales; and writes a fortnightly column in *Folha de S. Paulo.* He has written many books, including *As Revoluções Utópicas dos Anos 60* (1972), *O Colapso de uma Aliança de Classes* (1978), *Development and Crisis in Brazil* (1984), *A Sociedade Estatal e a Tecnoburocracia* (1980), *The Theory of Inertial Inflation* (with Yoshiaki Nakano, 1987), *Economic Reforms in New Democracies* (with Adam Przeworski and José Maria Maravall, 1993), *Economic Crisis and State Reform in Brazil* (1996), and his most recent one, *Macroeconomia da Estagnação: Crítica da Ortodoxia Convencional no Brasil pós-1994* (2007).

François Combarnous is Associate Professor at the University of Bordeaux and member of the Groupe de recherche en économie théorique et appliquée (GREThA-CNRS). His papers have been published in *Economie Appliquée*, *Brazilian Journal of Political Economy* and *Revue Tiers-monde*.

Robert W. Dimand is a Professor of Economics at Brock University, St. Catharines, Ontario, Canada. Educated at McGill and Yale Universities, he has written *The Origins of the Keynesian Revolution* (Edward Elgar and Stanford University Press, 1988) and more than 60 journal articles, and has edited ten books.

Philippe Dulbecco is Professor of Economics in the Department of Economics at the University of Clermont 1. His fields of research are in institutional economics, theory of the firm, and market process analysis. He has published in such journals as *World Development, Louvain Economic Review, Journal of International Development, Review of International Organizations, Review of International and Political Economy, European Journal of Development Research, Review of Austrian Economics, Revue Economique*, and *Revue d'Economie Politique*.

Claude Gnos is Associate Professor of Economics at the University of Burgundy and Director of the *Center for Monetary and Financial Studies* in Dijon, France. He is the author of *L'Euro* (Management et Société, 1998) and *Les grands auteurs en économie* (Management et Société, 2000), and co-editor of *Post-Keynesian Principles of Economic Policy* (Elgar, 2006, with Louis-Philippe Rochon) and *The Keynesian Multiplier* (Routledge, 2008, with Louis-Philippe Rochon). He has also published a number of articles on monetary economics, circuit theory, and the history of economic thought, which have appeared in books and refereed journals (*Journal of Post Keynesian Economics, Review of Political Economy, International Journal of Political Economy, Economie Appliquée, Revue d'Economie Politique, Economies et Sociétés*).

Eckhard Hein is a Senior Researcher at the Macroeconomic Policy Institute (IMK), Hans Boeckler Foundation, Duesseldorf, and an Adjunct Professor at Carl von Ossietzky University, Oldenburg, Germany. He is a co-organizer of the Research Network Macroeconomics and Macroeconomic Policies and a managing co-editor of *INTERVENTION: Journal of Economics*. His papers have been published in *Banca Nazionale del Lavoro Quarterly Review, Cambridge Journal of Economics, European Journal of the History of Economic Thought, International Review of Applied Economics, Metroeconomica* and *Structural Change and Economic Dynamics*. He is the author of *Money, Distribution Conflict and Capital Accumulation: Contributions to 'Monetary Analysis'* (Palgrave Macmillan, 2008).

Claudia Maya holds an MA from the National University of Mexico (UNAM) and is currently a doctoral student at the University of Missouri-Kansas City. She has contributed several chapters in various edited books on financing development, primarily investigating the financial globalization processes and their consequences for social and economic development. She has worked on different research projects related to the effects of the North American Free Trade Agreement (NAFTA) on the financial systems in Canada, the United States and Mexico, sponsored by the National Autonomous University in Mexico (UNAM).

Corinne Pastoret is Assistant Professor at Laurentian University, Sudbury, Canada. She holds a first doctorate from the University of Dijon, France, and is currently working on finishing her second doctorate at the University of Missouri, Kansas City. Her first doctorate dealt with post-Keynesian monetary theory, while her current doctorate is on full employment development policies and debt sustainability in developing countries, with an emphasis on Argentina. She is specialized in development and public employment guarantee policy, such as the Argentine Jefes program, on which she has written extensively.

Louis-Philippe Rochon is Associate Professor of Economics at Laurentian University, Canada. He has authored over 70 journal and book articles, and has written or edited numerous books, including *Credit, Money and Production* (Edward Elgar, 2005), *Modern Theories of Money: The Nature and Role of Money in Capitalist Economies* (Edward Elgar, 2003, co-edited with Sergio Rossi), *Monetary and Exchange Rate Systems: A Global View of Financial Crises* (Edward Elgar, 2006, co-edited with Sergio Rossi), *Credit, Money and Macroeconomic Policy* (Edward Elgar, 2008, with Claude Gnos; forthcoming) and *Employment, Growth and Development* (Edward Elgar, 2008, with Claude Gnos; forthcoming). His papers have appeared, among other places, in the *Review of Political Economy*, *International Journal of Political Economy*, *Metroeconomica*, *Journal of Economic Issues*, *Economie Appliquée*, and the *Journal of Post Keynesian Economics*. His research is on macroeconomic and monetary theory and policy, and post-Keynesian economics.

Sergio Rossi is Professor of Economics at the University of Fribourg, Switzerland. He has a DPhil degree from the University of Fribourg and a PhD degree from the University of London (University College). His publications include: *Money and Inflation: A New Macroeconomic Analysis* (Edward Elgar, 2001, reprinted 2003), *Modern Theories of Money: The Nature and Role of Money in Capitalist Economies* (Edward Elgar, 2003, co-edited with Louis-Philippe Rochon), *Monetary and Exchange Rate Systems: A Global View of Financial Crises* (Edward Elgar, 2006, co-edited with Louis-Philippe Rochon), *Money and Payments in Theory and Practice* (Routledge, 2007). He has also published several articles on monetary economics in the *International Journal of Political Economy*, *International Review of Applied Economics*, *Intervention: Journal of Economics*, *Journal of Asian Economics*, *Journal of Post Keynesian Economics*, *Public Choice*, *Review of Political Economy*, *Studi Economici* and the *Swiss Journal of Economics and Statistics*.

Eric Rougier is Associate Professor at the University of Bordeaux and member of the Groupe de recherche en économie théorique et appliquée (GREThA-CNRS). His research has been published in many French economics journals and in several books. He specializes in the fields of macroeconomics, growth analysis and international economics.

Malcolm Sawyer is Professor of Economics, University of Leeds, and Pro-Dean for Learning and Teaching for the Faculty of Business. He is managing editor of *International Review of Applied Economics* and the editor of the series *New Directions in Modern Economics* published by Edward Elgar. He is the author of 11 books, has edited 18 books and published over 70 papers in refereed journals and contributed chapters to nearly 100 books. His research interests are in macroeconomics, fiscal and monetary policy, the political economy of the European Monetary Union, the nature of money, causes and concepts of unemployment and the economics of Michal Kalecki. Recent publications include *Re-examining Monetary and Fiscal Policy for the 21st Century* (Edward Elgar, 2004, with Philip Arestis), *Alternative Perspectives on Economic Policies in the European Union* (Palgrave Macmillan, with Philip Arestis) and, most recently, *A Handbook Of Alternative Monetary Economics* (Edward Elgar, 2007, with Philip Arestis).

Domenica Tropeano is Associate Professor of Economics at the faculty of Economics of the University of Macerata, Italy. She has an MA from the University of Warwick and a doctorate from the European University Institute. She has studied and published in the fields of history of economic thought, history of macroeconomics and is currently working on the issue of macroeconomic policies and globalization.

Acknowledgements

We would very much to thank Edward Elgar for his continued and enthusiastic support of our work and the work of post-Keynesians everywhere. We would also like to thank his wonderful staff for their support during the development of this book. We are grateful to all those who helped with the logistics of the Dijon conference and especially to Isabelle Penet for her warm and strong devotion to the ongoing project of rebuilding Keynesian economics in France. Finally, we would like to thank Olawoye Omosalewa, a student at Laurentian University, for helping with the formatting, editing, checking over the final proofs of the book, and for her overall excellent work.

Claude Gnos
Louis-Philippe Rochon

Introduction: the growth of post-Keynesian economic policy

Claude Gnos and Louis-Philippe Rochon

Recently, Tom Palley (2006) lamented that post-Keynesians in general do not pay sufficient attention to economic policy, being too preoccupied by theory, a warning he has repeated on several other occasions. While this is certainly true, we cannot forget that economic policy is itself rooted in deep theory. In that sense, the so-called obsession we have for theory nurtures our thinking as well as the development of economic policy; and as much as post-Keynesian theory is fundamentally different from the mainstream approach, this should enable us to reach different policy conclusions.

This observation is certainly evident throughout this book. Readers will appreciate the deep theoretical tradition, while also acknowledging the richness and uniqueness of post-Keynesian policy. While Palley's criticism is correct, things have certainly changed over the last few years, propelled mainly, we would argue, by an interest in Taylor Rules, inflation targeting and the New Consensus. What is evident is that post-Keynesian economic policy is finally asserting itself as a hallmark of post-Keynesianism.

While the overall theme of the 2005 Dijon conference, from which these chapters are drawn, was on economic governance, some participants presented papers that touched upon other themes. We decided to focus on governance because we wanted post-Keynesians to reflect on this important topic. While post-Keynesians discuss monetary and fiscal policy abundantly, they have little to offer on a number of other topics. Ours was, to our knowledge, the first post-Keynesian conference to address governance. As you will see, a good many chapters address this topic, especially with respect to international institutions.

This book is the second in a series dealing with post-Keynesian policy that we have edited, the result of a conference held at the University of Burgundy (Dijon, France), in December 2005. These conferences are held every two years and are part of an effort to revive Keynesian thought in France. In addition to this book (the publication of which, for personal reasons, was delayed), two additional books will be published in early 2009, resulting from the December 2007 conference. Those books, entitled *Credit, Money and Macroeconomic Policy: A Post-Keynesian Approach* and *Employment, Growth and Development: A Post-Keynesian Approach* respectively, will also be published with Edward Elgar Publishing (see also Gnos and Rochon, 2006).

Structure of the Book

This book is divided into two sections. Part I, entitled 'Monetary and Macroeconomic Policy', addresses a number of issues dealing with wage determination and income distribution, as well as central bank governance. Many of these chapters share interesting points in common, in particular criticism of the usefulness of monetary policy in fighting or targeting inflation and the questions this raises for central bank governance.

In the lead contribution, Hein proposes a Kaleckian model of monetary distribution and growth coupled with conflict inflation in which the role of the NAIRU is assessed. He examines both the NAIRU's short-run stability by taking into account real debt effects of accelerating and decelerating inflation, as well as the short-run effectiveness of monetary policy interventions. The author also addresses the problem of the long-run endogeneity of the NAIRU by integrating the long-run distribution effects of monetary policy's real interest rate variations into the model. Hein concludes that in order to stabilize inflation monetary policy interventions are either unnecessary or costly in terms of employment in the short run. In the long run, these policies bear the risk of continuously increasing the NAIRU in order to keep inflation under control, which yields a horizontal long-run Phillips curve and latent stagflation. He suggests that instead of relying on monetary policies, the cause of inflation should be directly addressed and wage bargaining coordination should be applied as an appropriate tool.

In their contribution, Arestis and Sawyer propose an alternative to the Phillips curve relationship. Building on previous work, the authors offer a simple argument: an approach to inflation based on wage and price determination provides a different perspective; notably that the rate of change rather than the level of economic activity plays a role, that the level of economic activity has an impact through its influence on desired or target real wage (or equivalently profit share), and that any inflation barrier arises outside of the labour market and is subject to continuous change.

Dealing with central bank governance, Louis-Philippe Rochon, in Chapter 3, argues that the literature on good governance, although certainly welcomed, is misplaced in the traditional literature since it does not change the fact that the central bank's emphasis on inflation targeting is simply bad policy. Rochon argues that there is too much monetary policy dominance. Rather, the debate among post-Keynesians is whether monetary policy should be discretionary or follow a rule – between those Rochon and Setterfield (2007) have called the activist post-Keynesians and those who favour 'parking' the rate of interest. Good monetary policy should recognize the income-distributive nature of the rate of interest, and this leads to favouring a 'parking-it' approach to monetary policy: the Smithin Rule, the Kansas City Rule and the Pasinetti or Fair Rate Rule.

In Chapter 4, Angel Asensio argues that the economic policy of the 'New Consensus' may cause dysfunctions in a Keynesian context, which call for substantial changes in the macroeconomic governance of the eurozone. First, as the European Central Bank (ECB) cannot repress distributive inflationary pressures without having depressive effects, it should be recognized that the best way to control this type of inflation rests on a consensual income policy. Second, authorities should not refer to optimal rules aimed at stabilizing the economy around an imaginary natural position. Keynesian uncertainty rather suggests a pragmatic approach. In this perspective, the European Monetary Union (EMU) could take advantage of complementarities between monetary and fiscal instruments.

In Chapter 5, Sergio Rossi suggests that the monetary policy of the ECB is systematically biased against output stabilization, and lacks the flexibility that an inflation-targeting strategy grants. To further improve the ECB's monetary policy governance, Rossi proposes an institutional reform of its decision-making process, in order to make central bank independence compatible with democracy, to increase central bank accountability in respect of the population, including the possibility to dismiss malperforming central bankers, and to drop the regulation requiring that the ECB's Governing Council members have to be European Union (EU) nationals, so as to choose them in light of their actual economic performance rather than their passport.

Part II of this book addresses open economy issues such as capital flows, globalization, foreign direct investment and the Washington Consensus. For instance, in Chapter 6, Jean-Pierre Allegret and Philippe Dulbecco contend that faced with criticism regarding its governance, the International Monetary Fund (IMF) has to face two closely interlinked challenges: on the one hand, it needs to improve the domestic governance of economies connected to the global capital market, while on the other hand, it also needs to respect the governance standards of country members. These two challenges address the institutional dimension of the IMF, and its enforcement role in the global economy. The authors conclude that the question of IMF governance should not be limited to its internal decision-making structure, but rather expanded to include its ability to articulate global and domestic objectives successfully.

Eric Berr, François Combarnous and Eric Rougier, in Chapter 7, construct a unique quantitative measure of the depth and pace of all aspects of institutional financial institution (IFI) programmes – the Washington Consensus Index (WCI) – and investigate their whole impact on economic growth. Two main conclusions emerge. First, among observed countries, those who come up to Consensus expectations maintain a relatively high degree of government involvement. Second, when combined with usual explanatory variables, the WCI presents a significant non-linear relationship with the probability of getting higher growth than in other countries. Thus, it seems that a 'too fast' and/or a 'too far' implementation of IFI programmes, especially with respect to deregulation and monetary orthodoxy, can harm growth in developing countries

Chapter 8, by Luiz Carlos Bresser-Pereira, deals with global economic disgovernance, which characterizes the world economy today. In particular, the author emphasises the recurring balance-of-payments crises in developing countries, and the present enormous current account deficit in the United States. The emergent markets' crises are essentially the outcome of a strategy that the North proposed to the South: the growth cum foreign savings strategy. Given the fact that the inflow of capital influences the exchange rate, and that the countries did not face major investment opportunities in the 1990s, such strategy led not to increase in capital accumulation and growth but to large current account deficits and to balance-of-payments (financial) crises. On the other hand, the US current account deficit is a serious problem. The US is already a debtor country, but adjustment continues to be postponed. Thus, the probability of a soft landing is small. Both sources of instability are related to current account deficits and overvalued currencies. The political economy behind this scenario has a name: exchange rate populism, one of the two forms of economic populism (the other is fiscal populism). This is not surprising in developing countries, but could be in a developed country like the United States. Yet, when one considers the political and social retrocession that the American society has been experiencing since the end of World War II, it is not.

In Chapter 9, Robert Dimand reminds us that James Tobin's 'Proposal for Monetary Reform' was, in Tobin's opinion, misunderstood by both supporters and opponents of the Tobin tax on international currency transactions. The publication of *World Finance and Economic Stability: Selected Essays of James Tobin* (2003) provides an opportunity to investigate his analysis of how to increase the stability of the global financial system, to evaluate his analysis in light of developments since he first advanced his proposal in the 1970s (notably the financial crises of 1994–2001), and to compare his approach with those of Jagdish Bhagwati, Robert Mundell and Joseph Stiglitz. In this chapter, Dimand argues that the key to understanding Tobin's case against free capital mobility is his view of how financial markets function. However efficient in a mechanical sense (low transactions costs, rapid communications, arbitrage), they need not be efficient in any larger sense: 'there is only a singular path that leads from disequilibrium to equilibrium. If the markets are not on that path, or if they don't jump to it from wherever they are, they can follow any of a number of paths that lead away from equilibrium – paths along which, nonetheless, expectations are on average fulfilled.' In later years, Tobin emphasized the findings of his younger Yale colleague, Robert Shiller, on excessive volatility of asset prices. The linkage of the Tobin tax to Feige's Automated Payment Transaction Tax proposal is also noted.

In her contribution to this volume, Claudia Maya, a doctoral student at the University of Missouri, Kansas City, argues that for more than 30 years, mainstream economists have claimed financial liberalization is necessary for developing countries in order to increase domestic saving to have access to foreign saving. Foreign direct investment (FDI) has come to represent a major proportion of total investment and exports in many developing countries. Hence, in the last two decades, developing countries have made efforts and sacrifices to liberalize their economies in order to benefit from foreign flows. The author analyses the impact of FDI and capital flows on capital accumulation and growth in Mexico. She argues that financial liberalization has not been beneficial to the Mexican economy, the performance of which, especially the banking system, would have probably been less disappointing if state intervention had not been discouraged. She concludes that if the state wishes to influence growth and capital formation, this goal is best achieved through public spending rather than depending on foreign investment.

In Chapter 11, Domenica Tropeano argues that the rationale behind liberalization policies in general has been to get rid of distortions due to prices, which would be different from those that would prevail under competitive conditions. These distortions in turn encourage so-called rent-seeking activities by interest groups, which, in some cases, might reduce welfare. This logic should apply to all markets, although most studies refer to impediments to free trade via tariffs and quotas and resulting lobbying activities. The abolition of such distortions should improve welfare and according to some, through their direct effect on investment, favour growth and development. Further, it has been argued that development depends not only on real factors but also on the institutional environment. According to this view, both competitive markets and democracy would contribute to economic development. If conservative interest groups, which enjoyed rents from distortions, had lost their power because of liberalization, development would become more likely. The results of empirical studies on liberalization in developing countries, however, do not offer much support for such optimistic views. The general objective of her contribution is to discuss the issue of rents in relation to financial liberalization and growth.

Finally, in the last chapter of this book, Corinne Pastoret argues that while for many developing countries neoliberal economic policies might mean economic growth, this comes at the cost of increasing economic, political and financial fragility. When economic and financial crises occur, new safety nets are desperately needed to prevent the country from collapsing as a result of social unrest, increased poverty and historically high levels of unemployment. The author evaluates the impact of the Jefes y Jefas programme, a 'universal' public employment policy that the Argentine government implemented after the 2001 crisis to provide jobs to the poorest heads of households. She argues that this kind of programme (Employment of Last Resort (ELR) type) is not only a successful post-crisis emergency solution, but can also be a crucial element of a long-run strategy to support economic growth, human development and full employment in developing countries. The author also critically assesses the relationships between money and economic growth in the monetary theory behind the ELR programme.

REFERENCES

Gnos, C. and L.-P. Rochon (2006), *Post-Keynesian Principles of Economic Policy*, Cheltenham, UK and Northampton, MA, USA: Edward Elgar.

Palley, T. (2006), 'A post-Keynesian framework for monetary policy: why interest rate operating procedures are not enough', in Gnos, C. and L.-P. Rochon (eds), *Post-Keynesian Principles of Economic Policy*, Cheltenham, UK and Northampton, MA, USA: Edward Elgar.

Rochon, L.-P. and M. Setterfield (2007), 'Interest rates, income distribution and monetary policy dominance: post Keynesians and the "fair" rate of interest', *Journal of Post Keynesian Economics*, Fall, **30** (1), pp. 13–41.

Tobin, J. (2003), *World Finance and Economic Stability: Selected Essays of James Tobin*, (with a foreword by Janet Yellen), Cheltenham, UK, and Northampton, MA: Edward Elgar Publishing.

PART ONE

Monetary and Macroeconomic Policy

1. Wage bargaining and monetary policy in a Kaleckian monetary distribution and growth model: making sense of the NAIRU

Eckhard Hein

INTRODUCTION

The idea of a 'non-accelerating inflation rate of unemployment' (NAIRU) is at the core of modern New Keynesian and New Consensus models of monetary policy analysis.[1] In these models the NAIRU is determined by structural factors of the labour market, the wage bargaining process, and the social benefit system. Due to 'micro-founded' rigidities, short-run unemployment determined by the goods market may deviate from long-run equilibrium unemployment given by the NAIRU. However, New Keynesian and New Consensus models suppose a perhaps slow, but stable adjustment mechanism, either through a real balance effect or through a monetary policy reaction function. A downward sloping Phillips curve is valid in the short run, but in the long run effective demand and hence monetary policy has no effect on the NAIRU, and the long-run Phillips curve becomes vertical again. All that monetary policy can do is stabilize output and employment in the short run and stabilize inflation in the long run (Fontana and Palacio-Vera, 2005).

In the standard model, short-run unemployment has no effect on the NAIRU. However, within the New Keynesian approach some models have been advanced in which short-run unemployment determined by the goods market affects the NAIRU through the phenomenon of 'hysteresis' (Blanchard and Summers, 1987, 1988; Ball, 1999). Applying union wage bargaining or insider–outsider models, persistent unemployment and an increasing share of long-term unemployment in total unemployment with the associated loss of skills and access to firms by the long-term unemployed will decrease the pressure of a given rate of unemployment on labour unions' or insiders' target real wage and hence on nominal wage demands. This requires an increasing total rate of unemployment in order to stabilize inflation. The economic policy implications of this amended New Keynesian approach, however, are quite straightforward: prevent unemployment in the short run by means of applying appropriate monetary policies, and reduce the existing NAIRU by means of structural reforms in the labour market and the social benefit system, which reduce workers' nominal wage demands and hence inflation pressure, and allow for more expansive monetary policies.

Post-Keynesians have reacted differently to the New Keynesian NAIRU approach. On the one hand, some have rejected the idea of a NAIRU altogether and have insisted that unemployment in the short and in the long run is determined by the principle of effective demand (Galbraith, 1997; Davidson, 1998). On the other hand, in post-Keynesian models the cause of accelerating inflation is usually attributed to unresolved conflict over the distribution of income, in particular between capital and labour (Rowthorn, 1977; Lavoie, 1992, pp. 391–421; Lavoie, 2002; Sawyer, 2001a, 2002; Cassetti, 2002; Arestis and Sawyer, 2004, pp. 73–87; Arestis and Sawyer, 2005). This implies that, although employment is determined by effective demand in the short and in the long run, in every moment in time there may be some sort of 'inflation barrier' (Robinson, 1962, p. 59) for the increase in economic activity. In what follows, we attempt to contribute to an integration of a conflicting-claims theory of inflation with a long-run determination of unemployment by effective demand. This will give rise to a post-Keynesian interpretation of the NAIRU which will allow us to examine its short-run stability and long-run endogeneity properties.

Within post-Keynesian theory, Sawyer (2001a, 2002) has argued that the NAIRU may only be a weak attractor for actual unemployment determined by effective demand without analysing the stability of the adjustment process in detail. Stockhammer (2004) has investigated the stability of the NAIRU, focusing on distribution effects of employment variations – and not on inflation effects – within a post-Keynesian distribution and growth model in the tradition of Bhaduri and Marglin (1990). He has shown that only in a profit-led growth regime is the NAIRU generally stable. Sawyer (2001a, 2002) and Arestis and Sawyer (2004, pp. 73–99, 2005) have demonstrated that the NAIRU will become endogenous to actual unemployment if the long-run effects of current investment on capital stock and on productivity growth are taken into account. Lavoie's (2004) post-Keynesian amendment of the New Consensus model also relies on a positive relation between capital stock growth and productivity growth, and between output growth and labour supply, which makes the natural rate of growth and the NAIRU endogenous to actual growth and actual unemployment.[2]

Although post-Keynesian models of distribution and growth with conflict inflation, and also some modern New Keynesian and New Consensus NAIRU models, explicitly or implicitly rely on a credit economy in which credit and the stock of money are endogenous, they do not explicitly analyse the implications of debt and costs of debt (interest) on the stability and the endogeneity of the NAIRU. This is a serious limitation because the effects of accelerating inflation or disinflation/deflation on firms' debt–asset ratio might considerably affect their investment decisions. This has already been pointed out by Fisher (1933) and Keynes (1936 [1973], p. 264). Real debt effects might hence affect the stability of the NAIRU in the short run, and might contribute to endogeneity in the long run. And central banks' variations in the real interest rate, although perhaps effective in the short run when it comes to putting a halt to accelerating inflation, may have long-run effects on firms' costs of production and hence on the NAIRU which then might contradict the stabilization of inflation in the short run (Lavoie, 1992, pp. 402–4). We will address these problems using a monetary extension of a Kaleckian model of distribution and growth, as developed in Hein (2006), and integrating conflict inflation and monetary policy interventions into this model. The remainder of the chapter is structured as follows. Section 2 presents the basic model and derives the goods market equilibrium. Section 3 adds distribution conflict and inflation to the model and distinguishes the 'stable inflation rate of employment' (SIRE) from the 'goods market equilibrium rate of employment' (GERE). In Section 4 the short-run stability of the SIRE is investigated, without and with monetary policy interventions affecting the real interest rate, and it is shown that the SIRE is not generally stable. In Section 5 the long-run effects of variations in the real interest rate on the SIRE and the GERE are discussed and the endogeneity problem is addressed. Section 6 summarizes and derives some conclusions for monetary policies and wage bargaining.

THE BASIC MODEL

We assume a closed economy without economic activity of the state. Under given conditions of production, there is just one type of commodity produced that can be used for consumption and investment purposes. There is a constant relation between the employed volume of labour (L) and real output (Y), that is, there is no overhead labour and no technical change, so that we get a constant labour–output ratio and hence constant labour productivity (y). The capital-potential output ratio (v), the relation between the real capital stock (K) and potential real output (Y^v), is also constant. The capital stock is assumed not to depreciate. The rate of capacity utilization (z) is given by the relation between actual real output and potential real output. The basic model can be described by the following equations:

$$p = (1+m)\frac{w}{y}, \qquad m > 0 \tag{1.1}$$

$$h = \frac{\Pi}{pY} = 1 - \frac{1}{1+m} \tag{1.2}$$

$$r = \frac{\Pi}{pK} = \frac{\Pi}{pY}\frac{Y}{Y^v}\frac{Y^v}{K} = hz\frac{1}{v} \tag{1.3}$$

$$\Pi = \Pi^n + R = \Pi^n + iB \tag{1.4}$$

$$\lambda = \frac{B}{pK} \tag{1.5}$$

$$h = h(i), \qquad \frac{\partial h}{\partial i} \geq 0 \tag{1.6}$$

$$\sigma = \frac{S}{pK} = \frac{\Pi - R + S_R}{pK} = h\frac{z}{v} - i\lambda(1 - s_R), \qquad 0 < s_R < 1 \tag{1.7}$$

$$g = \frac{\Delta K}{K} = \frac{I}{K} = \alpha + \beta z + \tau\left(h\frac{z}{v} - i\lambda\right), \quad \alpha, \beta, \tau > 0, \tau < 1 \tag{1.8}$$

$$g = \sigma \tag{1.9}$$

$$\frac{\partial \sigma}{\partial z} - \frac{\partial g}{\partial z} > 0 \;\Rightarrow\; (1-\tau)\frac{h}{v} - \beta > 0 \tag{1.10}$$

Writing w for the nominal wage rate, we assume that firms set prices (p) according to a mark-up (m) on constant unit labour costs up to full capacity output with the mark-up being determined by the degree of price competition in the goods markets and by the relative powers of capital and labour in the labour market (equation 1.1) (Kalecki, 1954, pp. 11–27). The profit share (h),that is the proportion of profits (Π) in nominal output (pY), is therefore determined by the mark-up (equation 1.2). The profit rate (r) relates the annual flow of profits to the nominal capital stock (equation 1.3).

Introducing monetary variables into the model, we follow the post-Keynesian horizontalist monetary view developed by Kaldor (1970, 1982, 1985), Lavoie (1984; 1992, pp. 149–216; 1996), and Moore (1988; 1989), and assume that the interest rate is an exogenous variable for the accumulation process whereas the quantities of credit and money are determined endogenously by economic activity.[3] In this view, the central bank controls the base rate of interest. Commercial banks set the market rate of interest by marking up the base rate, and then supply the credit demand of consumers and investors they consider creditworthy at this interest rate. The central bank accommodates the necessary amount of cash. For the sake of simplicity, in what follows we suppose that the central bank's nominal interest rate policy controls – within certain limits discussed below – the real rate of interest, that is, the nominal interest rate corrected by the inflation rate. We follow Pasinetti's (1974, p. 47) recommendation to treat the rate of interest as an exogenous variable in the theory of effective demand.

The pace of accumulation is determined by the entrepreneurs' decisions to invest. We assume that long-term investment finance is supplied only by retained earnings or by long-term credit of rentiers' households (directly or through banks).[4] By means of this simplification we do not have to distinguish between creditor households receiving interest income, on the one hand, and shareholder households receiving dividend income, on the other hand, and their different saving propensities.[5] Introducing interest payments into the model, profit splits into profit of enterprise (Π^n) and rentiers' income (R) (equation 1.4).[6] Rentiers' income is determined by the stock of long-term credit (B) granted to firms and the exogenously given rate of interest (i). Equation (1.5) defines the firms' debt–capital ratio (λ)

Considering the distribution effects of interest rate variations (equation 1.6) we will assume that the mark-up is interest-inelastic in the short run but that it is interest-elastic in the long run.[7] As the mark-up on variable costs has to cover the firms' actual and imputed interest payments, the minimum mark-up is also affected by the interest rate. For the same reason, the rate of interest determines the minimum rate of profit on real investment in the long run. In the short run, there need not be an immediate positive impact of interest rate variations on the mark-up, the profit share and the profit rate, but we rather suppose a direct effect on internal funds of the firm and hence on investment and employment which will be discussed below. If changes in the interest rate are lasting, the mark-up and the profit share will have to change in the same direction, because in the long run firms can only sustain those production processes which yield the minimum rate of profit determined by the interest rate. Note that for a long-run effect on the mark-up and the profit share, it is, a change in the interest rate and not in the actual interest payments which is relevant, because we assume that firms are aware of imputed interest costs on own capital, that is, on accumulated retained earnings.

We assume a classical saving hypothesis, that is, workers do not save. The part of profits retained is completely saved by definition. The part of profits distributed to rentiers' households, that is, the interest payment, is used by those households according to their propensity to save (s_R). Therefore, total saving (S) comprises retained profits (Π-Z) and saving out of interest income (S_R). Taking equations (1.3), (1.4) and (1.5) into account, we get the saving rate (σ) in equation (1.7), which relates total saving to the nominal capital stock.[8] Note that an increase in the rate of interest, *ceteris paribus*, decreases the saving rate because income is transferred from firms with a saving propensity of unity to rentiers' households with a saving propensity of less than unity. An increasing debt–capital ratio of firms reduces the saving rate for the same reason.

Equation (1.8) for the accumulation rate (g), relating net investment (I) to the capital stock, follows the arguments in Kalecki (1954) and assumes that investment decisions are positively affected both by expected sales and by retained earnings.[9] Expected sales are determined by the rate of capacity utilization. Retained earnings, in relation to the capital stock, are given by the difference between the rate of profit and the rate of interest times the debt–capital ratio. Therefore, the rate of interest and the debt–capital ratio both have a negative impact on investment because they adversely affect internal funds. This also limits the access to external funds on imperfect capital markets, according to Kalecki's (1937) 'principle of increasing risk'.[10]

The goods market equilibrium is determined by the equality of saving and investment decisions in equation (1.9). The goods market stability condition in equation (1.10) requires that the saving rate responds more elastically to changes in capacity utilization than capital accumulation does. Note that the necessary condition for a stable equilibrium requires that $\tau < 1$, which means that the effects of internal funds on investment have to be restricted in order to achieve a stable goods market equilibrium. The goods market equilibrium values (*) for capacity utilization, capital accumulation, and the rate of profit are as follows:

$$z^* = \frac{i\lambda(1 - s_R - \tau) + \alpha}{\frac{h}{v}(1 - \tau) - \beta} \tag{1.11}$$

$$g^* = \frac{i\lambda\left[\beta(1 - s_R) - \tau\frac{h}{v}s_R\right] + \alpha\frac{h}{v}}{\frac{h}{v}(1 - \tau) - \beta} \tag{1.12}$$

$$r^* = \frac{\frac{h}{v}\left[i\lambda(1 - s_R - \tau) + \alpha\right]}{\frac{h}{v}(1 - \tau) - \beta} \tag{1.13}$$

EMPLOYMENT, WAGE BARGAINING AND INFLATION: THE GERE AND THE SIRE

With constant productivity of labour, capacity utilization determined by the goods market equilibrium also determines employment (L) and with a given labour force (LF) also the employment rate ($e = L/LF$), which, in what follows, we term the 'goods market equilibrium rate of employment' (GERE). An increase in capacity utilization is associated with a proportional increase in the GERE. Generally, in Kaleckian and post-Keynesian distribution and growth models full utilization of productive capacity determined by the capital stock will not mean full employment of labour. In order to keep things as simple as possible, however, we will assume in what follows that the rate of capacity utilization and the employment rate are equal ($z = e$) and that hence full utilization of capacity is associated with full employment.[11] Under these conditions the rate of unemployment [$u = (LF\text{-}L)/LF$] is determined by the rate of capacity utilization:

$$z = e = 1 - u \tag{1.14}$$

Inflation in Kaleckian and post-Keynesian models is determined by conflict over income distribution between capital and labour.[12] Figure 1.1 displays a simple 'conflicting-claims' model of employment and inflation assuming constant production coefficients and a constant mark-up.

Although wage bargaining is concerned with money wage rates, it is assumed that labour unions intend to achieve a certain real wage rate – and with labour productivity given or productivity growth correctly anticipated a certain wage share. The labour unions' target real wage rate (w^r_b) depends positively on the employment rate, and with our assumptions mentioned abovc therefore on the rate of capacity utilization, because unemployment has a negative impact on union bargaining power.

At this stage we assume that unions do not consider the macroeconomic effects of their nominal wage demands. There is coordination neither between unions in different firms or industries nor between wage–bargaining parties and monetary policy. Full employment is therefore associated with a union target real wage rate equal to labour productivity (y). Therefore, unemployment has the function to curtail distribution claims of workers (Kalecki, 1971, pp. 156-64).

$$w^r_b = \theta + \varepsilon z \tag{1.15}$$

The feasible real wage rate (w^r_p) is given by mark-up pricing of firms. From equation (1.1) we get for the 'target real wage rate' of firms:

$$w^r_p = \frac{w}{p} = \frac{y}{1+m}. \tag{1.16}$$

With the simplifying assumptions of a constant coefficient technology and a constant mark-up up to full capacity output the feasible real wage rate curve in Figure 1.1 is just a horizontal line. The unions' target real wage and the feasible real wage only coincide by accident. From equations (1.15) and (1.16), and making use of equation (1.2), we get for the employment rate (e^N), and hence the rate of capacity utilization (z^N), which allows for the consistency of the target real wage rate of labour unions and firms:

$$z^N = e^N = \frac{\frac{y}{1+m} - \theta}{\varepsilon} = \frac{y(1-h) - \theta}{\varepsilon} \tag{1.17}$$

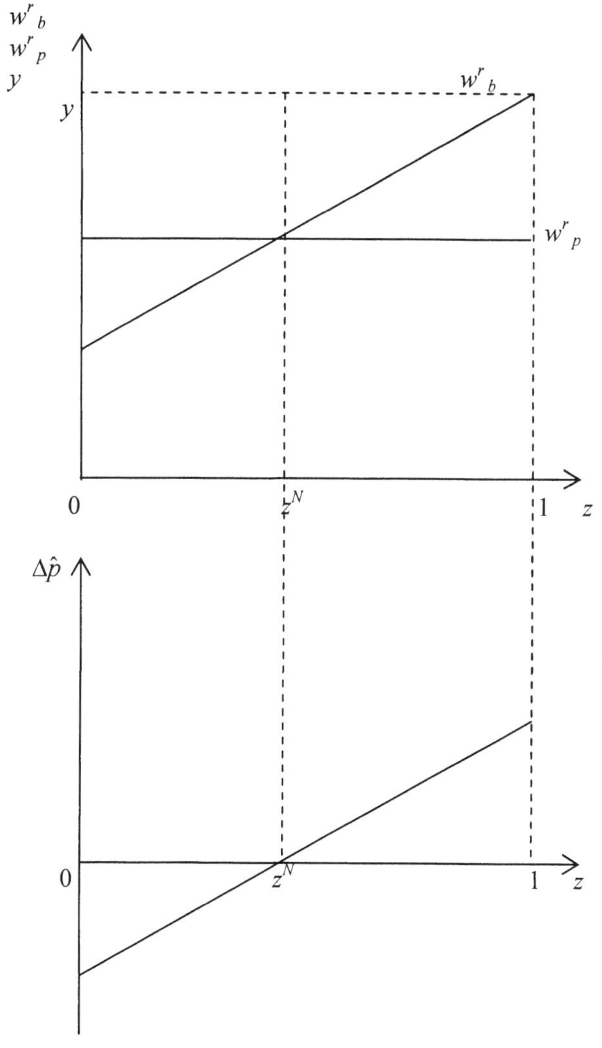

Figure 1.1 Employment rate and distribution conflict: no wage bargaining coordination

Only if the goods market equilibrium generates an employment rate of $z^* = z^N$, will the distribution claims of labourers and firms be compatible. Whenever the GERE deviates from z^N we get rising or falling inflation rates (and finally deflation). This can easily be shown as follows. Assume that wage bargaining parties determine the growth rate of nominal wages ($\hat{w}$) according to:

$$\hat{w}_t = \hat{p}_{t-1} + \hat{y}_t + \varepsilon\left(z_t^* - z^N\right) \tag{1.18}$$

Wage inflation is therefore determined by past inflation, (correctly anticipated) productivity growth, the attempt to improve distribution whenever the employment rate exceeds some threshold, and nominal wage moderation whenever the employment rate is below this threshold. Price setting of firms follows wage setting by wage bargainers. It is therefore firms' pricing decisions which determine distribution at any rate. From equation (1.1) we get for the inflation rate ($\hat{p}$):

$$\hat{p}_t = \left(1 \hat{+} m\right)_t + \hat{w}_t - \hat{y}_t \tag{1.19}$$

If firms do not vary the mark-up, and productivity growth is either correctly anticipated by firms and labour unions or zero, we get:

$$\hat{p}_t = \hat{p}_{t-1}, \text{ only if} : z_t^* = z^N = 1 - \text{NAIRU} \tag{1.20}$$

The unemployment rate $[u^N = (LF - L^N)/LF = 1 - e^N = 1 - z^N]$ associated with this 'stable inflation rate of employment' (SIRE) may therefore be termed 'non-accelerating inflation rate of unemployment' (NAIRU). It defines a distribution equilibrium between the claims of workers and those of firms.

THE SHORT-RUN STABILITY OF THE NAIRU/THE SIRE

In discussing the stability of the NAIRU or the SIRE, we will proceed in two steps. First, we will consider the issue of stability without monetary policy interventions. Then we will analyse the effects of monetary policy applying the interest rate tool whenever the GERE deviates from the SIRE.

No Monetary Policy Intervention

In older New Keynesian models with an exogenous stock of money, the stability of the NAIRU is achieved by a real balance effect.[13] Falling (rising) nominal wage and hence price inflation whenever unemployment is above (below) the NAIRU is assumed not to affect nominal demand but only real demand. This will then bring back real demand to a level consistent with the NAIRU. However, as in our model the stock of money is endogenous, Keynes and/or Pigou effects cannot work as stabilisers.

Stockhammer (2004) has discussed another potential stabilization mechanism of the NAIRU in a post-Keynesian distribution and growth model making use of the Bhaduri–Marglin (1990) distinction between wage-led and profit-led growth regimes. Following a suggestion by the late Kalecki (1971, pp. 156–64), distribution is assumed to be affected by unemployment: rising (falling) unemployment causes a falling (rising) wage share. Therefore, in a profit-led regime the NAIRU will always be stable, whereas in a wage-led regime stability depends on the relative adjustments of accumulation and distribution whenever unemployment deviates from the NAIRU. However, the distribution effects of a changing employment rate or rate of capacity utilization supposed by Stockhammer (2004) cannot be taken for granted: a rising employment rate will cause increasing nominal wage demands by workers, but it may also trigger rising profit claims by firms and hence rising mark-ups.[14] And as firms set prices in the goods markets after nominal wages have been set in the labour market, we could also suppose a rising profit share accompanying rising rates of capacity utilization and employment due to firms' improved sales conditions, at least in a closed economy. If this is assumed, the NAIRU in Stockhammer's (2004) model will be stable in the wage-led regime, whereas in the profit-led regime stability will depend on relative adjustments of accumulation and distribution.

We will not try to resolve this issue here and continue to assume that distribution between wages and gross profits is not affected by changes in the rates of capacity utilization and employment. In what follows we will rather discuss a presumably more important effect in a credit economy: the real debt effect associated with rising/falling inflation rates which has already been highlighted by Fisher (1933) and by Keynes (1936 [1973], p. 264).

Let us assume that the stock of firms' debt is not indexed to changes in the inflation rate. Accelerating inflation will therefore decrease the debt–capital ratio defined in equation (1.5); decelerating inflation will increase this ratio. If monetary policy does not respond to changes in the inflation rate, and does not vary the nominal interest rate accordingly, real interest rates will fall in the face of accelerating inflation and will rise when inflation decelerates. Taken together, this implies that the interest–capital ratio [$i\lambda = (iB)/(pK) = R/(pK)$] will fall when inflation rises, and will rise when inflation falls. Given that changes in the real interest rate do not affect the mark-up and hence the profit share in the short run, the effects of changes in the interest–capital ratio on the GERE can be determined from equation (1.11):

$$\frac{\partial z}{\partial(i\lambda)} = \frac{1 - s_R - \tau}{\frac{h}{v}(1-\tau) - \beta}. \tag{1.11a}$$

If only stable goods market equilibria are considered, equation (1.11a) shows that the effects of changes in the interest–capital ratio on the GERE depend on the parameters in the saving and investment function of the model. If the rentiers' propensity to consume ($1\text{-}s_R$) is smaller than firms' investment elasticity related to internal funds (τ), rising indebtedness and rising real interest payments will have a negative effect on the GERE. This can be called the 'normal case' (Lavoie, 1995), usually expected in post-Keynesian theory. An increasing interest–capital ratio of firms will have a negative impact on the goods market equilibrium. If the conditions of the 'normal case' prevail, the SIRE will be unstable. Whenever the GERE exceeds the SIRE, accelerating inflation will cause falling debt–capital ratios and falling real interest rates, and hence a rising GERE, moving the economy farther away from stable inflation. If the GERE falls short of the SIRE, decelerating inflation and finally deflation will cause a rising debt–capital ratio and rising real interest rates, and hence a falling GERE. The economy will be trapped in a downward spiral of disinflation/deflation, rising real indebtedness of the firm sector and a falling GERE. Therefore we get a macroeconomic 'paradox of debt' associated with cumulative inflation or disinflation/deflation.[15] With decelerating inflation and rising interest–capital ratios, firms individually reduce investment in order to confine the burden of debt, with the macroeconomic effect that disinflation or deflation is reinforced and the interest–capital ratio keeps on rising. With accelerating inflation, firms individually will increase debt and investment, with the macroeconomic effect of further acceleration of inflation and a further decrease in the interest–capital ratio.

If the rentiers' propensity to consume exceeds firms' investment elasticity with respect to internal funds, a rising interest–capital ratio of firms will be associated with an increasing GERE. This may be called the 'puzzling' case (Lavoie, 1995), usually not expected in post-Keynesian theory. If the conditions of the 'puzzling case' prevail, the SIRE will be stable. Rising (falling) inflation rates will trigger falling (rising) debt–capital ratios and falling (rising) real interest rates which will then cause a falling (rising) GERE.[16] The GERE will therefore adjust to the SIRE.

Monetary Policy Intervention

In our 'normal case', stabilizing the SIRE requires monetary policy intervention applying the monetary interest rate tool. Also modern New Keynesian and, in particular, the New Consensus models rely on monetary policy to adjust actual unemployment to the NAIRU and to stabilize the inflation rate.[17] In these models the (real) rate of interest is the monetary policy instrument which implies that it is no longer assumed that monetary policy controls the stock of (high-powered) money and that the latter is endogenous to the whole economic process (Arestis and Sawyer, 2004, pp. 10–72). Whenever unemployment falls short of the NAIRU, and inflation accelerates, the central bank is supposed to increase nominal interest rates such that real interest rates increase, which then adversely affects aggregate demand and hence employment. If unemployment is above the NAIRU the central bank should lower nominal interest rates such that real interest rates decrease, which increases aggregate demand and hence employment. In order to have a stable NAIRU, monetary policy interventions have to be symmetric and their effects have to be assumed to be symmetric as well. If these conditions are fulfilled, what central banks can achieve is output stabilization in the short run and stable inflation rates in the long run (Fontana and Palacio-Vera, 2005).[18]

In the 'normal case' in our model, however, in order to stabilize the SIRE central banks do not only have to change real rates of interest by means of varying the nominal rate, but the change in the real interest rate has to be sufficient to overcompensate the counter-effects of the change in the debt–capital ratio of firms on the GERE. In general, this is not a problem in a situation of rising inflation, because there is no upper limit for the nominal interest rate set by the central bank. But in a situation of falling inflation or even deflation, central banks may not be able to reduce the nominal rate of interest by a sufficient amount to decrease real rates and to overcompensate the restrictive demand effects of rising debt–capital ratios, because there is a zero lower bound for the nominal interest rate. Therefore, in this situation central banks may be unable to adjust the GERE to the SIRE, and the economy may be trapped in a deflationary recession. In the 'normal' case, therefore, the NAIRU can generally only be considered an 'inflation barrier' which has to be enforced by the central banks, but central banks may be incapable of adjusting actual unemployment to the NAIRU whenever the former exceeds the latter.

In the 'puzzling case', monetary policy interventions, which follow the New Keynesian/New Consensus advice and increase the real rate of interest in the face of rising inflation and decrease it in the face of falling inflation or deflation, will have a destabilizing effect. This may overcompensate the stabilizing effect exerted by the change in the debt–capital ratio and may cause a further deviation of the GERE from the SIRE. Table 1.1 summarizes our results with respect to short-run stability of the SIRE.

Table 1.1 The short-run stability of the 'stable inflation rate of employment' (SIRE)

	$1 - s_R - \tau$	
	- ('normal case')	+ ('puzzling case')
No monetary policy intervention	*unstable*	*stable*
Monetary policy intervention	*stable*, if change in real interest rate overcompensates change in the debt–capital ratio, otherwise *unstable*	*unstable*, if change in real interest rate overcompensates change in the debt–capital ratio, otherwise *stable*

THE LONG-RUN ENDOGENEITY OF THE NAIRU/THE SIRE

The endogeneity of the NAIRU – that is, the adjustment of the NAIRU to the actual rate of unemployment determined by the goods market in the case of a persistent deviation of the two rates – has been discussed within New Keynesian models under the heading of 'hysteresis' (Blanchard and Summers, 1987; Ball, 1999). Applying union wage bargaining or insider-outsider models, persistent unemployment and an increasing share of long-term unemployment in total unemployment with the associated loss of skills and access to firms by the long-term unemployed will decrease the pressure of a given rate of unemployment on labour unions' or insiders' target real wage and hence on nominal wage demands. The labour unions' target real wage curve in Figure 1.1 will rotate upwards (ε in equations (1.15), (1.17) and (1.18) will increase), the SIRE will decline, and the NAIRU will increase.

Sawyer (2001a, 2002) and Arestis and Sawyer (2004, pp. 73–99; 2005) have discussed another source of endogeneity of the NAIRU: the effect of current investment on capital stock and productivity growth.[19] Whereas investment in the short run determines effective demand and hence the GERE, net investment also increases the capital stock and therefore affects maximum employment if it is restrained by the capital stock. And it also affects the NAIRU or the SIRE if it is assumed that firms increase the mark-up when actual output approaches full capacity output. In order to simplify our model, we have excluded this by means of assuming a constant mark-up and full utilization of capital stock being associated with full employment. However, in the real world this is not necessarily the case and Arestis and Sawyer have therefore made an important point: low investment does not only cause a low GERE, but also decreases the SIRE by restraining the capital stock and output capacity. But investment does not only affect the size of the capital stock, it also affects productivity growth if we assume that technical progress is embodied in physical investment and/or that there are increasing returns to scale.[20] In our model, increasing productivity (growth) will shift the firms' target real wage curve in Figure 1.1 upwards and the SIRE in equation (1.17) will increase. This, however, supposes that labour unions do not adjust their target real wage rate when productivity (growth) increases. But this cannot be taken for granted, if labour unions target a certain wage share and can correctly anticipate productivity growth as we have assumed in equation (1.18). If this is the case, productivity growth will have no effect on the SIRE or the NAIRU. Therefore, the effect of productivity growth on the NAIRU depends on labour unions' or workers' aspirations to participate in increasing productivity (growth).

In what follows we will trace another source of endogeneity which is associated with the distributional effects of monetary policy responses to accelerating or decelerating inflation rates. Assume for the reasons given above that persistent changes in the real interest rate are in the long run accompanied by changes in the mark-up in the same direction. In our model this has two effects.

First, changes in the mark-up affect the firms' target real wage rate: an increasing (decreasing) mark-up shifts the firms' target real wage curve in Figure 1.1 downwards (upwards) and the SIRE decreases (increases). From equation (1.17) we get for the effect of a change in the mark-up and hence in the profit share on the SIRE:

$$\frac{\partial z^N}{\partial h} = -\frac{y}{\varepsilon} < 0 \quad (1.17a)$$

Second, changes in the mark-up and thus in distribution between wages and gross profits have an additional effect on the goods market equilibrium and hence on the GERE. From equation (1.11) we get:

$$\frac{\partial z}{\partial h} = -\frac{\frac{1-\tau}{v}z}{\frac{h}{v}(1-\tau)-\beta} < 0 \quad (1.11b)$$

The effect of a change in the mark-up and in the profit share on the GERE is negative. Raising the mark-up when interest rates increase will have a positive impact on firms' internal funds but will simultaneously reduce consumption demand, sales and hence capacity utilization (and the GERE), which will then negatively feed back on internal funds. Furthermore, lower capacity utilization will also have a negative impact on investment decisions.

Let us now discuss the implications for the effects of monetary policy interventions. We start with the 'normal case' from Table 1.1. Assume that the GERE exceeds the initial SIRE at $z^N{}_1$ in Figure 1.2. Since accelerating inflation and a falling interest–capital ratio of firms is a stimulus for effective demand, the GERE will further increase and inflation acceleration will speed up. In order to stabilize the rate of inflation, central banks have to increase nominal interest rates in order to raise real interest rates by a sufficient amount to overcompensate the demand stimulating effects of falling debt–capital ratios. Therefore, in the short run the central bank can bring back the GERE to the SIRE at $z^N{}_1$.

In the long run, however, a higher real interest rate will induce firms to increase the mark-up. This will shift the firms' target real wage curve down from $w^r{}_{p1}$ to $w^r{}_{p2}$ and reduce the SIRE to $z^N{}_2$. The redistribution at the expense of labour will also reduce the GERE. Three scenarios are possible depending on the relative effects of changes in distribution on the GERE and on the SIRE in equations (1.11b) and (1.17a):

- If, by accident, $\frac{\partial z}{\partial h} = \frac{\partial z^N}{\partial h}$, the reduction of the GERE caused by an increasing mark-up will make this new rate coincide with the SIRE at $z^N{}_2$ so that the economy gets to rest at a stable SIRE.

- If $\left|\frac{\partial z}{\partial h}\right| > \left|\frac{\partial z^N}{\partial h}\right|$, the effective demand effect of redistribution at the expense of labour will make the GERE fall below z^N_2 and we get falling inflation rates. This should then make monetary policies reduce real interest rates, making the GERE increase to z^N_2 in the short run. In the long run, firms then reduce mark-ups, the firms' target real wage curve shifts upwards, and effective demand is stimulated by redistribution in favour of labour. The SIRE as well as the GERE will increase, with the latter now overshooting the former and monetary policy will have to intervene again. This oscillation may converge to a stable SIRE between z^N_2 and z^N_1, but may also generate stable oscillation around that SIRE, or the oscillation may even explode, depending on the degree of over- and undershooting of the GERE with respect to the SIRE and the concomitant change in the real interest rate required for the short-run adjustment of the GERE to the SIRE.
- If $\left|\frac{\partial z}{\partial h}\right| < \left|\frac{\partial z^N}{\partial h}\right|$, the effective demand effect of redistribution at the expense of labour is weak so that the GERE remains above z^N_2. We will get accelerating inflation again inducing the central bank to increase real interest rates, forcing the GERE down to z^N_2 in the short run. In the long run, firms will again increase mark-ups, which will shift their target real wage curve down to w^r_{p3} and the SIRE will decline to z^N_3. The GERE will also decline because of the redistribution of income at the expense of labour but will remain above z^N_3, inflation will accelerate anew and central banks will have to intervene again.

Equation (1.11b) shows that the effective demand effect of redistribution between wages and gross profits becomes weaker when the GERE decreases. This implies that a development according to scenario 3 becomes the more likely the lower the GERE declines. This is shown in Figure 1.2: stable inflation is associated with a declining SIRE. The long-run 'Phillips curve' becomes horizontal because of the nature of monetary policy interventions.[21] In this scenario, monetary policy is only able to stabilize the inflation rate in the long run at the expense of a continuously decreasing GERE. Monetary policy interventions trigger a process in which stabilizing inflation in the short run by means of increasing real interest rates and slowing down the economy re-establishes the inflation problem in the long run when the full distribution effects of real interest rate variations are felt. In the long run, this scenario describes a latent tendency towards stagflation.

Note that scenario 3 also works in reverse: if the central bank intends to improve the GERE, in the short run lowering real interest rates will be associated with accelerating inflation. In the long run, however, a falling mark-up increases the SIRE. And since the demand effect of redistribution in favour of labour is not too strong so that the GERE does not exceed the SIRE, there is again room for manoeuvre for the central bank to cut real interest rates.

Let us now briefly discuss the short-run 'puzzling case' from Table 1.1. In this case a deviation of the GERE from the SIRE is self-correcting in the short run without monetary policy intervention. If the GERE exceeds z^N_1 in Figure 1.2, the reduction in consumption demand caused by the devaluation of rentiers' assets will overcompensate the stimulation of firms' investment demand caused by a falling interest–capital ratio. If central banks simply hold the nominal interest rate constant, they will support this adjustment process and the economy will approach z^N_1.

If, however, central banks try to fight accelerating inflation rates by means of increasing the real interest rate as recommended by the New Keynesian and the New Consensus models, they will delay the convergence process towards z^N_1 in the short run.[22] The long-run effect of an increasing real interest rate will reduce the SIRE to z^N_2. This will again accelerate inflation. The redistribution at the expense of labour caused by an increasing mark-up, however, will have a dampening effect on the GERE, shifting it towards z^N_2. Again, we have three scenarios depending on the relative effects of changes in distribution on the GERE and on the SIRE (equations (1.11b) and (1.17a)):

- If, by accident, $\left|\frac{\partial z}{\partial h}\right| = \left|\frac{\partial z^N}{\partial h}\right|$, the GERE will coincide with z^N_2 and the economy will get to rest in this lower stable SIRE.
- If $\left|\frac{\partial z}{\partial h}\right| > \left|\frac{\partial z^N}{\partial h}\right|$, the GERE falls below z^N_2 and we will get disinflation, short-run real interest rate cuts delaying the convergence process towards z^N_2, which will in the long run decrease the mark-up moving the SIRE upwards. Redistribution in favour of labour will stimulate demand and employment and will make the GERE exceed the SIRE, and so on. The outcome of this process will again depend on the degree of over- and undershooting of the GERE with respect to the SIRE and on the degree of (now disturbing) monetary policy interventions.

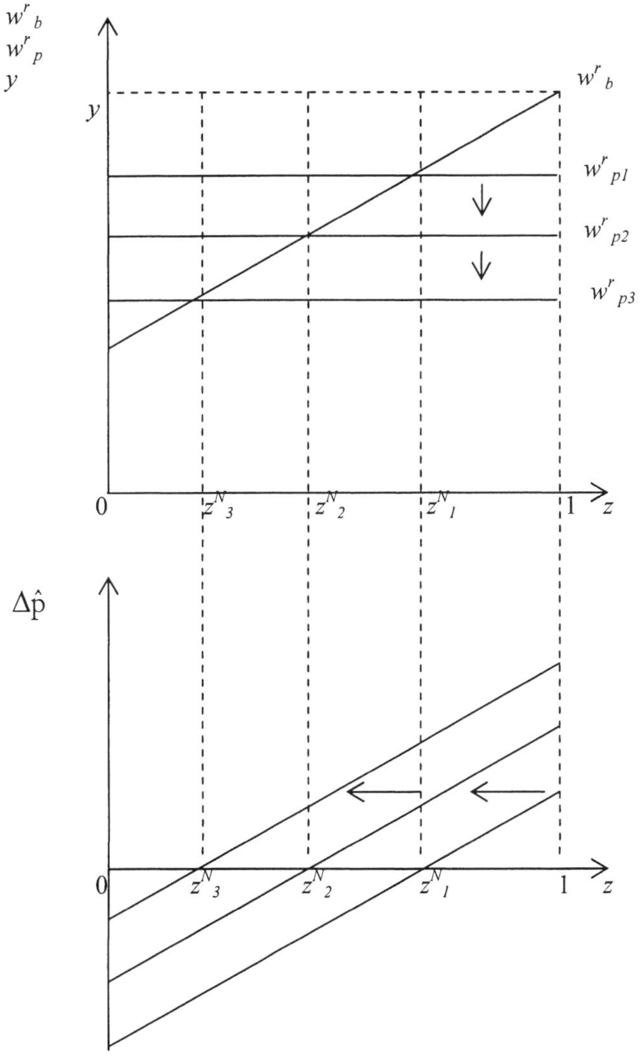

Figure 1.2 Long-run endogeneity of the stable inflation rate of employment (SIRE) caused by monetary policy intervention: the horizontal long-run Phillips curve

- If $\left|\frac{\partial z}{\partial h}\right| < \left|\frac{\partial z^N}{\partial h}\right|$, the redistribution effect at the expense of labour income on demand is weak, the GERE will remain higher than z^N_2. Inflation will accelerate, central banks will increase real interest rates disturbing the short-run convergence process towards z^N_2 and decreasing the SIRE to z^N_3.

Since the effective demand effect of redistribution between wages and gross profits becomes weaker when the employment rate goes down (equation (1.11b)), we get again that scenario 3 becomes the more likely the lower the GERE drops: the long-run 'Phillips curve' again becomes horizontal, as in Figure 1.2.

Let us finally add that, whatever case we consider and whatever scenario comes into existence, in the long run the SIRE and hence the NAIRU are endogenous to monetary policy's real interest rate manipulation in our model. Therefore, in our approach the NAIRU is a direct result of monetary policy interventions.

RESULTS AND IMPLICATIONS FOR MONETARY POLICY AND WAGE BARGAINING

In a Kaleckian distribution and growth model with endogenous money and inflation generated by distribution conflict we have shown that monetary policy is either an unnecessary or a costly tool to control inflation in the short run. Taking into account the real debt effects of inflation acceleration or deceleration, the NAIRU will be stable in the 'puzzling case' with a propensity to consume out of rentiers' income exceeding the sensitivity of investment with respect to internal funds. Inflation-targeting monetary policies raising real interest rates in the face of accelerating inflation will disturb adjustment to stable inflation rates in this case. In the 'normal case' of a rentiers' propensity to consume falling short of firms' elasticity of investment with respect to internal funds, the NAIRU will be unstable. Inflation-targeting monetary policies applying the interest rate tool will be able to contain accelerating inflation. There are, however, some doubts whether monetary policies will be able to fight decelerating inflation and finally deflation because there is a zero bound for the nominal interest rate. In this case, therefore, the NAIRU is merely an 'inflation barrier' enforced by monetary policies, but there is no guarantee that monetary policies will always be able to adjust unemployment determined by the goods market to the NAIRU, as is assumed in New Keynesian or New Consensus models.

In the long run, variations in the real interest rate will affect the firms' target real wage rate and the NAIRU becomes endogenous to monetary policy. This direct channel of endogeneity supplements those channels already discussed in the literature: labour market hysteresis and capital stock effects on the NAIRU. In the 'normal case' as well as in the 'puzzling case', inflation-targeting monetary policies raising the real interest rate in the face of accelerating inflation will raise the NAIRU. This bears the risk of a continuously increasing NAIRU in order to keep inflation under control, which may yield a horizontal long-run Phillips curve and latent stagflation. Taking these effects into account, monetary policy raising real interest rates can be considered an inappropriate tool to control inflation in the long run.

According to our analysis, monetary policy should rather aim at low real interest rates in the short and in the long run. This allows for a long-run increase in the SIRE and hence a reduction in the NAIRU, in any case. In the 'puzzling' case, lower real interest rates will decrease the GERE in the short run, but the real debt effects associated with disinflation will finally adjust the GERE to the higher SIRE in the long run. In the 'normal case', lowering real interest rates will increase the GERE in the short run which might trigger acceleration of inflation. This, however, will be dampened or even be wiped out as soon as the long-run increase in the SIRE becomes effective.

If short-run accelerating inflation in the face of an increasing GERE is to be avoided, the causes of inflation should be addressed directly. Therefore, policy-makers should resort to wage bargaining coordination as an appropriate tool. As recent research on the interaction of independent central banks and wage bargaining institutions has shown, effectively coordinated wage bargaining is able to internalize negative macroeconomic wage externalities (Franzese, 2001a, 2001b; Hein, 2002, 2004): in economies with a high degree of 'effective' wage bargaining coordination, the reduction of inflation rates has been accompanied by less employment losses than in economies with a low degree of coordination.

Effective wage bargaining coordination is characterized by a high degree of horizontal bargaining coordination between industries (pattern bargaining, state-imposed or -sponsored coordination, intra-associational coordination). In order to solve the implementation problem of collective agreements and to prevent wage dumping or positive wage drift, 'effective' bargaining coordination also has to include a high degree of vertical coordination within industries (high level of union and bargaining agreement coverage, legal enforceability of collective agreements, peace obligations) (Kittel and Traxler, 2001). The influence of effective coordination of wage bargaining on the SIRE in our model is shown in Figure 1.3.

With effective wage bargaining coordination, the labour unions' target real wage curve has a horizontal part. Between z^N_1 and z^N_2 the bargaining parties are able to accept the feasible real wage and to exhaust the scope for distribution, taking into account the inflation objective of the central bank. By means of effectively coordinated wage bargaining a constant inflation rate becomes compatible with a range of GEREs. The SIRE or the NAIRU as the short-run limit to employment are no longer unique. Contrary to prevailing propositions, in our Kaleckian approach a reduction of the NAIRU and an increase in the SIRE can be attained by means of organizing the labour market and coordinating the bargaining parties, and does not require decentralization of wage bargaining and deregulation of labour markets, as in New Keynesian or New Consensus models. A high degree of effective wage bargaining coordination should also have the additional virtue that increasing unemployment will not cause immediate disinflation or deflation with its potentially negative impacts on effective demand and the GERE in the 'normal' case of our model.

ACKNOWLEDGEMENTS

This chapter was presented at conferences in Berlin and Dijon in 2005, and in Bilbao and Kansas City in 2006. For helpful comments I would like to thank the participants and, in particular, Philip Arestis, Giuseppe Fontana, Geoff Harcourt, Gustav Horn, Malcolm Sawyer, Achim Truger and the referees of *Intervention: Journal of Economics*. Remaining errors are mine. The original version was published in *Intervention: Journal of Economics*, 2006, **3** (2), 305–29. I am grateful to the editors for the permission to reprint.

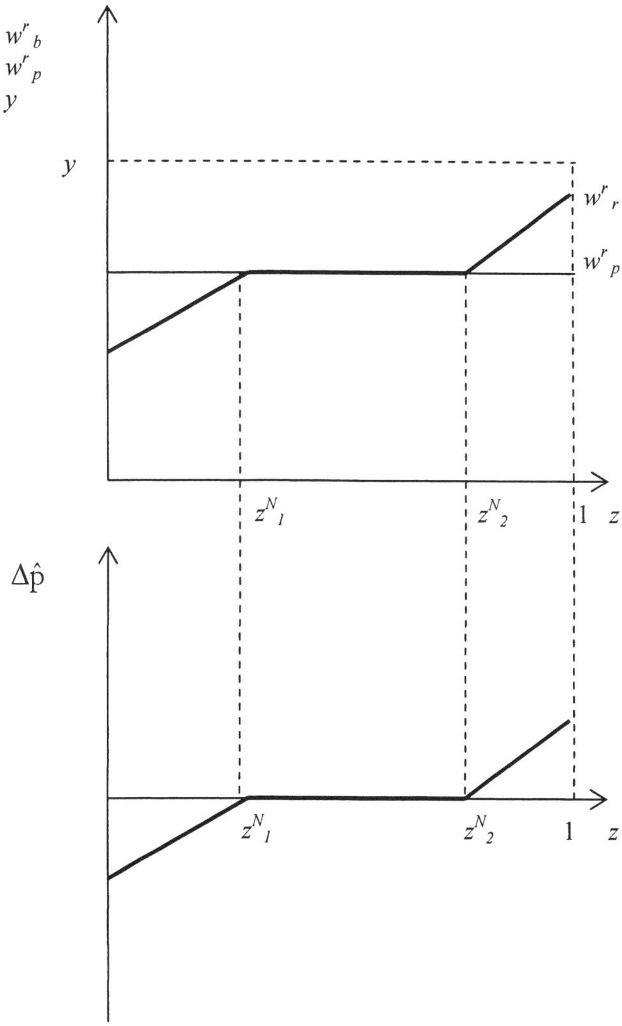

Figure 1.3 Employment rate and distribution conflict: effective wage bargaining coordination

NOTES

1. See Carlin and Soskice (1990, 133–66), Layard et al. (1991, 361–96), Blanchard and Katz (1997), Stiglitz (1997), Mankiw (2001) and Ball and Mankiw (2002) for New Keynesian discussion of the NAIRU and Clarida et al. (1999), McCallum (2001), Meyer (2001), Walsh (2002), Snowdon and Vane (2005, 419–27) and Carlin and –Soskice (2006, 27–172) for New Consensus models. These models are basically characterized by three equations: (1) an aggregate demand function derived from households' and firms' optimization behaviour which relates the output gap inversely to the real interest rate; (2) an expectations-augmented Phillips curve which makes the rate of inflation positively dependent on the output gap in the short run; and (3) a central bank reaction function in which the nominal interest rate set by the central bank is determined by the equilibrium real interest rate, by the output gap, and by the deviation of actual inflation from the inflation target (Taylor rule).
2. Setterfield's (2004) post-Keynesian extension of the New Consensus model, however, assumes away an inflation barrier and hence a NAIRU. He asserts that there is a long-run stable relationship between the rate of growth and the inflation rate, and hence no acceleration of inflation at a certain point.
3. See for a similar procedure with respect to the introduction of monetary variables into post-Keynesian models of distribution and growth Lavoie (1992, 347–71; 1993; 1995), Dutt and Amadeo (1993), Dutt (1989; 1992), Taylor (1985; 2004, 272–78); and Hein (1999; 2006; 2007).
4. The distinction between short-term finance for production purposes and long-term finance for investment purposes, not dealt with in the present chapter, can be found in the monetary circuit approach (Graziani, 1989; 1994; Lavoie, 1992, 151–69; Seccareccia, 1996; 2003).
5. Of course, our simplification implies that profits net of interest payments are all reinvested into the firm.
6. In what follows the terms 'profit', 'profit share' and 'profit rate' are related to gross profits as the sum of profit of enterprise and interest paid to rentiers.
7. According to Kalecki (1954, 18), the degree of monopoly, and hence the mark-up, may – but need not – increase when overhead costs, including interest costs, increase.
8. This saving function is similar to the one used by Lavoie (1992, 365; 1995, 160), the only difference is that we explicitly consider the debt–capital ratio.
9. On different accumulation functions in Kalecki's work see also Steindl (1981).
10. On Kalecki's 'principle of increasing risk' see Arestis (1996) and Sawyer (1985, 101–06; 2001b). A similar view was taken by Robinson (1962, 86) and Steindl (1952, 107–38). Recent empirical work has shown that the interest rate has important effects on investment through its impacts on internal funds and hence on the access to external borrowing in imperfect capital markets (Fazzari et al., 1988; Hubbard, 1998; Schiantarelli, 1996).
11. This simplification precludes that the size of the capital stock may have an effect on the NAIRU, as in Sawyer (2001a; 2002) and Arestis and Sawyer (2004, 71–99; 2005).
12. See Rowthorn (1977), Lavoie (1992, 391–421, 2002), Sawyer (2001a; 2002), Cassetti (2002), Arestis and Sawyer (2004, 73–87; 2005) for models of distribution conflict and inflation.
13. See Carlin and Soskice (1990, 159–60), and Layard et al., (1991, 362–64) who rely on a Keynes-effect within an IS-LM-framework. Blanchard and Summers (1987) take nominal demand as given and implicitly rely on a Pigou-effect.
14. See Arestis and Sawyer (2004, 73–87; 2005) for a conflicting claims model with an increasing mark-up when high levels of capacity utilization are achieved. See also Lavoie (1992, 391–7) for a discussion of different cases with respect to relative bargaining power of firms and labour unions.
15. For a macroeconomic paradox of debt in Kaleckian and post-Kaleckian distribution and growth models with constant prices see Lavoie (1995) and Hein (2006; 2007).

16. Even if we concede that in the face of accelerating inflation the behaviour of rentiers and firms may change, this will only temporarily inhibit the convergence process of the GERE towards the SIRE. Rentiers' consumption behaviour may change and the saving propensity out of rentiers' income may decline when inflation accelerates. For the 'puzzling' case to exist, however, the saving propensity of rentiers already has to be very low so that there is only small room for manoeuvre. The same argument applies to the responsiveness of investment with respect to interest payments.
17. For the modern New Keynesian and New Consensus view see Clarida et al. (1999), Romer (2000), Taylor (2000), McCallum (2001), Meyer (2001), Walsh (2002), Snowdon and Vane (2005, 419–27), and Carlin and Soskice (2006, 27–172).
18. For a more extensive discussion of the New Consensus model from a post-Keynesian view see Arestis and Sawyer (2004), Lavoie (2004), Setterfield (2004), Fontana and Palacio-Vera (2005), and Palacio-Vera (2005).
19. See also Rowthorn (1995; 1999), Arestis and Mariscal Biefang-Frisancho (2000) and Arestis et al. (2006).
20. The productivity-enhancing effects of investment in capital stock is pointed out in demand-led growth models. See Kaldor (1957), Leon-Ledesma and Thirlwall (2002), Dutt (2003; 2006), and the chapters in Setterfield (2002). Growth is primarily demand–driven because labour force and productivity growth respond to demand. This view has been applied by Lavoie (2004) in his post-Keynesian alternative to the New Consensus models in which the natural rate of growth is endogenous to the actual rate of growth.
21. Our argument is different from Freedman et al.'s (2004) who also derive a horizontal long-run Phillips curve. They use the labour market hysteresis argument: in order to keep inflation down, a certain amount of short-term unemployment is required irrespective of long-term unemployment. But as short-term unemployed in the process of time inevitably become long-term unemployed, the total rate of unemployment required to stabilize inflation has to increase.
22. Of course, central banks raising the real interest rates may also prevent the adjustment process as we have argued above.

REFERENCES

Arestis, P. (1996), 'Kalecki's role in post-Keynesian economics: an overview', in King, J.E. (ed.), *An Alternative Macroeconomic Theory: The Kaleckian Model and Post-Keynesian Economics*, Boston, MA: Kluiwer, 11–34.

Arestis, P., M. Baddeley, and M. Sawyer (2006), 'Is capital stock a determinant of unemployment?', in Hein, E., A. Heise and A. Truger (eds), *Wages, Employment, Distribution and Growth: International Perspectives*, Basingstoke: Palgrave-Macmillan, 49–66.

Arestis, P. and I. Biefang-Frisancho Mariscal (2000), 'Capital stock, unemployment and wages in the UK and Germany', *Scottish Journal of Political Economy*, **47** (5), 487–503.

Arestis, P. and M. Sawyer (2004), *Re-Examining Monetary and Fiscal Policy for the 21st Century*, Cheltenham, UK and Northampton, MA, US: Edward Elgar.

Arestis, P. and M. Sawyer (2005), 'Aggregate demand, conflict and capacity in the inflationary process', *Cambridge Journal of Economics*, **29** (6), 959–74.

Ball, L. (1999), 'Aggregate demand and long-run unemployment', *Brookings Papers on Economic Activity*, **2**, 189–251.

Ball, L. and G. Mankiw (2002), 'The NAIRU in theory and practice', *Journal of Economic Perspectives*, **16** (4), 115–36.
Bhaduri, A. and S. Marglin (1990), 'Unemployment and the real wage: the economic basis for contesting political ideologies', *Cambridge Journal of Economics*, **14** (4), 375–93.
Blanchard, O. and L. Katz (1997), 'What we know and do not know about the natural rate of unemployment', *Journal of Economic Perspectives*, **11** (1), 51–72.
Blanchard, O. and L. Summers (1987), 'Hysteresis in unemployment', *European Economic Review*, **31** (1–2), 288–95.
Blanchard, O. and L. Summers (1988), 'Beyond the natural rate hypothesis', *American Economic Review*, **78** (2), 182–7.
Carlin, W. and D. Soskice (1990), *Macroeconomics and the Wage Bargain. A Modern Approach to Employment, Inflation and the Exchange Rate*, Oxford: Oxford University Press.
Carlin, W. and D. Soskice (2006), *Macroeconomics: Imperfections, Institutions and Policies*, Oxford: Oxford University Press.
Cassetti, M. (2002), 'Conflict, inflation, distribution and terms of trade in the Kaleckian model', in Setterfield, M. (ed.), *The Economics of Demand-Led Growth*, Cheltenham, UK and Northampton, MA, US: Edward Elgar, 189–211.
Clarida, R., J. Gali and M. Gertler (1999), 'The science of monetary policy: a new Keynesian perspective', *Journal of Economic Literature*, **37** (4), 1661–707.
Davidson, P. (1998), 'The macroeconomics of OECD unemployment', *Economic Journal*, **108** (448), 817–31.
Dutt, A.K. (1989), 'Accumulation, distribution and inflation in a Marxian/post-Keynesian model with a rentier class', *Review of Radical Political Economics*, **21** (3), 18–26.
Dutt, A.K. (1992), 'Rentiers in post-Keynesian models', in Arestis, P. and V. Chick (eds), *Recent Developments in Post-Keynesian Economics*, Aldershot, UK and Brookfield, US: Edward Elgar, 95–122.
Dutt, A.K. (2003), 'New growth theory, effective demand, and post-Keynesian dynamics', in Salvadori, N. (ed.), *Old and New Growth Theories: An Assessment*, Cheltenham, UK and Northampton, MA, US: Edward Elgar, 67–100.
Dutt, A.K. (2006), 'Aggregate demand, aggregate supply and economic growth', *International Review of Applied Economics*, **20** (3), 319–36.
Dutt, A.K. and E. Amadeo (1993), 'A post-Keynesian theory of growth, interest and money', in Baranzini, M. and G.C. Harcourt (eds), *The Dynamics of the Wealth of Nations*, London: Macmillan, 181–205.
Fazzari, S. M., R. Hubbard, and B.C. Petersen (1988), 'Financing constraints and corporate investment', *Brookings Papers on Economic Activity*, **1**, 141–95.
Fisher, I. (1933), 'The debt–deflation theory of great depressions', *Econometrica*, **1** (4), 337–57.
Fontana, G. and A. Palacio-Vera (2005), 'Are long-run price stability and short-run output stabilization all that monetary policy can aim for?' Working Paper No. 430, Levy Economic Institute of Bard College.
Franzese, R.J. (2001a), 'Institutions and sectoral interactions in monetary policy and wage/price-bargaining', in Hall, P.A. and D. Soskice (eds), *Varieties of Capitalism.*

Institutional Foundations of Comparative Advantage, Oxford: Oxford University Press, 104–44.

Franzese, R.J. (2001b), 'Strategic interaction of monetary policymakers and wage/price bargainers: a review with implications for the European common-currency area', *Empirica*, **28** (4), 457–86.

Freedman, C., G. Harcourt and P. Kriesler (2004), 'Has the long-run Phillips Curve turned horizontal?', in Argyrous, G., M. Forstater and G. Mongiovi (eds), *Growth, Distribution, and Effective Demand. Alternatives to the Orthodoxy: Essays in Honor of Edward J. Nell*, Armonk, NY: M.E. Sharpe, 144–62.

Galbraith, J.K. (1997), 'Time to ditch the NAIRU', *Journal of Economic Perspectives*, **11** (1), 93–108.

Graziani, A. (1989), 'The theory of the monetary circuit', *Thames Papers in Political Economy*, spring.

Graziani, A. (1994), 'Monetary circuits', in Arestis, P. and M. Sawyer (eds), *The Elgar Companion to Radical Political Economy*, Aldershot, UK and Brookfield, US: Edward Elgar, 274–78.

Hein, E. (1999), 'Interest rates, income shares and investment in a Kaleckian model', *Political Economy. Review of Political Economy and Social Sciences*, **5**, 5–22.

Hein, E. (2002), 'Monetary policy and wage bargaining in the EMU: restrictive ECB policies, high unemployment, nominal wage restraint and inflation above the target', *Banca Nazionale del Lavoro Quarterly Review*, **55** (222), 299–337.

Hein, E. (2004), 'Die NAIRU – eine post-keynesianische Interpretation', *Intervention: Zeitschrift für Ökonomie*, **1** (1), 43–66.

Hein, E. (2006), 'Interest rate, debt and capital accumulation – a Kaleckian approach', *International Review of Applied Economics*, **20** (3), 337–52.

Hein, E. (2007), 'Interest rate, debt, distribution and capital accumulation in a post-Kaleckian model', *Metroeconomica*, **58** (2), 310–39.

Hubbard, R.G. (1998), 'Capital–market imperfections and investment', *Journal of Economic Literature*, **36** (1), 193–225.

Kaldor, N. (1957), 'A model of economic growth', *Economic Journal*, **67** (268), 591–624.

Kaldor, N. (1970), 'The new monetarism', *Lloyds Bank Review*, **97**, July, 1–17.

Kaldor, N. (1982), *The Scourge of Monetarism*, Oxford: Oxford University Press.

Kaldor, N. (1985), 'How monetarism failed', *Challenge*, **28** (2), 4–13.

Kalecki, M. (1937), 'The principle of increasing risk', *Economica*, **4** (16), 440–47.

Kalecki, M. (1954), *Theory of Economic Dynamics*, London: George Allen.

Kalecki, M. (1971), *Selected Essays on the Dynamics of the Capitalist Economy, 1933–70*, Cambridge: Cambridge University Press.

Keynes, J.M. (1936) [1973], *The General Theory of Employment, Interest, and Money*, *The Collected Writings of John Maynard Keynes*, Vol. 7, London, Basingstoke: Macmillan.

Kittel, B. and F. Traxler (2001), 'Lohnverhandlungssysteme und Geldpolitik', *Wirtschaft und Gesellschaft*, **27** (1), 11–40.

Lavoie, M. (1984), 'The endogenous flow of credit and the post-Keynesian theory of money', *Journal of Economic Issues*, **18** (3), 771–97.

Lavoie, M. (1992), *Foundations of Post-Keynesian Economic Analysis*, Aldershot, UK and Brookfield, US: Edward Elgar.
Lavoie, M. (1993), 'A post-classical view of money, interest, growth and distribution', in Mongiovi, G. and C. Rühl (eds), *Macroeconomic Theory: Diversity and Convergence*, Cambridge: Cambridge University Press, 3–21.
Lavoie, M. (1995), 'Interest rates in post-Keynesian models of growth and distribution', *Metroeconomica*, **46** (2), 146–77.
Lavoie, M. (1996), 'Horizontalism, structuralism, liquidity preference and the principle of increasing risk', *Scottish Journal of Political Economy*, **43** (3), 275–300.
Lavoie, M. (2002), 'The Kaleckian growth model with target return pricing and conflict inflation', in Setterfield, M. (ed.), *The Economics of Demand-led Growth*, Cheltenham, UK and Northampton, MA, USA: Edward Elgar, 172–88.
Lavoie, M. (2004), 'The New Consensus on monetary policy seen from a Post-Keynesian perspective', in Lavoie, M. and M. Seccareccia (eds), *Central Banking in the Modern World: Alternative Perspectives*, Cheltenham, UK and Northampton, MA, USA: Edward Elgar, 15–34.
Layard, R., S. Nickell and R. Jackman (1991), *Unemployment: Macroeconomic Performance and the Labour Market*, Oxford: Oxford University Press.
Leon-Ledesma, M. and A. Thirlwall (2002), 'The endogeneity of the natural rate of growth', *Cambridge Journal of Economics*, **26** (4), 441–59.
Mankiw, N.G. (2001), 'The inexorable and mysterious tradeoff between inflation and unemployment', *Economic Journal*, **111** (471), C45–C61.
McCallum, B. (2001), 'Monetary policy analysis in models without money', *Federal Reserve Bank of St. Louis Review*, **83** (4), 145–60.
Meyer, L.H. (2001), 'Does money matter?', *Federal Reserve Bank of St. Louis Review*, **83** (5), 1–15.
Moore, B.J. (1988), *Horizontalists and Verticalists: The Macroeconomics of Credit Money*, Cambridge: Cambridge University Press.
Moore, B.J. (1989), 'The endogeneity of credit money', *Review of Political Economy*, **1** (1), 65–93.
Palacio-Vera, A. (2005), 'The 'modern' view of macroeconomics: some critical reflections', *Cambridge Journal of Economics*, **29** (5), 747–67.
Pasinetti, L.L. (1974), *Growth and Income Distribution*, Cambridge: Cambridge University Press.
Robinson, J. (1962), *Essays in the Theory of Economic Growth*, London, New York: Macmillan.
Romer, D. (2000), 'Keynesian macroeconomics without the LM curve', *Journal of Economic Perspectives*, **14** (2), 149–69.
Rowthorn, R. E. (1977), 'Conflict, inflation and money', *Cambridge Journal of Economics*, **1** (3), 215–39.
Rowthorn, R.E. (1995), 'Capital formation and unemployment', *Oxford Review of Economic Policy*, **11** (1), 26–39.
Rowthorn, R.E. (1999), 'Unemployment, wage bargaining and capital–labour substitution', *Cambridge Journal of Economics*, **23** (4), 413–25.

Sawyer, M. (1985), *The Economics of Michal Kalecki*, Armonk, New York: M.E. Sharpe.
Sawyer, M. (2001a), 'The NAIRU: a critical appraisal', Arestis, P. and M. Sawyer (eds), *Money, Finance and Capitalist Development*, Cheltenham, UK and Northampton, MA, USA: Edward Elgar, 220–54.
Sawyer, M. (2001b), 'Kalecki on money and finance', *European Journal of the History of Economic Thought*, **8** (4), 487–508.
Sawyer, M. (2002), 'The NAIRU, aggregate demand and investment', *Metroeconomica*, **53** (1), 66–94.
Schiantarelli, F. (1996), 'Financial constraints and investment: methodological issues and international evidence', *Oxford Review of Economic Policy*, **12** (2), 70–89.
Seccareccia, M. (1996), 'Post Keynesian fundism and monetary circulation', in Deleplace, G. and E. Nell (eds), *Money in Motion*, London: Macmillan, 400–16.
Seccareccia, M. (2003), 'Pricing, investment and the financing of production within the framework of the monetary circuit: some preliminary evidence', in Rochon, L.-P. and S. Rossi (eds), *Modern Theories of Money*, Cheltenham, UK and Northampton, MA, US: Edward Elgar, 173–97.
Setterfield, M. (ed.) (2002), *The Economics of Demand-led Growth. Challenging the Supply-side Vision of the Long Run*, Cheltenham, UK and Northampton, MA, US: Edward Elgar.
Setterfield, M. (2004), 'Central banking, stability and macroeconomic outcomes: a comparison of New Consensus and Post-Keynesian monetary macroeconomics', in Lavoie, M. and M. Seccareccia (eds), *Central Banking in the Modern World. Alternative Perspectives*, Cheltenham, UK and Northampton, MA, US: Edward Elgar, 35–56.
Snowdon, B. and H. Vane (2005), *Modern Macroeconomics: Its Origins, Development and Current State*, Cheltenham, UK and Northampton, MA, US: Edward Elgar.
Steindl, J. (1952) [1976], *Maturity and Stagnation in American Capitalism*, 2nd edition, New York, London: Monthly Review Press.
Steindl, J. (1981), 'Some comments on the three versions of Kalecki's theory of the trade cycle', in Lois, J. (ed.), *Studies in Economic Theory and Practice*, Amsterdam: Elsevier, 125–33.
Stiglitz, J. (1997), 'Reflections on the natural rate hypothesis', *Journal of Economic Perspectives*, **11** (1), 3–10.
Stockhammer, E. (2004), 'Is there an equilibrium rate of unemployment in the long run?' *Review of Political Economy*, **16** (1), 59–77.
Taylor, J.B. (2000), 'Teaching modern macroeconomics at the principles level', *American Economic Review*, **90** (2), 90–4.
Taylor, L. (1985), 'A stagnationist model of economic growth', *Cambridge Journal of Economics*, **9** (4), 383–403.
Taylor, L. (2004), *Reconstructing Macroeconomics. Structuralists Proposals and Critiques of the Mainstream*, Cambridge, MA, London: Harvard University Press.
Walsh, C.E. (2002), 'Teaching inflation targeting: an analysis for intermediate macro', *Journal of Economic Education*, **33** (4), 333–46.

2. Price and wage determination and the inflation barrier: moving beyond the Phillips curve

Philip Arestis and Malcolm Sawyer

INTRODUCTION

The Phillips curve relationship continues to play a key role in macroeconomic analysis, and this is evidenced by its central position in the recent literature of the New Consensus Macroeconomics (NCM).[1] In the simplest representation of the NCM the Phillips curve is one of the three key equations (in this case the Phillips curve is generally represented in terms of price inflation depending on expected inflation and deviations of output from trend). In this chapter we use the term 'Phillips curve' to signify a single-equation relationship between some measure of inflation (price or wage) as a function of expected inflation and some measure of economic activity.

At least implicitly, notions of the Phillips curve underlie the orthodox approach to monetary policy in two senses. First, the use of interest rates to target inflation draws on the linkage:

interest rate → aggregate demand → economic activity → inflation

and the Phillips curve is the final link in that chain. The sole use of monetary policy in the form of interest rates to target the rate of inflation would be difficult to justify without that final link in the chain (and it also requires the assumption that interest rates do have a significant impact on aggregate demand, on which see Arestis and Sawyer, 2004a, 2004b). Second, the notion of the trade-off between inflation and unemployment has been used to argue the case for independence of central banks on the grounds that politicians are tempted to stimulate the economy to reduce unemployment without regard for the longer-term inflationary consequences. Further, the supply-side equilibrium is portrayed as unaffected by the path of demand and as a position towards which the economy moves; the classical dichotomy is embedded which enables the argument to be put for the focus of monetary policy on inflation without regard to longer-term effects on the level of economic activity.

In this chapter we build on previous work we have undertaken, and one which was intended as a critique of the Phillips curve by advancing a positive alternative in terms of a perspective on inflation. This approach draws on some of our previous work (notably Arestis and Sawyer, 2005) as well as work of authors such as Layard, Nickell and Jackman (1991). The simple argument of this chapter is that an approach to inflation based on wage and price determination provides a different perspective, and specifically that the rate of change rather than the level of economic activity plays a role, that the level of economic activity has an impact through influence on desired or target real wage (or equivalent profit share), and that any inflation barrier arises outside of the labour market. Further, the role of investment is crucial in first determining the change in capacity and then the position of any inflation barrier which is seen as subject to continuous change.

AN ALTERNATIVE APPROACH

We discuss in this section an alternative approach based on Arestis and Sawyer (2005, 2007a). We begin by a discussion of the Phillips curve and its perceived weaknesses, before developing a price and wage determination model, which we see as superior to the Phillips curve approach.

The Phillips Curve

In Arestis and Sawyer (2007a) we discussed the theoretical foundations of the Phillips curve. We noted in that paper that the Phillips curve has been variously defined and given different theoretical foundations, but there was a general notion of a relationship between some measure of inflation (whether in prices or wages) to some measure of the level of economic activity (for example, output relative to trend, unemployment) and some relevant set of inflationary expectations. In that paper, we argued that there is little theoretical justification for the Phillips curve (as defined above). One starting point for this argument is the view that economic relationships are generally specified in terms of level of variable upon level of variable and, specifically in microeconomics, these relationships generally involve level of (relative) prices and level of demand (or supply). Indeed, we will argue below that there are significant macroeconomic relationships involving prices and wages, which are expressed in level form. That simple observation would seem to provide a case for investigating whether there is something different in macroeconomic terms for looking at the rate of change of prices on the level of economic activity. In one sense it could be said that the pace of inflation is a level variable (of inflation) and that inflation is much more a matter of concern than the price level. But that does not directly answer the question as to the justification of inflation as related to the level of economic activity. In Arestis and Sawyer (2007a) it was argued that the justification for the Phillips curve (whether in terms of wage change or of price change) arising from viewing inflation as price adjustment in the face of excess demand did not provide a solid theoretical basis for the Phillips curve, specifically that the mapping from excess demand to an observable variable (for example, unemployment, output gap) was unsafe. Further, we argued that the more recent New Keynesian Phillips curve was also flawed on the grounds that it relied on the assumption of rising marginal costs for which the empirical evidence is weak, and on sluggish price adjustment, with no mention of wage determination. In both cases, it can be argued that the theoretical derivation of the Phillips curve is flawed.

Two related issues concerning the usual specification of the Phillips curve are that the rate of change of economic activity is not included as impacting on the rate of inflation, and that there is no form of 'catch-up' or error correction mechanism. The latter feature is a notable one when so much econometric attention is given to error correction mechanisms, and in a situation where it could be expected that the level of wages and of prices were co-integrated.

The Phillips curve is generally used as a reduced-form equation in which the underlying inflation mechanisms are not spelt out clearly. This, in part, can be related to the point made above on the lack of theoretical justification. Further the Phillips curve (in its expectations-augmented mode with unit coefficient on expected inflation) contains an equilibrium level of economic activity, and for policy purposes insights into the nature and determinants of that equilibrium level of economic activity are important.

The Phillips curve has two features which attract our attention. First, it relates the rate of inflation to the level of economic activity, and through the inclusion of expected inflation this translates into an 'accelerationist' relationship between the change in inflation (that is, acceleration in the price level) and the level of economic activity. Second, there is an implied 'supply-side equilibrium' such as the 'natural rate of unemployment'. In its reduced-form representation, the nature and determinants of this supply-side equilibrium are left unstated. In order for the 'supply-side' equilibrium to operate as a determinant of the actual level of economic activity, there has to be some (at least implied) adjustment process, which leads the economy to the supply-side equilibrium. In other words, there has to be some mechanism by which the level of aggregate demand adjusts to support this supply-side equilibrium. We argue in section 2.5 below that the adjustment processes which are generally proposed do not operate.

The Alternative Approach

In Arestis and Sawyer (2005), we set out what we described as a structuralist approach to inflation, and we draw on that model to suggest an alternative view. The approach to inflation has to be more sophisticated than that indicated by the reduced-form Phillips curve, and the links between the economic activity and inflation much more complex than suggested in the Phillips curve.

One general notion which underlies this approach is that we may theorize about the nature of the relationship between the price-wage ratio (or equivalently the wage–price ratio) and the level of economic activity (rather than the change in price and the level of economic activity). The second notion is that the determination of wages and prices should be set out with sufficient 'structural' detail to provide clear indications of the determinants of any 'supply-side equilibrium' (though we prefer to regard any such position in terms of being an inflation barrier). The third is that the adjustment process, which does (or does not) guide the economy to the supply-side equilibrium, should be clearly stated and evaluated.

The basis of that approach involves the following.

Wage determination

An underlying positive relationship between real wages and the rate of employment is reflected in a wage equation of the general form (cf. Blanchflower and Oswald, 1994):

$$w - p = \mathrm{H(E)} = \mathrm{h(U)} \qquad (2.1)$$

where p is log of price level, w log of wage level, E employment rate and U unemployment rate. This equation can be derived from a range of models, for example, efficiency wages (Shapiro and Stiglitz, 1984), union bargaining models (Layard et al. 1991, chapter 2), target real wage bargaining (Sawyer, 1982, 2002). This equation clearly has the feature that it relates level of real wages with level of (un)employment. A significant feature of an equation such as (2.1) is that the relationship between real wage and employment is positive.

From this equation an adjustment process can be postulated of the general form where money wages are the adjustment variable in the context of wage determination. Hence change in money wages depends on expected change in prices and an adjustment element depending on the difference between actual and 'desired' real wage from the wage equation, and hence:

$$\dot{w} - \dot{p}^{e} = \lambda\,[w(-1) - p(-1) - h(U)] \tag{2.2}$$

where $w(-1)$ and so on refers to one period lag on log wages, and the superscript e denotes expectations and λ the adjustment coefficient taken to be negative. This adjustment process embodies two elements: a move of actual real wage towards previous desired real wage, and accounting for the change in the desired real wage, which follows from the change in the level of unemployment.

An alternative formulation for the wage change equation would come from viewing wage changes as based on expected price changes (to maintain real wage), the change in the 'desired' real wage (which is given by $h'(U)dU/dt$) and a catch-up element. This would give:

$$\dot{w} = \dot{p}^{e} + h'(U)\frac{dU}{dt} + \lambda[w(-1) - p(-1) - h(U)] \tag{2.3}$$

This equation contains some obvious elements, but ones which are particularly relevant for the arguments below are the inclusion of the rate of change of a quantity (here the unemployment rate) and of an 'error correction' mechanism. Further it can be noted that the level of unemployment rate enters (with a negative sign) in this equation so that it could be said that there is a partial Phillips curve relationship. However, it has to be noted that this role of unemployment comes via the effect of unemployment (and employment) on the 'desired' real wage.

Price determination

There are numerous formulations of the relationship between output price relative to input price and the level of output. Models of monopoly, oligopoly, imperfect competition and mark-up pricing all point in that direction (cf. Sawyer, 1983). The precise form of the relationship will differ, and indeed some mark-up pricing models would stress the constancy of the mark-up of price over costs with respect to the level of output. Here we use a general specification whereby the relationship between output price (relative to input prices) and the level of output is treated as non-linear (approximately quadratic) whereby price initially declines as output increases but later price increases with output. This reflects a combination of an underlying (traditional) U-shaped cost curve and the dependence of the price–cost margin on the level of economic activity. There are obviously issues of aggregation involved here. For simplicity a closed economy is assumed for the present, and hence at the aggregate level wages are the only costs. We postulate a relationship of the form:

$$p - w = j(q) \tag{2.4}$$

where q is a measure of output relative to some notion of capacity output. The relationship between unit labour costs and output (relative to capacity), also that between the desired mark-up of price over wages and output (relative to capacity) may be non-monotonic. In the first case, unit labour costs may initially fall as output increases, and then rise. In the second case, there has been some debate over how the mark-up may vary (and in a profit maximizing case how the elasticity of demand changes as the demand curve facing firms shifts).

From a price equation of the form given above, again an adjustment equation can be postulated of the general form:

$$\dot{p} = \dot{w}^{e} + \psi((p(\text{-}1) - w(\text{-}1) - j(q)) \tag{2.5}$$

Alternatively as before:

$$\dot{p} = \dot{w}^{e} + j'(q)\frac{dq}{dt} + \chi((p(\text{-}1) - w(\text{-}1) - j(q-1)) \tag{2.6}$$

Interaction of price and wage determination

From $w - p = H(E)$ and $p - w = j(q)$, with an assumed mapping between employment rate E and output relative to capacity q, these provide equations from which $w - p$ and E and q can be solved. The mapping between E and q will change over time as, for example, the total capacity changes through investment. There is no presumption here that the level of employment corresponding to $q = 0$ (that is, output at capacity or trend level) is full employment or any other desired level of employment.

These two notions can be combined into Figure 2.1 by taking the simple case where labour is the only cost of production and there is a mapping between output and employment. No particular significance should be given to the precise position of the intersection between the two curves, or to the focus on a unique equilibrium position (for further discussion on this see Sawyer, 2002).

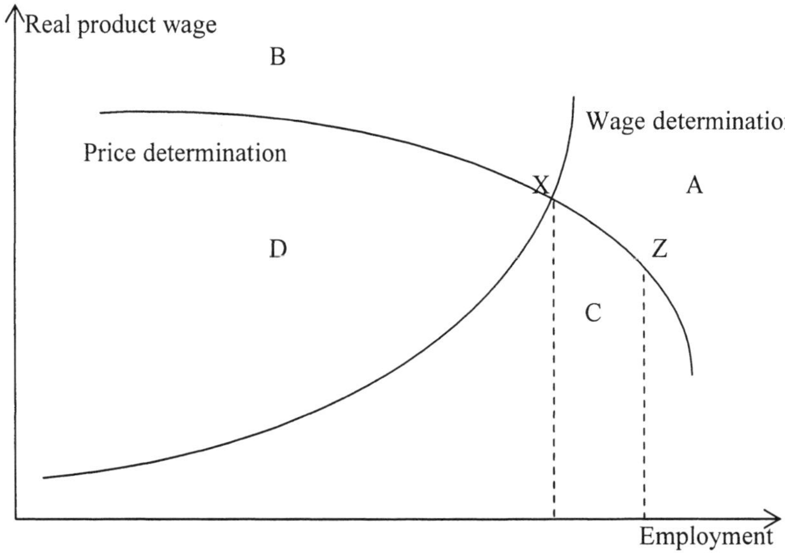

Figure 2.1 Interaction of price and wage determination

In contrast to the Phillips curve approach (and reflecting a point made above) here the relationships are between levels – level of real wages and level of employment. The intersection point is a form of NAIRU in the sense that at that point since the ratio of wages to prices is constant, prices and wages would rise at the same rate with no tendency for inflation to rise.

The pace of inflation may well depend on the speed of the adjustment process in the sense that if wages respond quickly to prices, and vice versa, then a more rapid increase in the inflationary situation would arise (as compared with slow responses in each case).

This approach (unlike the simple Phillips curves) involves both wage and price determination in the inflationary process. It is in effect the presence of the determination of both wages and prices which generates inflation. For example, consider Figure 2.1 without the wage determination curve, and the economy at point Z. Output would be above capacity output, but the real product wage would be that desired by enterprises, given the level of output. Prices and wages would be rising in line, and there would be no pressures to raise (or lower) prices relative to wages and no pressure for inflation to rise.

We have argued (Arestis and Sawyer, 2005; Sawyer, 1995) that in order to map out a relationship between price (and costs) and output, there has to be some variation in exogenous variables, for simply from firms' decision-making perspective for a given set of exogenous variables there would be a single price chosen and a single level of output. We argued that the obvious approach to use in the context of macroeconomic analysis was the inclusion of the level of aggregate demand in the demand curve facing each firm, and allow shifts in aggregate demand to be the required change in the exogenous variables. For a given level of aggregate demand, a firm (and then by aggregation) would choose a level of output (and thereby level of employment) and a price (and thereby real product wage) which served its interests (for example, maximized profits). As the level of aggregate demand is conceptually varied, a locus of points (as described by the price determination curve in Figure 2.1) would be mapped out. The price determination curve cannot be understood without reference to a movement in a variable treated as exogenous to the firm (and we choose the level of aggregate demand).

In terms of the determination of supply-side equilibrium (that is point X in Figure 2.1), we have argued elsewhere (Sawyer, 2002; Arestis and Sawyer 2005) that the position of the price determination curve is dependent on the investment decisions which firms make and so on. It is a simple proposition that the supply capability of firms depends on their capital stock. The price determination curve is the flip side of the (aggregated) cost curves of firms (along with the relationship of the price–cost margin with output) and the position of the cost curves depends on the size of the capital stock. As investment proceeds, the capital stock changes, and the supply-side equilibrium changes.

The supply-side equilibrium position, which is always on the move, is unlikely to be a 'strong attractor' for the actual level of employment (economic activity). There is no strong reason to think that the level of aggregate demand will be compatible with that supply-side equilibrium position. The 'automatic' adjustments of the real balance effect are here denied, and interest rate manipulation by the central bank not potent enough to secure aggregate demand in line with the supply-side equilibrium, as discussed further below.

There are three aspects of this approach, which we now highlight. First, the level of economic activity does not have a direct impact on the rate of inflation, but rather an indirect one coming from the effect of the level of economic activity on the target or desired price–wage ratio. For example, from consideration of the efficiency wage, for a given level of employment, there is a real wage which can be set in the overall interests of the firms (taking into account the effects of wages on work effort and productivity). In respect of wage determination, a higher level of employment would be associated with a higher wage–price ratio. Indeed, whether or not it was associated with a higher rate of wage inflation (relative to price inflation) would depend on whether the wage–price ratio was above or below the wage determination curve. If the wageprice ratio fell on the wage determination curve, then wage inflation would equal price inflation.

Second, the approach which we have sketched here can be interpreted to some degree in a Phillips curve setting. For example, if employment is above point X and the economy is in zone A then wage and price inflation would be tending to rise; conversely if employment is below point X and the economy is in zone D, the wage and price inflation would be tending to fall. Employment may be above point X but inflation need not tend to rise: if the economy were in zones B or C, then inflation would not tend to rise (in zone B real wage would be tending to fall as wages rise less quickly than prices, and in zone C tending to rise as prices rise less quickly than wages). As indicated in the equations above the inflationary mechanism comes from a difference between a target and a desired (optimal) outcome. The desired outcome may itself be dependent on the level of economic activity, as indeed is reflected in the price determination and wage determination curves in Figure 2.1. But the equations given above indicate that wage (price) inflation is seen to depend on expected price (wage) inflation, the change in employment (output), and the adjustment process. We can of course note that in zones B and C, a high level of economic activity is not necessarily associated with rising inflation. In zone A, the underlying cause of rising inflation could be seen as an inherent conflict over income shares, represented here as differences over the desired pricewage ratio. In the absence of that conflict (for example, if the wage determination and price determination lines coincided), there would be no effect of the level of economic activity on inflation.

Third, it is the change in economic activity that is viewed to have an effect on inflation. We can first note that, in respect of price changes, the effect of a change in economic activity may be positive or negative. The sign of the relationship would depend on the way in which unit costs and the mark-up of price over costs varies with the level of output. This suggests that the speed of changes in economic activity may have significant impacts on the rate of inflation. Further, since firms are often observed to operate where unit costs are declining or constant with respect to output, increases in the level of economic activity could serve to restrain or reduce the pace of inflation.

THE NATURE OF THE INFLATION BARRIER

A major reason for seeking to approach inflation through a rather less reduced-form approach than the simple Philips curve was to enable some more attention to be given to the nature of the inflationary process, and for particular significance for this section to the nature of a 'supply-side equilibrium'. A point such as X in Figure 2.1 has some attributes of being such a supply-side equilibrium. However, an equilibrium position brings the connotation that there is a process which pushes the economy towards the equilibrium. In the next section we argue that there is not a point such as X that is a 'strong attractor' (or even a 'weak attractor') for the level of economic activity. Further, although away from point X wages and prices are changing, and hence the pricewage ratio is also changing, that does not imply that the ratio is moving towards point X.

We would then view a point such as X as more akin to an inflation barrier, with no implication that the economy will tend towards that point. A diagram such as Figure 2.1 is intended to indicate what is predicted to happen to wage and price inflation, rather than express the view that X constitutes a 'strong attractor' or equilibrium position.

There are two features of Figure 2.1 and the inflation barrier X to which we point. First, although the axes are labelled 'real wage' and 'employment', there should be no implication that this represents in any way a 'labour market'. Figure 2.1 is presented to indicate where real wages and employment based on price determination and wage determination notions may be consistent. The price determination curve cannot provide a 'demand for labour curve'. The price-wage ratio depends on decisions which firms make on prices, and the employment decision arises from the level of aggregate demand.[2] The wage determination curve reflects firms' wage decisions, when account is taken of the effects of wages on work effort and productivity. In no way can it be thought of as a 'supply of labour curve'.

Thus, any notion that, if the point X in Figure 2.1 corresponds to an unfavourable level of economic activity – that is, one involving significant levels of unemployment – then the policy measures relate to making the labour market more 'flexible' is not tenable.

Second, it could be anticipated that the inflation barrier (point X) is always on the move. A major reason for this comes from consideration of the price determination curve and also the relationship between output and employment. Sawyer (2002) shows how costs, and thereby price determination, depends on the general level of productive capacity. It is shown there that new productive capacity will shift the equivalent of the price determination curve. The output produced and the employment offered in total by the enterprises depends on the amount of capacity which the enterprises have. Thus, the position of the price determination curve in Figure 2.1 depends on the amount of productive capacity. An increase in the capital stock, which represents an increase in the capital-intensity of production, will raise labour productivity and shift the price determination curve downwards. Output is a function of the capital stock, employment and material inputs. An increase in the capital stock raises the productivity of labour, reduces unit costs and thereby shifts the price determination curve. Investment is an addition to the capital stock, and clearly investment is always occurring (at different rates) and additions are being made to the capital stock (the term 'additions' will be used but it is noted that the capital stock may be diminishing through depreciation which is not covered by gross investment).

The implications of the simple observation that investment serves to shift the equivalent of the price determination curve rest on the way in which the determinants of investment are viewed. The approach (following authors such as Kalecki) here is to view investment decisions as influenced by factors such as capacity utilization and changes in utilization, and profitability (influencing both the incentive to invest and the availability of internal funds). It may be added that the execution of those investment decisions rests on sufficient finance being forthcoming from the banking system. The approach leads to two implications. First, investment (and thereby additions to the capital stock) is path dependent. There is no notion of a pre-existing optimal capital stock depending on relative prices towards which adjustment is made through investment. It is rather that the 'long run is a collection of short runs'. Second, investment depends on the level of economic activity. Hence when economic activity is high, investment is relatively high and more additions are being made to the capital stock.

(NON-)ADJUSTMENT PROCESSES

When the Phillips curve is used, it is generally assumed that the 'supply-side equilibrium' embedded in that curve (for example, the 'natural rate of unemployment') is a strong attractor for the actual level of economic activity. The implicit assumption is then made that the level of demand will adjust to the supply-side equilibrium. Two mechanisms have been invoked. The first, which is present in Friedman (1968), is a real wage adjustment to excess demand/supply in the labour market. His approach to the Phillips curve is to express it as a real wage adjustment process, and hence that the real wage guides the labour market to the 'natural rate of unemployment'. The second, which has been much more widely used, is the real money effect, that is, given a nominal money stock the price level will change (rise when demand is high, fall when demand is low), thereby shifting the *LM* curve and perhaps via the real balance effect the *IS* curve. In the New Keynesian approach, the level of demand is often represented by the real money stock, and hence again adjustment can take place through changes in that real money stock, albeit in the New Keynesian case prices adjust sluggishly and hence the changes in the real money stock take some time.

However, those mechanisms do not in practice operate. The movement in real wages is the outcome of two separate processes, namely the movement in prices and the movement in wages. However it can be seen, by reference to Figure 2.1, that at a given level of output (and hence of aggregate demand) real wages may rise or fall. The movement in real wages would depend on the initial starting point for real wages and the relative strengths of the movements in prices and wages. The movement in real wages would have some effect on the profit margin and hence on the level of aggregate demand. From these considerations there is no clear direction in which income distribution would change (that is, wage share might rise or it might fall). Even if income distribution changed in the 'right' direction, that is when demand is relatively high, profit share rises, thereby reducing the level of demand; there is no reason to think that the changes would lead demand to a level consistent with the supply-side equilibrium.

The operation of the real money stock effect is based on the assumption of exogenous money which constitutes net worth. But money is clearly now endogenous, and credit money created by the banking system does not constitute net worth. Money is created through the loan creation process, with the actual stock of money tending to the level determined by the demand for money. A change in the price level does not have any real balance effect since net worth of money is zero. It is then clear that there is a lack of automatic 'market' forces, which serve to bring demand into line with supply. Say's Law does not operate over any length of time. How then do the demand side and the supply side relate to one another?

In terms of Figure 2.1, if the economy were operating in zone A, then inflation would tend to rise. Whether real wages would rise or fall would depend on the relative strengths of the wage adjustment and the price adjustment processes. Would there be any mechanism by which the level of economic activity would then tend to fall towards point X? We could consider this under two headings. First, do the price and wage changes have any effect? There are two elements involved. The first element is that real wage is changing, but the direction of change is ambiguous. If prices were rising faster than wages, the profit share would be rising, and this may have a dampening effect on the level of demand (depending, as above, on certain conditions). Conversely, if wages were rising faster than prices, then real wages would be rising, and this may tend to raise the level of demand. The second element is that inflation is rising. One effect of that would be to lower the real rate of interest, thereby tending to raise demand. Insofar as rising inflation has a negative effect on confidence and so on, there may be forces which tend to lower demand (but this is not something which is clear from the model presented above).

Second, there may be policy responses. The only such attitude which is currently most frequently discussed would be the monetary policy response in a regime where the (often independent) central bank is given the objective of achieving a target rate of inflation with interest rate as the policy instrument. This raises the issue of the significance of economic policy, which we turn our attention to discussing next.

SIGNIFICANCE FOR ECONOMIC POLICY

The approach to inflation which has just been outlined has several points of significance for economic policy:

- Insofar as there is a 'supply-side equilibrium', which is akin to an inflation barrier, then a prime determinant of the position of that barrier will be the level of productive capacity in the economy. As can be seen by reference to Figure 2.1, the claims on real wages arising from wage determination are also important. However, the position of the inflation barrier cannot in a simple sense be ascribed to the nature and working of the labour market.

- The use of deflationary measures to address the issue of inflation rests on the view that a lower level of economic activity will lead to a reduction in the rate of inflation. The approach outlined above suggests that the relationship between the level of economic activity and the pace of inflation is not as straightforward as indicated by the Phillips curve. Further, there is a range of causes of inflation in addition to any which are associated with the level of demand. We have not explored this above, but we would argue that, for example, increases in world commodity prices would lead to domestic inflation upswings.
- The use of deflationary measures (for example, raising interest rates) to address inflation may have longer-term adverse consequences. Insofar as the deflationary measures impact on investment, then future productive capacity will be that much reduced (and in terms of Figure 2.1 the price determination curve is a more adverse position). Specifically in the context of monetary policy, interest rate changes have an effect through those components of demand which are sensitive to monetary conditions, whether in the form of price effects (interest rate) or quantity effects (credit rationing). Investment is, of course, a major form of demand which falls into that category.
- Following on from that point, the complex relationship between the level of economic activity and inflation undermines simple notions such as that a higher level of economic activity now leads to future inflation. It may be that a lower level of economic activity now leads to lower future economic activity and a worsening inflation position. It was, though, the former notion (as reflected in the Phillips curve), which lies behind much of the argument with regard to problems of time inconsistency. It also lies behind much of the argument for independence of central banks, which are presumed to be less likely than politicians to engage in short-run stimulation of the economy which is perceived to have longer-term inflationary consequences.
- The supply-side equilibrium (inflation barrier as point X in Figure 2.1) does not have any connotation of being an optimal position. In general, it would not correspond to either full employment or full capacity utilization. Thus, the notion of using the supply-side equilibrium as some idea of an optimal position (as in, for example, the optimizing approach to monetary policy, Svensson, 2003) does not carry through.

CONCLUSION

In this chapter we have argued for the replacement of a Phillips curve approach to inflation by an alternative structuralist view based on the interaction of price and wage determination. The latter approach generates a more complex relationship between inflation and economic activity as compared with the Phillips curve, and we have discussed the implications of that specifically for the conduct of monetary policy. But more significantly the latter approach focuses on the role of productive capacity in the determination of an inflation barrier and the weak forces which would lead the economy to the inflation barrier.

NOTES

1. We have dealt with the nature of the NCM approach in separate papers (see, for example, Arestis, 2007; Arestis and Sawyer, 2007b) and in a book (Arestis and Sawyer, 2004a).
2. For a particular set of aggregate demand and cost conditions facing the enterprise, a particular price (hence real product wage equal to wage divided by price) and a particular level of output (and hence level of employment to produce that output) will be chosen by the enterprise. As the level of aggregate demand varies, so will the amount of output produced and employment offered. As output varies, the costs of production may change, so that at low levels of output, unit costs may well fall as output increases, though at high levels of output it could be expected that unit costs begin to rise.

REFERENCES

Arestis, P. (2007), 'What is the new consensus in macroeconomics?' in P. Arestis (ed.), *Is There a New Consensus in Macroeconomics?* Basingstoke: Palgrave.

Arestis, P. and M. Sawyer (2004a), *Re-examining Monetary and Fiscal Policy for the 21st Century*, Aldershot, UK: Edward Elgar.

Arestis, P. and M. Sawyer (2004b), 'Can monetary policy affect the real economy?' *European Review of Economics and Finance*, **3** (3), 9–32.

Arestis, P. and M. Sawyer (2005), 'Aggregate demand, conflict and capacity in the inflationary process', *Cambridge Journal of Economics*, **29** (6), 959–74.

Arestis, P. and M. Sawyer (2007a), 'The weak theoretical foundations of the Phillips curve', mimeo.

Arestis, P. and M. Sawyer (2007b), 'A critical reconsideration of the foundations of monetary policy in the new consensus macroeconomics framework', mimeo.

Blanchflower, D.G. and A.J. Oswald (1994), *The Wage Curve*, Cambridge, MA: MIT Press.

Layard, R. S. Nickell, and R. Jackman (1991), *Unemployment: Macroeconomic Performance and the Labour Market*, Oxford: Oxford University Press.
Phillips, A.W. (1958), 'The relation between unemployment and the rate of change of money wages in the United Kingdom', *Economica*, **25**, 283–89.
Sawyer, M. (1982), 'Collective bargaining, oligopoly and macro-economics', *Oxford Economic Papers*, **34**, 428–48.
Sawyer, M. (1983), *Business Pricing and Inflation*, London: Macmillan.
Sawyer, M. (1995), *Unemployment, Imperfect Competition and Macroeconomics: Essays in the Post Keynesian Tradition*, Aldershot UK and Brookfield, US: Edward Elgar.
Sawyer, M. (2002), 'The NAIRU, aggregate demand and investment', *Metroeconomica*, **53** (1), 66–94
Shapiro, C. and J. Stiglitz (1984), 'Equilibrium unemployment as a worker discipline device', *American Economic Review*, **74** (3), 433–44.
Svensson, L.E.O. (2003), 'What is wrong with Taylor Rules? Using judgement in monetary policy through targeting rules', *Journal of Economic Literature*, **41** (2), 426–77.

3. Central bank governance, the euthanasia of the rentier and interest rate policy: a note on post-Keynesian monetary policy after Taylor

Louis-Philippe Rochon[1]

INTRODUCTION

In the last two decades, central banks have attained a level of prominence rarely seen of any public institution. Indeed, this policy or institutional prominence followed a period of relatively high inflation rates, which renewed concern over inflation and its possible implications for economic outcomes. At the root of this rise in inflation, some economists believe, are the large fiscal deficits of the previous decades, creating the illusion that fiscal deficits and inflation were correlated. This led to scepticism and suspicion over the usefulness of fiscal policy in controlling output.

In light of this phenomenon, we have witnessed a dramatic policy switch away from fiscal policy and towards monetary policy, where central banks have been given the (quasi) exclusive policy rights to combat rising inflation and regulate the economy: fiscal policy has been downgraded and seen as monetary policy's poor cousin.

This modern policy switch is exemplified in the latest incarnation of mainstream economics, under the guises of the New Consensus. Indeed, as advocates of Taylor Rules and inflation targeting will admit, central banks are given a prominent role in these models, to the detriment of fiscal policy. In fact, it is specifically stated that 'fiscal dominance' should be avoided at all costs. As Debelle et al. (1998, p. 2) summarize: 'if fiscal dominance exists, inflationary pressures of a fiscal origin will undermine the effectiveness of monetary policy by obliging the central bank to accommodate the demands of the government, say, by easing interest rates to achieve fiscal goals'. By adhering moreover to an inflation target, advocates believe this will inevitably force 'fiscal policy to align with monetary policy' (Mishkin, 2000, p. 2).

There are three underlying notions at play here. First, there is the idea that inflation is always caused by excess demand; second, fiscal deficits lead to inflationary pressures through artificially increasing demand or by monetizing the public debt. Public sector borrowing from the central bank should therefore remain low or non-existent. Fiscal policy therefore should never be allowed to dictate monetary policy. Proponents of inflation targeting and other mainstream economists therefore insist on disciplined fiscal policy and balanced budgets (at least over the whole business cycle). Third, inflation is the only legitimate concern: other variables are not deemed 'economic' variables. For instance, unemployment is rarely mentioned as a legitimate policy goal; it is considered a social problem to be fixed by changing generous social programmes.

In accordance with this philosophy, price stability or inflation targeting is increasingly the central bank's sole objective in many countries – or what Meyer (2001, p. 1) dubs the 'hierarchical principle', with inflation at the top of the hierarchy. In fact, this goal is so important that central banks are required to be independent, that is, out of the reach of the political class, and their actions closely monitored. Hence, a clear mandate on how central banks ought to conduct themselves, as well as a framework within which they can outline their strategy for attaining their objective, is of paramount importance. As a result, an entire literature over their behaviour has developed in recent years in economic circles, but also in the legal and political science circles, emphasizing in particular their governance.

But the discussion over governance cannot be made without referring to the objective of the central bank. This is especially the case within neoclassical theory: 'The conduct of monetary policy forms the primary task of a central bank. Hence, institutional arrangements ensuring good governance must first and foremost relate to this function' (Amtenbrink, 2004, p. 9). Yet, for neoclassical economists, governance has become synonymous with free-market ideology. It is often discussed alongside notions of efficiency and minimal government intervention.

However, the concept of governance in itself is not ideological. While it is undeniably a central theme of neoclassical and otherwise mainstream economic theory and policy, the notion of governance simply sets out rules of behaviour that institutions and firms ought to adopt to govern themselves. As such, it is not governance in itself that we should fear. Rather, it is the combination of governance and free-market policies. In the case of central banks specifically, the combination of independence and inflation targeting make for a particularly dangerous mix. It is therefore the use neoclassical economists make of the concept that attracts wide criticism from heterodox economists and other critics.

At the root of neoclassical economics, as stated above, is an unshaken belief that inflation is always a monetary phenomenon, or at least demand-driven, and as such, only central banks can fight it. It therefore stands to reason, neoclassical economists claim, that central banks ought to be given all the necessary tools. Yet, two arguments should be made at this stage. First, nowhere does it state that central bank independence, accountability and transparency – the so-called pillars of good governance – must be associated with inflation control or targeting. Second, this literature rests on the demand-determined nature of prices: 'The problem is that both the monetary targeting and inflation targeting regimes are based on a demand explanation of inflation that blames overexpansion of money and credit for inflation' (Lim, 2006, p. 1). Yet, what if this is not the case? What if prices are determined according to another process altogether? This carries obvious implications for monetary policy and its governance.

In light of these arguments, the objective of this chapter is to show that it is possible to develop a post-Keynesian or heterodox alternative to central bank governance. And while this topic is a very wide one, I wish to specifically address but a minuscule component of it. In particular, I wish to address central bank monetary policy within the confines of good governance. This objective requires a careful understanding of the causes of inflation and how the role played by both fiscal and monetary policies.

The chapter is divided into the following four sections. Section two briefly discusses the rise of inflation targeting and Taylor Rules in the last decade, and the importance of implementing good central bank governance. Section three takes a more critical look at these arguments and at inflation targeting in particular. In a sense, two important questions must be asked. First, what are the causes of inflation? Second, how can central banks, through their institutional infrastructure, affect the inflation rate and, de facto, achieve their inflation target? These questions are fundamental and intrinsically tied to central bank governance. In this section, contrary to the dominant view of inflation, it is argued that inflation is determined primarily by costs of production and conflict over the proper distribution of income among the social classes. If this view is correct, then central bank policy is at best misguided and a new approach is required. Section four presents a post-Keynesian monetary policy, in the spirit of

Keynes. Indeed, resting on Keynes's 'euthanasia of the rentier', it calls for the elimination of 'monetary policy dominance' (Rochon and Setterfield, 2007) and for a 'reswitching' away from monetary policy back to fiscal policy. The emphasis is placed on a policy of low real interest rates as well as the role of the central banks as clearing house in a multi-bank sector and minimizing systemic risk. Good governance is refined at the very least as behaving according to the real world, and not according to a fictitious view of the world. Section five concludes.

INFLATION TARGETING, TRANSPARENCY, ACCOUNTABILITY, INDEPENDENCE AND ALL THAT

The short history of central banking, both in economic theory and in practice, can be summarized as variations on a single and familiar theme. Indeed, in the last several decades, central banks have been primarily interested in some sort of price stability. The policy instrument or intermediate target used to achieve this goal may have changed over the years, but the overall objective or final target has remained the same. The emphasis on price stability – price-level or inflation targets – relies on traditional mainstream arguments that inflation:

- makes it more difficult for agents, firms and households to identify changes in relative prices of goods and services, given that they are obscured by fluctuations in the general price level. In turn, this can lead to ill-informed and incorrect production and consumption decisions, and to the non-efficient allocation of scarce resources;
- leads to increased investment speculation; as a result, productive investment falls, largely because nominal interest rates are a component of an 'inflation risk premium' that compensates creditors for the risks associated with holding longer-term nominal assets;
- makes it more plausible that individuals and firms will divert resources away from productive uses to hedge against inflation, which hinders economic growth.
- breeds inflation, which then leads to higher inflation rates, encourages capital outflows, and can even create social and political instability since it is often the weakest social groups who suffer the most from inflation, since they have limited opportunities to hedge against it.

And while central banks may claim that they are also concerned about output and financial stability, it is clear that they believe these can only be reached once price stability has been achieved (Bernanke, Laubach, Mishkin and Posen, 1999); stated otherwise, price stability is the precondition for output and financial stability. Inflation is seen as immensely disruptive to markets and their allocative abilities. For this reason, inflation remains the central bank's primary – and in many cases its sole – objective.

In sum, we can identify the following three constants. First, central banks have always strived to achieve some degree of price stability; today, in many countries, inflation is the primary, if not only, objective of central banks. Second, inflation has always been explained through demand forces. As Lavoie (1996, p. 535) says: 'In mainstream economics, inflation is mainly an excess demand phenomenon, induced by an excess supply of money.' Finally, monetary policy has always been considered neutral in the long run. In this sense, while the pursuit of price stability may have some unfortunate costs in the short run (which 'sacrifice ratios' are intended to measure), in the long run, high interest rate policies are considered as having no long-run consequences.

The rise of the New Consensus (Taylor, 1993, 2000; Meyer, 2001; Romer, 2000) has changed very little, despite possible first appearances. The New Consensus comprises of two key features, each carrying important implications for macroeconomic policy. The first feature is an interest rate rule that emphasizes the exogenous nature of the short-run (real) interest rate (the Taylor Rule; see Taylor, 1993, 2000), while the second feature is an inflation-targeting policy where the central bank agrees to keep inflation at a given level or within a given range. In this sense, the central bank-controlled interest rate is the intermediate target while the inflation rate remains the final objective of monetary policy.

Since Taylor's (1993) original paper, interest rates rules are now firmly established in a number of central banks around the world, as are specific inflation targets, in one form or another.[2] Recognizing the exogenous nature of interest rates, central banks now tightly control nominal (and perhaps even real) interest rates in an effort to hit their monetary policy target.

As for inflation targeting, it has become a very fashionable policy in the last decade or so. Indeed, since the adoption of this policy by New Zealand in 1990 and Canada in 1991, a number of countries have now adopted it as an official policy of their central bank. Yet, interestingly enough, at the time New Zealand and Canada adopted inflation targeting, there was very little research on the topic. Indeed, I could find very little in terms of research papers undertaken at the time in major central banks or international institutions such as the World Bank and the International Monetary Fund (IMF). We can safely conclude that perhaps no other policy was adopted with such little theoretical and empirical research in support of it: 'In some respects, inflation targeting in the industrialized economies emerged in an ad hoc fashion. Economic theory in the early 1990s did not provide a definitive guide to the most suitable specification for an IT [inflation targeting] regime' (Paulin, 2006, p. 16).

Similarly, King (2002, p. 460) claims that the data from the inflation targeting experiment in the United Kingdom so far show that 'not only has inflation been lower since inflation targeting was introduced, but that, as measured by its standard deviation, it has also been more stable than in recent decades. Moreover, inflation has been less persistent – in the sense that shocks to inflation die away more quickly – under inflation targeting than for most of the past century.'

Fraga et al. (2004, p. 365) also maintain that 'the performance of inflation-targeting regimes around the world has been positive. Average inflation in both emerging markets and developed economies is substantially lower after the adoption of the inflation-targeting regime than immediately before its adoption', even though the authors observe that 'emerging market economies have had a relatively worse performance'.

In short, as Bernanke et al. (1999, p. 288) put it, 'one of the main benefits of inflation targets is that they may help to "lock in" earlier disinflationary gains, particularly in the face of one-time inflationary shocks ... In each case, the re-announcement of inflation targets helped to anchor the public's inflation expectations and to give an explicit plan for and direction to monetary policy'.

In this sense, the New Consensus is simply a continuation of the ideas advocated in recent years by proponents of the New Keynesian school and, in many respect, of the Neoclassical Synthesis Keynesians before them. In a sense, they are 'second-generation' New Keynesians. We can find in fact in the New Keynesian literature of the late 1980s and early 1990s glimpses of the current New Consensus views (see for instance Blinder, 1987; Bernanke and Blinder, 1992; for a review of these earlier New Keynesian views, see also Rochon, 1999). They continue the research begun by their first-generation counterparts by emphasizing the importance of the credit channel (balance sheet effect) in the monetary transmission mechanism, yet under interest rate targeting rather than money supply targeting. Yet, the 'second-generation' New Keynesians seem to have abandoned some key elements of the New Keynesian literature. Indeed, gone are all references to credit rationing and asymmetric information. These arguments have either been abandoned altogether in the New Consensus version, or they have yet to be integrated within a fully coherent model.

Despite abandoning the control of the growth of the money supply in favour of interest rate control, much remains the same. For instance, inflation is still considered a result of excessive demand. In fact, there is still a link between inflation and money creation. There may not be a direct causality between money and prices as in the monetarist approach, but the current analysis is quite similar to Wicksell's discussion of prices and money creation (see Rochon, 2005, for a discussion over the Wicksellian roots of the New Consensus). If the central bank rate is set below the natural rate of interest, for example, then bank loans will increase and contribute to the inflationary process. The transmission mechanism is through the banking system and its affect on money creation and demand: the growth in production and output is fuelled by bank loans. Inflation is 'always and everywhere' a demand phenomenon. It is the fundamental belief that money is caused by demand that makes the central bank the steward of inflation: the supposed impact of interest rates on investment and output, through the loans market.

To be fair, of course, New Consensus theory does account for supply shocks, although these are considered transitory in nature and tend to cancel each other out. In the end, they are not given much weight. As Blanchard (2005, p. 414) explains: 'Cost shocks are present, but their effect works through the natural level of output, and so through the output gap. Put another way, the output gap is a sufficient statistic for the effect of real activity on inflation.' Arestis and Sawyer (2003, p. 14) note this clearly: 'The position taken by IT on cost inflation is that it should either be accommodated, or that supply shocks come and go – and on average are zero and do not affect the rate of inflation.'

Supply shocks, however, are not the same as a supply, or cost-determined, theory of inflation, as advocated by post-Keynesians.[3] Hence, if inflation is primarily caused by costs (see Lavoie, 1992 for instance), then monetary policy based on a demand-determined approach, the primary goal of which is to fight inflation, may lead to bad monetary policy. If this is the case, then the obvious question is: what constitutes a good monetary policy? This question will be answered later in the chapter.

Central Bank Governance

For mainstream economists, the current low inflation rates enjoyed by many countries is attributed specifically to inflation targeting policies, but also to the adoption of a governance framework that has allowed central banks to pursue inflation targeting in an open, transparent fashion (see Arestis and Angeriz, 2006; and Rochon and Rossi, 2007, however, for a rejection of this claim).

In discussing governance, an important issue must be kept in mind: the objective of the central bank cannot be disassociated from its overall institutional make-up. A central bank will necessarily adopt regulations to facilitate its stewardship in order to reach its objectives better. Governance is therefore discussed in light of central banks' objective of price stability or inflation targeting. This is precisely what Mendis (2005, p. 1) suggests when he writes that:

> Strategic planning plays a very important role in assisting the central banks to effectively and efficiently utilise the limited resources at their disposal to achieve such objectives [price stability] and accomplish the given tasks. However, the successful implementation of strategic plan will mainly depend on the legal framework governing a central bank, which provides for its independence, accountability and transparency.

Similarly, Amtenbrink (2004, p. 1) claims that 'good central bank governance means that the objectives and tasks delegated to an institution are performed effectively and efficiently, thus avoiding misuse of resources, which is crucial for establishing a good track record'.

The ingrained belief that inflation is always and everywhere a demand phenomenon has led many economists to argue in favour of the exclusive role of the central bank in combating inflation. Since central banks are entrusted with this role, then they must be given proper authority to do so, and the proper institutional framework, which includes central bank independence, accountability and transparency. According to Ribeiro (2002, p. 3): 'Most economists agree that CBI [central bank independence] is desirable because it helps the long-term goal of price stability.'

Central bank independence – in terms of both political independence and goal independence – is seen as perhaps the most important key in fighting inflation. The need for an independent central bank arises because neoclassical economists believe that politicians would otherwise use the central bank to further their political interests to (reduce unemployment in times of elections, for instance), and lead inevitably to inflationary pressures. Independence is seen as a key policy feature to reduce – or in fact to eliminate – the time-inconsistency problem, that is, the pursuit of short-run improvements in output to the detriment of prices in the long run.

In fact, numerous studies have shown that there exists a correlation between the degree of central bank independence and inflation (for an extensive review of this literature, see Berger, De Haan and Eijffinger, 2000). As Amtenbrink (2004, p. 3) argues: 'by leaving it to the discretion of an independent central bank to conduct monetary policy, the focus can be on long-term stability rather than short-term monetary temptations'. Some economists even go so far as to argue that central banks should become a 'fourth branch of government, whose main purpose should be to continuously counter potentially damaging fiscal policy' (see Zilioli and Selmayr, 2000).

The arguments behind this reasoning are that central banks are sensitive to how they are perceived on international financial markets. In this sense, the increased attention toward the concepts of governance in recent years is directly related to the reputation of the central bank on international financial markets (reputation risk). There are 'good' and 'credible' central banks and there are 'bad' ones. Good central banks are those that can maintain low stable prices. Central banks want to be perceived as 'credible' and 'good' by international standards, by adopting official inflation targets. This, they argue, reduces interest rates in the long run.[4] Yet, the goal itself is no longer seen as sufficient, as central banks also want to be judged on their ability to meet those goals, by adopting rules of transparency and accountability. Hence independence, though necessary, is no longer sufficient. The fight against inflation is so important that central banks must be supervised. Hence, independence requires transparency and accountability so that they can be properly judged.

According to the rules of transparency and accountability, the public must be made aware of central bank operations with timely and accurate information. In this sense, central banks are encouraged to announce not only their inflation goals, but also provide information regarding the steps and policies they adopt to meet their objectives, reveal the responsibilities of their personnel, and make regular disclosures regarding the central banks' financial status, based on professional accounting practices. The aim is to give as much information to the public and market participants as possible to minimize any possible unwanted shocks. In a sense, transparency is a prerequisite of accountability.

Disclosure of performance (such as in annual reports), and, in some cases, clear mechanisms for removing officials for non-performance, are seen as key elements of transparency and accountability. Accordingly, Perry (2001, p. 34) claims that 'monetary and financial policies can be made more effective if the public understands the goals and instruments of policy and if the authorities take a credible commitment to meeting them. Secondly, good governance calls for central banks to be accountable to shareholders (which for central banks may be a diverse group), particularly where monetary authorities are granted a high degree of autonomy.' This is echoed by Amtenbrink (2004, p. 6) who argues that 'central banks have discovered transparency [i]s an ally both in meeting demands of more openness and accountability and in communicating monetary policy'. In 1999, the IMF argued that the central bank must operate within 'an environment in which the objectives of policy, its legal, institutional and economic framework, policy decisions and their rational, data and information related to monetary ... policies, and the terms of agencies accountability, are provided to the public on an understandable, accessible and timely basis'.

With accountability, of course, the public needs some sort of 'yardstick' by which they measure the central bank's operations. An inflation target is such a yardstick. By adopting an inflation target, it further imposes the necessity for independence, and reduces the possible conflicts between central banks and governments.

Good governance is important not just for fighting inflation, according to the mainstream, but also for minimizing risk. In the end, it all comes down to concern over the credibility of central banks, given that this then filters through to the reputation risk. Hence, central banks must be seen as credible on international financial markets. Policies that are not deemed credible are not considered optimal. This is why inflation targeting, along with good governance, are seen by many economists as a superior monetary policy. Wray (2004, p. 18) quotes from FOMC minutes from 1994 to make this point: 'I really think the System's anti-inflationary stance has done a great deal to increase our credibility in recent years' (attributed to Federal Governor J. Alfred Broaddus).

TRANSPARENCY, ACCOUNTABILITY AND INDEPENDENCE: AND SO WHAT?

As stated above, the discussion over good governance and its three pillars of accountability, transparency and independence should not pose problems for post-Keynesians. After all, we can imagine a central bank targeting exclusively, say, a low, non-NAIRU unemployment rate with all the required institutional features of good governance. Indeed, in these circumstances, central banks would have to announce a specific unemployment target (which in itself can be quite controversial), and make those announcements clear and frequent.

Yet, the governance literature emphasizes that central banks ought to 'effectively and efficiently utilise the limited resources at their disposal' in order to achieve their objective. With respect to central banks, however, it is not made clear what resources are at play. How is this linked to the setting of interest rates and, more importantly, how is it related to achieving an inflation target?

The problem with the governance literature is that it is linked to an inflation target, or a commitment to fight inflation. As some post-Keynesians have shown, such a strategy can lead to a lower rate of growth in the long run. For instance, according to Lavoie (2004, p. 31): 'Government cannot avoid a long-run trade-off between inflation and economic growth. It shows that monetary policy affects more than the inflation rate: zero-inflation or low-inflation targeting has a negative impact on the real economy, bringing about high real rates of interest and low real rates of growth.' In the same spirit of this analysis, Rochon and Rossi (2007) have looked at the impact of interest rate policy, more specifically inflation targeting strategies, on income distribution. As predicted, they found that inflation targeting strategies lead to higher interest rates that would otherwise exist and, as a result, to a decrease in the labour share: inflation targeting negatively affects the distribution of income.

The task before post-Keynesians, therefore, is two fold. First, we must show that the causes of inflation are not rooted in excess demand, but rather in supply; more specifically, inflation is cost-induced.[5] If this is correct, then central bank policies are based on flawed reasoning. This is a perfect example of what Keynes meant when he wrote, in the first chapter on the *General Theory*, that given neoclassical theory does not represent 'the economic society in which we actually live ... its teaching is misleading and disastrous if we attempt to apply it to the facts of experience'.

Indeed, whereas for neoclassical economists inflation is always and everywhere caused by excess demand, irrespective of whether the source of the increased demand is money or otherwise, post-Keynesians see prices determined primarily by costs of production, that is, as a mark-up over costs. More generally, we can argue that inflation is the result of conflict over the proper distribution of income. What is specifically rejected is the notion that monetary factors affect inflation. Since money is endogenous, prices cannot be caused by the growth in the money supply. Rather, given that the economy is essentially a wage economy, inflation is determined by the cost of wages. Of course there are other possible costs as well, such as oil shocks, payroll and production taxes, and the effects of exchange rates (the exchange rate pass-through), which are all beyond the control of the central banks. This implies that central banks are unable to control costs directly and that they may not be best suited to deal with the issue of inflation (Arestis and Sawyer, 2003). In this sense, inflation is a conflict over the appropriate distribution of income. This is what Davidson (1972 [1978], p. 347) argued when stating that: 'The distribution of income is both a cause and a consequence of inflationary processes.' Scarcity plays no role.

Second, post-Keynesians need to show that central banks are inefficient in fighting inflation. Here, two arguments can be made, both highlighting the flaws in neoclassical thinking. First, in the short run, increases in the rate of interest may contribute to higher costs of borrowing. Given these higher costs, and the arguments presented above, these may in turn raise prices. Contrary to neoclassical theory, therefore, in the short run there may be a positive correlation between interest rates and inflation. This is in stark contradiction to mainstream thinking. Second, in the long run, higher rates of interest eventually collapse the economy and, with it, prices. As Lavoie (1996, p. 539) indicates: 'therefore, any attempt at restraining inflation through changes in the rate of interest would require drastic steps to be effective'.

But this eventuality is not the direct result of a change in demand per se. Rather, as the interest rate is a distributive variable, increases in the rate of interest will worsen the distribution of income, and lead to a fall in demand, higher unemployment and a general decrease in wages, which will lessen pressures on prices. As Lavoie (1996, p. 537) writes: 'the rate of interest is an important determinant of the distribution of income between social classes and presumably between individuals'. Wray (2004, p. 25) agrees: 'distributional effects of rate hikes, though little studied and poorly understood [by the Federal Reserve], are probably significant and pernicious'.

The fight against inflation comes therefore at a great cost. Interest rates should be avoided also because of the various time-lags involved in the process. This is the same conclusion reached by Kriesler and Lavoie (2007) who argue that: 'Post-Keynesians … believe that monetary policy takes a considerable amount of time to have any effect, especially on the inflation rate, unless interest rates are changed by drastic amounts (that may jeopardize the stability of the financial system) … Monetary policy acts upon inflationary forces by weakening aggregate demand and labour conditions' (see also Arestis and Sawyer 2004a). In this sense, the central bank and interest rate policy do not fine-tune the economy: they simply collapse the economy to reach the objective of price stability (or to reach an inflation target).

If this is the case, then monetary policy should perhaps not be used for the purpose of fighting inflation. It is an inefficient and costly tool of economic policy.

These arguments go beyond the old debates of rules versus discretion: the central bank is ineffective, irrespective of the methods used, in controlling output and prices. The solution is neither to adopt a rule for monetary policy nor to have the central bank use its discretion in setting the rate of interest. As I have also argued, setting an inflation target is also not the solution since the cost of reaching the target is too great.

A POST-KEYNESIAN INTEREST RATE POLICY: KEYNES AFTER TAYLOR

The discussion in the previous section has shown that central banks have been rather inefficient in their fight against inflation. As argued, central banks have tended toward the collapse of the economy in order to slow down the rate of inflation. Some mainstream economists have indeed argued that the fight against inflation (or the adoption of inflation targeting policies) comes at a definite cost. Sacrifice ratios, for instance, are presented to show the unemployment cost of fighting inflation. Ironically, the new Governor of the American Federal Reserve Bank seems to be in favour of inflation targeting, despite having shown in a study (see Bernanke et al., 1999, p. 258) that for three of the four inflation targeting countries he considered (Canada, New Zealand and the United Kingdom), the sacrifice ratio associated with these inflation targeting regimes was indeed higher than the average sacrifice ratio during all the disinflation episodes that occurred in these countries under other monetary policy regimes. Moreover, the sacrifice ratio was even higher than what the authors could predict using sophisticated econometric techniques (Bernanke et al., 1999, pp. 255–7). Among post-Keynesians, Epstein (2003, p. 2) reaches the same conclusion: 'Among the greatest disappointments for proponents of inflation targeting has been its apparent inability to reduce the so-called *sacrifice ratio*, the unemployment costs of fighting inflation'.

Yet, the argument presented here goes beyond the discussion of sacrifice ratios, which tend to argue that such sacrifices are merely short-term discomfort – or rather short-run pain for long-term gain. Indeed, even the advocates of sacrifice ratios would admit that in the long run, money is still neutral and that monetary policy is an effective tool to fight inflation.

Taylor Rules have forced post-Keynesians to clarify their position further regarding the proper role of central banks in setting monetary – or interest rate – policy. These were explored in greater detail in a recent symposium in the *Journal of Post Keynesian Economics*, in which Mark Setterfield and Rochon (2007) discuss what they describe as the 'activist' versus 'parking-it' approaches within post-Keynesian theory.

According to the activist policy, interest rates would still be used for fine-tuning the economy with respect to a given target, say unemployment, or perhaps capacity utilization. In this sense, interest rates would fall, say, whenever unemployment, for instance, rose above a given target. This is certainly a legitimate approach, as defended by Epstein (2003).

Another approach, however, emphasizes the real rate of interest in the long run. It finds its inspiration in Keynes's notion of the euthanasia of the rentier, who Keynes (1936, p. 376) called the 'functionless investor'.

In a famous passage in his 'Concluding notes' of *The General Theory*, Keynes (1936 [1973], p. 372) argues that 'the outstanding faults of the economic society in which we live are its failure to provide for full employment and its arbitrary and inequitable distribution of wealth and incomes'. This is an observation that is relevant especially in discussing monetary and interest rate policies.

Keynes's argument was simple: savings do not depend on the rate of interest, but rather on investment, which itself depends on lower rates of interest. In order to promote full employment, it was necessary, according to Keynes, to let the rate of interest fall to a suitably low level, or as low as possible. This, Keynes (1936 [1973], p. 376) wrote, 'would mean the euthanasia of the rentier, and, consequently, the euthanasia of the cumulative oppressive power of the capitalist to exploit the scarcity value of capital'.

Keynes's insights into the euthanasia of the rentier mesh well with an overall post-Keynesian view on interest rates. However, while the notion of the euthanasia of the rentier is a well-known and indeed well-referenced concept among many post-Keynesians, it can have a few interpretations. When post-Keynesians call for the euthanasia of the rentier, they are calling for lowering the rate of interest for a short period of time. Yet, what is becoming increasingly clear now is that in fact some post-Keynesians are now advocating permanent lower rates of interest.

In line with Smithin's warnings about the 'revenge of the rentier', therefore, I would propose that post-Keynesians follow through with the meaning of the euthanasia of the rentier, which I believe means that central bank policy should be removed from fine-tuning the economy, and as such from the realm of economic policy all together. This does not mean of course that central banks stop setting the rate of interest or all their other functions, but rather that they stop using the rate of interest as a tool of economic fine-tuning.

This then requires us to have an interest rate policy for long-run purposes. We must therefore have a value for the real rate of interest (not the Wicksellian natural rate). As Smithin (2004, p. 63) asks: 'If the level of the real rate of interest finally boils down to a target chosen by the central bank … what should the target be?'

There is in fact some precedence for this position in post-Keynesian theory. There are, I believe, three versions of this policy. First, Smithin (2004) advocates a policy of 'low but still positive' real rates. Accordingly, the author argues that this would imply adjusting the nominal policy rate one-for-one with observed inflation, and he is careful to note that his policy does not recognize the existence of a natural rate of interest, à la Wicksell.[6] His policy of low, but positive, real rates is analogous 'to an incomes policy of a sort, albeit an incomes policy for rentiers rather than for workers or entrepreneurs' (Atesoglu and Smithin, 2006, p. 686).

Lavoie and Seccareccia (1999) for their part, advocate a slightly different version of the same approach. The authors advocate using Pasinetti's approach of a 'fair' rate of interest. For Lavoie and Seccareccia (1999, p. 543), a 'fair' interest rate is the real rate that leaves 'unchanged the distribution of income between interest and non-interest income groups, regardless of lending and borrowing activities'. They claim that this scenario is achieved only when the central bank sets the real interest rate equal to labour (multi-factor) total productivity.

Finally, there is another, albeit perhaps more extreme position. Wray refers to a 'neutral' rate where 'indeed, a very good case could be made that the neutral rate is a Japan-like zero – but exploration of that issue would take us too far afield'. Hence, the Kansas City rule advocates setting the nominal rate of interest to zero.

By setting real or nominal rates at zero or close, this neutralizes interest rates as a tool of economic policy and indeed minimizes the role of the rentier class in influencing the direction of the central bank: it minimizes monetary policy dominance. The role of monetary policy should not be to affect output, but rather to give us the best possible distribution of income, given the distributive nature of the rate of interest. In this spirit, Lavoie (1996, p. 537) writes: 'It then becomes clear that monetary policy should not be so much designed to control the level of activity, but rather to find the level of interest rates that will be proper for the economy from a distribution point of view. The aim of such a policy should be to minimize conflict over income shares, in the hope of simultaneously keeping inflation low and activity high'.

Implications of the Euthanasia of the Rentier

If monetary policy is not used for fine-tuning, then what other tool would policy makers have to affect the economy? Given the discussion above and in the tradition of Keynes, fiscal policy would have to be, once again, elevated to its former prominence. As Keynes (1936 [1973], p. 378) writes: 'the State will have to exercise a guiding influence'. Indeed, Setterfield (2007) makes a compelling argument showing that fiscal policy, if necessary, is sufficiently efficient in fighting inflation, as it is in promoting growth, reducing unemployment and directly affecting the distribution of income by the adoption of some incomes policy. In using a fiscal policy version of a Taylor Rule – where the 'public sector borrowing requirement' adjusts to the inflation and output gaps – Setterfield shows that fiscal policy can be an effective tool in regulating inflation. Yet, it also carries additional benefits as it can be targeted to help specific segments of society. Setterfield in fact shows that his model is flexible, thereby allowing fiscal policy to depart from the 'pseudo' Taylor Rule without jeopardizing the stability of the model: in other words, fiscal policy can do more than simply react to inflation and output gaps.

While this approach places fiscal policy squarely at the centre of economic policy, it differs significantly from its Keynesian counterpart, however, inasmuch as it does not see fiscal policy as having a short-run role, but rather a prominent role in the long run as well. As Atesoglu and Smithin (2006, p. 686) clearly spell out: 'If further "activist" policy is required, on either the growth or inflation fronts, this would have to be the realm of fiscal policy, as in traditional Keynesian economics, or a conventional incomes policy.'

There is a remaining, important question. Would such a policy of low rates of interest lead to inflation? This is an important question and perhaps, within the context of this chapter, the most important one indeed. It is, however, beyond the immediate scope of this chapter.

CONCLUSION

The purpose of this chapter was to review the issues of governance in central banks within the context of inflation targeting. One of the main arguments is that discussion over good governance arose along with inflation targeting, following the high-inflation periods of the 1970s and 1980s accompanied with the large fiscal deficits.

Yet, the literature on governance is linked inextricably to the monetary policy goal of inflation control or targeting. The mainstream literature over governance arose specifically to give the central bank the institutional independence and structure to meet its inflation target. Yet, nothing prevents central banks from couching governance within an argument of full employment, although central bankers will tell us that this would harm their credibility on international markets.

There are two ways to achieve this: one way is to advocate a policy rule with an unemployment gap, for instance, and still use monetary policy to fine-tune the economy. Yet, there are problems with this approach altogether, since it relies on a calculation of a hypothetical NAIRU.

There is a second approach, which relies rather on the avoidance of 'monetary policy dominance', and thereby avoids resting monetary policy on calculations of a hypothetical variable. Rather, as advocated by a growing number of post-Keynesians, this policy would be to adopt a 'passive' monetary policy and minimize (or eliminate) monetary policy fine-tuning. This approach is based on the following Keynesian notions. First, the rate of interest is a distributive variable, and changes in the rate affect the distribution of income, and thereby aggregate demand and output. Second, inflation is largely cost-determined. This suggests that current monetary policy is based on an erroneous view of prices, and hence is at best misguided. Finally, monetary policy does not fine-tune: it simply collapses the economy until inflation is restored, and labour's negotiating advantage is broken. This implies therefore that the use of monetary policy to fight inflation is costly, both in the short and the long run.

In its stead, this chapter advocates setting the real rate of interest at a low level, in accordance with Keynes's 'euthanasia of the rentier', and using fiscal policy not only to stabilize output, but also to control inflation.

NOTES

1. I would like to thanks Claude Gnos, Eckard Hein, Ingrid Rima, Tom Palley and Sergio Rossi for their constructive comments. All usual disclaimers apply.
2. Inflation targets are firmly established in 29 countries currently, and a possible 30th soon with the appointment of Bernanke at the Federal Reserve.
3. As Arestis and Sawyer (2003) correctly argue, cost-push inflation cannot be incorporated within the New Consensus model. Although some may claim that they could be accommodated in the

stochastic term imbedded in the Phillips curve, wage increases and other increases in costs that may affect inflation are not stochastic in nature.

4. This is the reason, for instance, in the recent – although now defunct – discussion over dollarization.
5. I do not deny that inflation can be caused by demand factors (although not by excess demand). As demand increases, this may encourage firms to adjust their mark-up to reflect more historical levels of the rate of profit (Lavoie, 1992, p. 376).
6. There are I believe three overwhelming ideas that distinguish post-Keynesians from New Consensus proponents. First, money is endogenous because of the nature of money as debt. Second, post-Keynesians reject natural values, such as the natural rate of interest and the natural rate of unemployment (NAIRU). Finally, demand plays both a short-run and a long-run role in post-Keynesian theory.

REFERENCES

Arestis, P. and A. Angeriz (2006), 'Has inflation targeting had any impact on inflation?' *Journal of Post Keynesian Economics*, Summer, **28** (4), 559–72.

Arestis, P. and M. Sawyer (2003), 'Inflation targeting: a critical appraisal', Levy Economics Institute, Working Paper 388 (September), Annandale-on-Hudson.

Abraham-Frois, G. (2003), 'Pour en finir avec IS-LM', *Revue d'Economie Politique*, **113** (2), March–April, 155–70.

Allsopp, C. and D. Vine (2000), 'The assessment: macroeconomic policy', *Oxford Review of Economic Policy*, **16** (4), April, 1-32.

Amtenbrink, F. (2004), 'The three pillars of central bank governance – towards a model central bank law or a code of good governance', IMF LEG Workshop on Central Banking, Washington, DC, March.

Atesoglu, S. and J. Smithin (2006), 'Inflation targeting in a simple macroeconomic model', *Journal of Post Keynesian Economics*, Summer, **28** (4), 673–88.

Berger, H., J. De Haan and S.C.W. Eijffinger (2000), 'Central bank independence: an update on theory and evidence, CESifo Working Paper Series No. 255, February.

Bernanke, B.S. and A. Blinder (1992), 'The federal funds rate and the channels of monetary transmission', *American Economic Review*, September, **82** (4), 901–21.

Bernanke, B., T. Laubach, F.S. Mishkin and S. Posen (1999), *Inflation Targeting: Lessons from the International Experience*, Princeton, NJ: Princeton University Press.

Blinder, A. (1987), 'Credit rationing and effective supply failures', *Economic Journal*, June, **97**, 327–52.

Carlstrom, C. and T. Fuerst (2003), 'The Taylor rule: a guidepost for monetary policy?' *Federal Reserve Bank of Cleveland Economic Commentary*, (July), 1-4.

Davidson, P. (1972), *Money and the Real World*, New York: John Wiley & Sons. 2nd edition, 1978.

Debelle, G., P. Masson, M. Savastano and S. Sharma (1998), 'Inflation targeting as a framework for monetary policy', *International Monetary Fund Economic Issues* No. 15, Washington.

Epstein, G. (2003), 'Alternatives to inflation targeting monetary policy for stable and egalitarian growth: a brief research summary', University of Massachusetts Political Economy Research Institute Working Paper No. 62 (July), Amherst.

Fontana, G. and A. Palacio-Vera (2002), 'Monetary policy rules: what are we learning?', *Journal of Post Keynesian Economics*, **24** (4) (Summer), 547–68.

Fraga, A., J. Goldfajn and A. Minella (2004), 'Inflation targeting in emerging market economies', in Gertler, M. and K. Rogoff (eds), *NBER Macroeconomics Annual 2003*, Cambridge, MA: MIT Press, 365–400.

Kaldor, N. (1982), *The Scourge of Monetarism*, Oxford: Oxford University Press.

Keynes, J.M. (1936) [1973], *The Collected Writings of John Maynard Keynes. Volume vii: The General Theory of Employment, Money and Interest*, D. Moggridge (ed.), London: Macmillan and St-Martin's Press.

King, M.A. (2002), 'The inflation target ten years on', *Bank of England Quarterly Bulletin*, Winter, **42** (4), 459–74.

Kriesler, P. and M. Lavoie (2007), 'The new view on monetary policy and its post-Keynesian critique', *Review of Political Economy*, July, **19** (3), 397–404.

Lavoie, M. (1992), *Foundations of Post-Keynesian Economic Analysis*, Aldershot, UK and Brookfield, US: Edward Elgar.

Lavoie, M. (1996), 'Monetary policy in an economy with endogenous credit money', in Deleplace, G. and E. Nell (eds), *Money in Motion*, London: Macmillan.

Lavoie, M. (2004), 'The new consensus on monetary policy seen from a post-Keynesian perspective', in Lavoie, M. and M. Seccareccia (2004), *Central Banking in the Modern World: Alternative Perspectives*, Cheltenham, UK and Northampton, MA, US: Edward Elgar, 15–34.

Lavoie, M. and M. Seccareccia (1999), 'Interest rate: fair', in O'Hara, P. (ed), *Encyclopedia of Political Economy*, Vol. 1, London: Routledge, 543–5.

Lim, J. (2006), 'Alternatives to inflation targeting: central bank policy for employment creation, poverty reduction and sustainable growth', PERI, working paper 10.

McCallum, B. (2001), 'Monetary policy analysis in models without money', *Federal Reserve Bank of St Louis Review*, July–August, 145–60.

Mendis, S. (2005), 'Central bank governance and how such governance is related to strategic planning in central banks', Opening Remarks, Third SEACEN EXCO Seminar and Meeting.

Meyer, L.H. (2001), 'Does money matter?' *Federal Reserve Bank of St Louis Review*, **83** (4), 1–15.

Mishkin, F. (1999), 'International experiences with different monetary regimes', *Journal of Monetary Economics*, **43**, 579–606.

Mishkin, F.S. (2000), 'What should central banks do?' *Federal Reserve Bank of St Louis Review*, November–December, **82** (6), 1–13.

Monvoisin, V. and L.-P. Rochon (2005), 'Post-Keynesian theories of endogenous money, the new consensus and Keynes', in Gnos, C. and L.-P. Rochon (eds), *Post-Keynesian Principles for Economic Policy*, Cheltenham, UK and Northampton, MA, US: Edward Elgar, 59–80.

Moore, B. (1988), *Horizontalists and Verticalists: The Macroeconomics of Credit–Money*, Cambridge: Cambridge University Press.

Palley, T. (2005),'A post-Keynesian framework for monetary policy: why interest rate operating procedures are not enough', in Gnos, C. and L.-P. Rochon (eds), *Post-Keynesian Economic Policy*, Cheltenham, UK and Northampton, MA, US: Edward Elgar, 79-99.

Paulin, G. (2006), 'Credibility with flexibility: the evolution of inflation-targeting regimes, 1990–2006', *Bank of Canada Review*, Summer , 5–18.

Perry, R. (2001), 'Central bank corporate governance, financial management, and transparency', *Reserve Bank of New Zealand Bulletin*, **64** (1), 33–41.

Ribeiro, F. (2002), 'Central bank: independence, governance and accountability', Working Paper, Institute of Brazilian Studies, The George Washington University.

Robinson, J. (1956), *The Accumulation of Capital*, London: Macmillan.

Rochon, L.-P. (1999), *Credit, Money and Production: An Alternative Post-Keynesian Approach*, Cheltenham, UK and Northampton, MA, US: Edward Elgar.

Rochon, L.-P. (2005), 'Wicksell after the Taylor rule: A post-Keynesian critique of the new consensus', Laurentian University Working Paper.

Rochon, L.-P. and S. Rossi (2007), 'Central banking and post-keynesian economics', *Review of Political Economy*, October, **19** (4), 539-54.

Rochon, L.-P. and Rossi, S. (eds) (2006), *Monetary and Exchange Rate Systems: A Global View of Financial Crises*, Cheltenham, UK and Northampton, MA, US: Edward Elgar.

Rochon, L.-P. and M. Setterfield (2007), 'Interest rates, income distribution and monetary policy dominance: post Keynesians and the "fair" rate of interest', *Journal of Post Keynesian Economics*, Fall, **30** (1), pp. 13-41.

Romer, D. (2000), 'Keynesian macroeconomics without the LM curve', *Journal of Economic Perspectives*, **14** (2) Spring, 149–69.

Setterfield, M. (2004), 'Central banking, stability and macroeconomic outcomes', in Lavoie, M. and M. Seccareccia (eds), *Central Banking in the Modern World: Alternative Perspectives*, Cheltenham, UK and Northampton, MA, US: Edward Elgar, 35–56.

Setterfield, M. (2007), 'Is there a stabilizing role for fiscal policy in the new consensus?' *Review of Political Economy*, July, **19** (3), 405–18.

Smithin, J. (2004), 'Interest rate operating procedures and income distribution', in Lavoie, M. and M. Seccareccia (eds), *Central Banking in the Modern World: Alternative Perspectives*, Cheltenham, UK and Northampton, MA, US: Edward Elgar, 57–69.

Taylor, J. (1993), 'Discretion vs Policy Rules in Practice', *Carnegie-Rochester Conference Series on Public Policy*, December, **39**, 195–214.

Taylor, J. (2000), 'Teaching macroeconomics at the principles level', *American Economic Review*, **90** (2), 904.

Villieu, P. (2004), 'Une macroéconomie sans LM? Un modèle de synthèse pour l'analyse des politiques conjoncturelles', *Revue d'Economie Politique*, **114** (3), May–June, 289-332-37.

Woodford, M. (2001), 'The Taylor rule and optimal monetary policy', *American Economic Review*, May, **91** (2), 232–7.

Wray, R. (2004), 'The Fed and the new consensus: the case of rate hikes, part two', Public Policy Brief No. 80, The Levy Economics Institute of Bard College.

Zilioli, C. and M. Selmayr (2000), *The European Central Bank: An Independent Specialized Organization of Community Law*, **37**, CML Review, 591–644.

4. The macroeconomic governance of the European Monetary Union: a Keynesian perspective

Angel Asensio

INTRODUCTION

During the 1970s, the floating of the main currencies modified macroeconomic policy-making significantly: free from the obligation to defend their exchange rate, policies were more reactive, but also more inflationary, causing public deficits, and finally they were less efficient against unemployment. That supported the idea that markets work better without macroeconomic policies, and encouraged academic research that postulated the efficiency of the competitive mechanisms and delivered of course a negative vision of monetary and fiscal policies: either they were useless, or they were inflation-biased because of the temptation to monetize deficits or get extra output. That literature gave rise to new standards for macroeconomic governance, such as monetary policy conservatism, and strong public deficit limitations.

The new governance rules of the eurozone aim basically to weaken the discretionary power of economic policy, in order to protect the credibility of the euro against the 'inflationary temptation'. They work through a two-pillar institutional architecture: central bank independence and the Stability and Growth Pact. There is a close connection between the clauses concerning monetary and fiscal policies and the theoretical developments of the New Classical and New Keynesian macroeconomics. These developments are fundamentally based on the 'rational expectations hypothesis', with the result that the rules of governance they recommend have been designed for a world in which uncertainty (not risk) does not have a substantial impact on economic decisions. In such a world, the competitive adjustment of prices, wages and interest rates is largely admitted to be efficient, which ensures the predictability of the economic trajectory, given the structural data.

These theories had much success in the academic and politic arenas; they today have significant effects on the conduct of macroeconomic policies, especially in the European Union where they have been formalized into a treaty. However, the trials of the European stability pact or of the USA public finances show that it is difficult to hold the line of conduct in the real world. In both cases, the willingness of counter an unfavourable conjunction of circumstances has been pragmatically invoked in order to depart the policy-making from the medium to long-run objectives.[1] Those events suggest that the New Consensus macroeconomics (NCM) governance has heavy drawbacks when it is implemented in the real world. They show moreover that discretionary power has not been completely crowded out of European policy-making, in spite of the new institutional framework.

The chapter first presents the theoretical foundations of the anti-inflationary governance with respect to the kind of world for which it has been designed. Then, extending Asensio's theoretical framework (2006, 2007) to a monetary union, it examines the dysfunctions that the new governance may provoke in a Keynesian context where competitive forces do not ensure efficiency, as well as the pragmatic principles which could make macroeconomic policy more adequate. In accordance with Arestis and Sawyer's (2003) position, fiscal policies will occupy a central place, but attention will be paid to their interactions with the monetary policy of the Union.

In the next section, we present the NCM and Keynesian general equilibrium equations of a two-country monetary union model. In the third section, we discuss the consequences of the NCM governance in both systems, and explore the outlines of the Keynesian macroeconomic governance. The conclusion draws some lessons about the current fiscal and monetary rules of the eurozone.

MODELLING A MONETARY UNION

Starting with the usual four-macro-market structure of the closed economy, we move towards a two-country monetary union by assuming perfectly integrated markets for bonds and unique money. Consequently, the system comprises six markets (the two labour markets – immobile factor; the two markets for goods – imperfect substitutes; the market for bonds; and the market for money), which supposes five relative prices (two real wages in terms of goods, the international relative price of goods, the rate of interest and the real price of money in terms of goods, the inverse of which is the nominal price of goods). Because of the aggregate balanced-budget equality, the equilibrium condition for the market of bonds will remain implicit.

Variables are expressed in terms of relative variations from their initial value, excepting the rate of interest and the tax rate, which are expressed as variations. We focus on the short-run behaviour of the system, in the sense that productive physical stock of capital is assumed to be constant during the period considered. All the parameters (generally in small Greek letters) have the same value in the two countries so as to make the algebra tractable.

The NCM will be analysed through the equilibrium properties of the supply and demand aggregate behaviours. Then, behaviours in the face of uncertainty will be considered so as to put forward, within the same macro-market structure, the general equilibrium properties of a Keynesian system.[2]

Monetary Union Modelling within the NCM

After Keynes had demonstrated the decisive importance of expectations for macroeconomic analysis, the rational expectations hypothesis gave a new impulse to the (neo)classical economics during the 1970s. It was shown that, in stochastic stationary regimes, the main properties of the classical system continued to work, provided that market efficiency was postulated. The 'New Keynesian' economics shares most of this revitalized New Classical framework, even though it puts forward nominal and real rigidities, which prevent the competitive process from working perfectly in the 'short run'. If nominal wages, for example, are imperfectly flexible, inflationary shocks temporarily move real wages and employment from their natural level. Demand policies may be useful in this case, but only to the extent that they use the surprise-inflation channel. However, while money can influence the relative prices and other real variables temporarily, it plays a limited role in the New Keynesian macroeconomics because rational expectations make it possible to predict the future values of the economic variables without making systematic errors. Hence, as far as stochastic shocks are supposed to produce only temporary deviations in ergodic regimes,[3] the long-run behaviour of the system is basically the same as in the New Classical macroeconomics.

Labour markets

At equilibrium, variations in real wages and employment compensate for the marginal disutility of labour (supply side) and furthermore ensure profit maximization (demand side). The marginal productivity equalization to the real cost of labour induces a negative relation between employment and real wage:

$$n_i = -\rho(w_i - p_i) + d_i,\ i = 1,2$$

n_i is the relative variation in employment level in country i
w_i is the relative variation in nominal wage in country i
p_i is the relative variation in the price of goods in country i

It is possible to introduce fiscal distortion effects by supposing that in the short run they work through the price of the variable input: replacing the nominal cost of labour (W) by $W(1+\xi t)$, where $0 \leq \xi < 1$ measures the (weakened) impact of the tax rate on the labour cost, profit maximization requires $\partial Y/\partial N = W(1+\xi t)/P$. The demand for labour relative variation (n) then takes the form of a function of the fiscally corrected labour cost, which relative variation can be approximated by $(p - w - \xi \hat{t})$ for small values of $\hat{t}$ (variation in t):

$$n_i = -\rho(w_i - p_i - \xi \hat{t}_i) + d_i \tag{4.1}$$

We will suppose that labour contracts have been negotiated, at the starting point of the period, on the basis of the expected rate of inflation for the current period (p^a). The supply of labour results from the equalization of marginal disutility of labour to the expected real wage, which supposes a positive relation between n_i and $w_i - p_i^a$. It will be useful to reverse this relation in order to express the (expected) real wage as a function of the level of employment given by equation (4.1):

$$w_i - p_i^a = \theta n_i \tag{4.2}$$

From (4.1) we get:

$$w_i = p_i + \frac{\theta d_i - (p_i - p_i^a) - \theta\rho\xi\hat{t}_i}{1 + \rho\theta}$$

$$n_i = \frac{\rho(p_i - p_i^a) + d_i - \rho\xi\hat{t}_i}{1 + \rho\theta}$$

If $p_i^a = p_i$ (which is assumed to be true in the 'long run', as a result of rational expectations in ergodic regimes), employment (and production; see below) only depends on structural and technological data (plus the fiscal distortion effect), but in case of inflationary surprise ($p_i \neq p_i^a$), demand shocks influence the level of employment through the prediction error ($p_i - p_i^a$).

Goods markets

The supply of goods in each country depends on the quantity of inputs, especially the labour in the short run, and therefore the country's i technology will be represented as:

$$y_i = \alpha n_i + c_i \tag{4.3}$$

y_i is the relative variation in output in country i, c_i represents other exogenous technological factors. We assume $\alpha<1$ (diminishing marginal product of labour).

From the expression of n, we get y as a function of the prediction error:

$$y_i = \frac{\alpha\rho(p_i - p_i^a) + \alpha d_i - \alpha\rho\xi\hat{t}_i}{1 + \rho\theta} + c_i$$

Apart from taxes and public expenditure changes ($\hat{t}_i$, g_i), the demand for goods varies in both countries with the rate of interest ($\hat{i}$), the international relative output price ($p_j - p_i$) and an exogenous component (a_i), so the market clearing conditions have the form:[4]

$$y_i = -\gamma\hat{t}_i - \sigma\hat{i} + \kappa(p_j - p_i) + \lambda(\varphi g_i + a_i),\ i = 1,2,\ j = 1,2,\ i \neq j$$

which can be expressed as:

$$p_i = p_j - \frac{1}{\kappa}(y_i + \gamma\hat{t}_i + \sigma\hat{i}) - \lambda(\varphi g_i + a_i) \tag{4.4}$$

As far as monetary authorities are credible, the expected variations in the national price indexes follow the long run commitment ($p_i^a = \overline{p}_i$), which is assumed to be the initial level (so as $\bar{p}_i = 0$). However, as short-run deviations are allowed for stabilization purposes, p_i may differ from $\bar{p}_i$, with the result that $p_i - p_i^a \neq 0$. Equation (4.4) shows how the monetary and fiscal policy instruments influence the price indexes and, thereby, the output level.

The money market

In the former Classical view, money was simply a transaction device, and the demand for money was assumed to vary according to the volume and the price of transactions, but more sophisticated (short-run) demand for money is often preferred so as to take risk into account:[5]

$$m = \frac{1}{2}(y_1 + y_2) + \frac{1}{2}(p_1 + p_2) - \eta \hat{i} \tag{4.5}$$

where m is the quantity of money.

The system therefore turns into an extended two-country IS–LM model (equations 4.4 and 4.5), which contains a supply set of equations for the determination of wages and prices. However, as Lavoie (2006) pointed out, in recent versions of the New Consensus the monetary policy consists in controlling the rate of interest rather than the quantity of money, which has to be considered an endogenous variable. In this case, the LM function only determines the quantity of money, and therefore it is possible to solve the model for real magnitudes without it (see Romer, 2000).[6]

Keynesian Equilibrium in a Non-Ergodic Monetary Union

Equation (4.5) admits different interpretations depending on the definition of uncertainty. In ergodic regimes, risk makes money a useful portfolio diversification device, as we have just mentioned. This is a step towards the Keynesian monetary theory, but it does not capture its essential features. Indeed, there is a fundamental difference in the way to manage uncertainty when dynamic stability is not ensured, compared with a system where agents may predict the future without making systematic errors. The Keynesian concept of liquidity preference is not captured in equation (4.5); the liquidity preference does not result from any optimal decision concerning risk and return, which could make sense in ergodic regimes but does not ensure that it is the 'best' solution in a Keynesian world. According to *The General Theory* (Chapter 12), its magnitude results from the confidence level that people give to their expectations (whatever the distribution of probabilities they may make use of).

This Keynesian specificity will be formally underlined through considering η_k as an exogenous variable which is subject to the kind of volatility that usually affects expectations:

$$m = \frac{1}{2}(y_1 + y_2) + \frac{1}{2}(p_1 + p_2) - \eta_k \hat{i} \qquad (4.5_k)$$

When aggregate demand, and prices, decrease, the need for transaction money falls, and the rate of interest decreases; that increases the demand and the price of goods and moves the real wages towards their full-employment level.[7] But, in Keynesian contexts, the magnitude of the decrease in interest rate (the so-called 'Keynes effect') and of any positive real balance effect (people do not want to hold idle cash balances and therefore increase the demand for goods) depends on speculative decisions concerning the demand for money, with the result that income and employment eventually depend on the degree of confidence of the moment and on its impact on the demand for money. Hence, competitive forces do not necessarily adjust the economy to the ideal outcome.

Markets articulation at equilibrium

Labour markets

The demand for labour will not be determined here by equation (4.1), but by equation (4.3), which gives the variation in labour that makes the better use of the technology for a given demand of goods.

Since the level of labour is fixed by the demand of firms, the supply-side equation of the labour market must determine the equilibrium wage. In the Classical world, as well as in the NCM 'long run', nominal wages adjustment, together with the real-balance effect, drives the real wages so as to ensure equality between the supply and demand of labour. The 'invisible hand' simultaneously drives the rate of interest so as to ensure that the aggregate demand absorbs the full-employment supply of goods. In such a world, money only can induce short-run 'noises', but in a Keynesian world, shifts of the speculative demand for money may keep the 'invisible hand' away from full employment. Hence, insofar as nothing in these conditions ensures the equalization of the equilibrium real wages and marginal disutility of labour attached to a given level of effective demand, equation (4.2), which represents the second 'Classical postulate', must be abandoned.

How then is the equilibrium nominal wage determined? The *General Theory* pointed out that a decrease in wages does not systematically increase employment, because of the negative demand effects it may provoke through the expected return on capital. Notice that, in our autarkic monetary union, a positive external demand effect due to a wage decrease in country *i* supposes a negative effect in country *j*, with the result that the competitive adjustment of wages does not solve the problem at the union level.[8] Unemployment at equilibrium means that the self-regulatory process failed either the wages decrease has not been able to stimulate the effective demand or has amplified the depression (but in this case wages should continue to fall),[9] or workers have been able to stop the decrease in wages. We will therefore suppose that nominal wages are anchored in an exogenous (though variable) threshold ($\overline{w}_i$). The current wage however may deviate from this threshold when certain events occur, such as a rise in unemployment rate or exogenous disturbances:

$$w_i = \overline{w}_i - \theta_k (n_{fi} - n_i), \ i = 1,2 \qquad (4.2_k)$$

where n_{fi} is the rate of change of the labour force in country *i*.

Goods markets

As the markets equilibrium requires that firms adjust production y_i to the effective demand (equation 4.4) and then technology determines employment (equation 4.3), employment does not result from equation (4.1). This does not mean that firms cannot adjust the marginal productivity of labour to the factor real cost, but it is not through the choice of the output level that they can do it. Equation (4.1) actually gives the price index that makes firms able to remain on their labour demand curve, despite the fact that the demand for labour is constrained by the demand for goods. When demand increases, it is through inflation that the real wage variation is made equal to the marginal productivity decline, prompting firms to respond to the increasing demand.

Without changing the formal condition expressed in equation (4.1), we can rewrite it in accordance with the Keynesian approach to inflation:

$$p_i = w_i + n_i - y_i - \dot{\alpha}_i + \xi \hat{t}_i \qquad (4.1')$$

where $-\dot{\alpha}_i + \xi \hat{t}_i$ is the rate of variation of the mark-up on unit labour cost.[10]

Inflation may be caused by interest rate variations through their impact on aggregate demand and output, but in contrast to the NCM model, this does not require inflation surprises. In addition, inflation reveals its connection with the labour costs, including taxes, and with the mark-up. Equation (4.1') also indicates that a positive shift in output, which reduces the productivity of labour in the absence of technological change,[11] does not necessarily imply a decline of real wages; it depends on the mark-up behaviour. Thus real wages may vary pro-cyclically.

The money market

Following the post-Keynesian approach to endogenous money, we will suppose that banks deliver the quantity of money that is demanded at the current rate of interest, which is influenced by central bank decisions. However, despite the formal resemblance, the functioning of the market differs from the NCM one, notably because of the speculative demand instability. Hence, the transmission of short-term interest rate variations, through which the central bank may influence the long-term interest rates, is made uncertain. For example, lower short-term rates (increases in high-powered money) aiming to extend credit do not produce the same decline in long-term rates depending on whether the liquidity preference changes or not. When it rises, banks may be able to sell more credit without having to reduce their interest rates, for non-bank loan rates in this case tend to rise in order to compensate for the increasing liquidity preference. Moreover, speculative behaviours may also block the transmission process when the current rates are considered as very low (liquidity trap). Thus automatic monetary rules à la Taylor turn out to be excessively optimistic in a Keynesian context.

Formal similarities and fundamental discrepancies

From a formal point of view, the differences between the two models concern equations (4.2_k) and (4.2) as long as equation LM is not explicitly represented. If, as usually supposed, the labour force is constant in the short run ($n_{fi} = 0$, $i = 1{,}2$), differences are restricted to wages determinants ($\overline{w}_i$ or p_i^a) and parameters (θ or θ_k) that have different definitions in the two models.

Thus, apart from the postulate that the specified shocks (c_i, α_i, p_i^a, a_i) produce temporary deviations around a predictable long-run trajectory in the NCM model, the modelling of the short-run behaviour of non-ergodic systems looks approximately like the modelling of the short-run behaviour of ergodic systems with rational expectations. However, this formal similarity hides fundamental differences about the general equilibrium properties. First, the volatility of the demand for money (equation 4.5_k) threatens the interest rate ability to push aggregate demand up to full employment at the union level (whatever way it might take: spontaneous competitive forces or monetary policy). Second, Keynesian equilibrium is driven by effective demand; there is no force of attraction towards any predetermined 'long-run' or 'natural' position (in that sense, Keynesian equilibrium is not a temporary situation). Third, that unemployment does not tend to reduce nominal wages beyond some exogenous limit is not a cause of unemployment; in certain circumstances, it can even be viewed as a protection against cumulative depressive forces (but a shift in unemployment may weaken the workers' resistance, as in equation 4.2_k).

Other fundamental discrepancies concern the signification of inflation and the role of monetary policy. We have mentioned the connection between cost-pushed inflation and demand-led inflation. Indeed, inflationary effects associated to wages, mark-up and/or tax pressures ($\overline{w}_i > 0, \dot{\alpha}_i > 0, \hat{t}_i > 0$) in equation (4.1') depend on the way monetary authorities will pass them on effective demand. Since cost pressures come with higher demand for transaction money, inflation can develop only if the central bank satisfies the additional demand of money, in order for example to stabilize the rate of interest. If on the contrary monetary authorities aim to stabilize the price index, they do not prevent the rise of interest rates, so as to offset the inflationary effects of increasing costs through a depressive impact on effective demand. Hence, recurrent distributive conflicts, whatever the reason (wage-profit sharing, fiscal pressures), force monetary policy into a dilemma: to accept the inflationary consequences and preserve economic activities, or to depress economic activity in order to stabilize the real value of money through a non-temporary pressure of unemployment on wages. In the Keynesian context, monetary policy is involved in the determination of equilibrium and income distribution; it is not a simple stabilization device for self-regulated systems.

ALTERNATIVE MACRO-GOVERNANCE APPROACHES

According to the NCM, debt monetization and the willingness to get extra output are the primary causes of inflation. Solutions stem from governance principles like central bank independency and public deficit limitation, which aim to prevent central banks from creating more money than is needed for making transactions at current prices. Whereas such principles seem suitable in an ergodic system, they can deteriorate the situation in the presence of Keynesian uncertainty. This section compares the main implications of the NCM governance in both contexts.

NCM Governance

The type of governance that is suggested by the NCM is based on targets that are defined in relation to the expected 'natural' trajectory of the economy. Temporary deviations of the rate of interest may be decided for stabilization purposes, in such a way that, in the long run, the quantity of money evolves in concert with the demand induced by the economic growth, without inflation pressures. Conversely, policies that aim systematically to get extra output through inflation surprise or debt monetization are fully predictable and therefore inefficient; they only feed the inflation core. Consequently, the New Consensus pleads in favour of central bank political independence and low-inflation targeting. In addition, according to the 'unpleasant monetary arithmetic' of Sargent and Wallace (1981), public deficit limitations are necessary for the credibility and effectiveness of monetary policy.

NCM governance within the New Consensus representation of the world

In order to draw some analytical conclusions from the model, let us assume that credible institutions have removed the inflation bias, with the result that active monetary policy aims to stabilize the system by means of (non-systematic) inflation surprise.[12] Since the central bank is credible, private agents anchor their expectation on the announced long-run inflation target. However, in the face of a shock, monetary authorities deviate from the target in order to stabilize employment at the union level, with a magnitude which depends on their degree of 'conservatism' about inflation.

The governments for their part have long-run budget balance targets related to their financial policy and debt management constraints. Like monetary authorities, they can temporarily deviate from the target for stabilization purposes.

Let us suppose that the average price index and budget balance deviations from initial values are decided with respect to the employment deviations:

$$\frac{1}{2}(p_1 + p_2) = -\beta\frac{1}{2}(n_1 + n_2) \tag{4.6}$$

$$b_i = \psi n_i,\ i = 1,2 \tag{4.7}$$

where $b_i \equiv \varphi(y_i - g_i) + \hat{t}_i$ (see Appendix 4.B).[13]

Equation (4.6) for example means that, in order to stabilize the economic activity, a positive (negative) temporary deviation of the average price index is accepted in case of a negative (positive) deviation from the natural rate of employment. The parameters $\beta \geq 0$ and $\psi_i \geq 0$ represent respectively the monetary degree of 'conservatism' and the fiscal degree of 'Orthodoxy'. $B = 0$ means that there are no short-run deviations from the inflation target (full 'conservatism'). $\psi_i = 0$ means that the budget deficit (or surplus) in country i depends only on financial long-run considerations, and do not participate in stabilization operations. The two conditions above suppose that the rate of interest and the budget balance move so as to weaken the impact of the shock on employment; considering equations (4.1'), (4.2), (4.3) and (4.4), they determine the required deviation of the policy instruments $\hat{\imath}$ and g (or $\hat{t}$) at equilibrium. Notice that if, for example, governments adjust expenditure, the impact of the shocks on the budget balances can in principle be controlled by means of the tax rates. Actually, the following monetary and fiscal policy rules:

for $i = 1,2$

$$\hat{t}_i = \frac{1}{2}\frac{(\lambda-\gamma)-4\kappa\xi}{\xi(2\kappa\xi-(\lambda-\gamma))}(p_i^a-\dot{\alpha}_i)+\frac{1}{2}\frac{(\lambda-\gamma)}{\xi(2\kappa\xi-(\lambda-\gamma))}(p_j^a-\dot{\alpha}_j)+$$
$$\frac{1}{2}\frac{4\kappa\xi-(1-\lambda\varphi)\xi-(\lambda-\gamma)}{\xi(2\kappa\xi-(\lambda-\gamma))}c_i+\frac{1}{2}\frac{(1-\lambda\varphi)\xi-(\lambda-\gamma)}{\xi(2\kappa\xi-(\lambda-\gamma))}c_j+$$
$$\frac{1}{2}\frac{\lambda}{\xi(2\kappa\xi-(\lambda-\gamma))}(a_i-a_j)$$

$$g_i = \frac{1}{2}\frac{(\lambda-\gamma)-4\kappa\xi}{\xi\varphi(2\kappa\xi-(\lambda-\gamma))}(p_i^a-\dot{\alpha}_i)+\frac{1}{2}\frac{(\lambda-\gamma)}{\xi\varphi(2\kappa\xi-(\lambda-\gamma))}(p_j^a-\dot{\alpha}_j)+$$
$$\frac{1}{2}\frac{4\kappa\xi(1-\xi\varphi)-(1+\varphi(\lambda-2\gamma))\xi-(\lambda-\gamma)}{\xi\varphi(2\kappa\xi-(\lambda-\gamma))}c_i+\frac{1}{2}\frac{(1-\lambda\varphi)\xi-(\lambda-\gamma)}{\xi\varphi(2\kappa\xi-(\lambda-\gamma))}c_j+$$
$$\frac{1}{2}\frac{\lambda}{\varphi(2\kappa\xi-(\lambda-\gamma))}(a_i-a_j)$$

$$\hat{\imath} = -\frac{1}{2}\frac{\lambda-\gamma}{\sigma\xi}(p_1^a-\dot{\alpha}_1+p_2^a-\dot{\alpha}_2)+\frac{1}{2}\frac{\lambda-\gamma-\xi(1-\lambda\varphi)}{\sigma\xi}(c_1+c_2)+\frac{1}{2}\frac{\lambda}{\sigma}(a_1+a_2)$$

together with equations (4.1'), (4.2), (4.3) and (4.4), yield:

$$\frac{1}{2}(p_1 + p_2) = n_i = b_i = 0,\ i = 1,2$$

which means that both the governments and the central bank reach their ideal output.[14]

That is the reason why, in the NCM, the deficit limitation is not really considered an obstacle to economic stabilization.

NCM governance in a Keynesian world

What kind of consequences may such governance principles have in a Keynesian unemployment situation? In order to answer the question, let the exogenous variable q_i represent the labour force variation that is initially required for full employment in country i. Since n_i is the variation in employment for the current period, $q_i - n_i$ measures the level of unemployment at the end of the period. As authorities think that q_i reflects the natural rate of unemployment ($\overline{w}_i$, c_i, $\dot{\alpha}_i$ and a_i are supposed to provoke temporary deviations from the assumed trajectory), they do not take it as a stabilization matter, and make the policy discussed earlier.

The formal results of the previous section can easily be adapted to the present configuration when the labour force remains unchanged during the current period ($n_{fi} = 0$), provided we replace equation (4.2) by equation (4.2$_k$), which only supposes that $\overline{w}_i$ and θ_k replace p_i^a and θ. It follows that, in the most favourable case where authorities can completely stabilize the prices and the activity without deteriorating their budget balance, unemployment remains blocked at its initial level ($q_i - n_i = q_i$). Thus, as long as the actual level of unemployment is the target level, the policy mix tends to perpetuate unemployment.

In less favourable cases, the authorities do not have enough room for manoeuvre as concerns the adjustment of taxes, expenditure and interest rates, with the result that the effective demand depressions cannot be totally offset. The problem is all the more serious since Keynesian unemployment does not tend spontaneously towards any long-run value, contrary to what authorities think, with the result that they take the new rate of unemployment as the new natural one. That suggests a different explanation of what New Keynesians have referred to as unemployment hysteresis:[15] restricted policy-mix reactions to the effective demand depressions only weaken the rise of unemployment, but subsequently neither the market forces nor the economic policy tend to restore the initial level. Actually, as far as wages respond to the variations in unemployment, not to its level, the NCM concludes to real wages rigidity, hiding by the way what in fact is a lack of policy mix flexibility (remember that wage flexibility does not ensure better results in a Keynesian system).

Things may even be made worse when recurrent distributive tensions exist, because the central bank tends to raise the rate of interest according to the conflict intensity. Indeed, as long as persistent inflationary pressures are interpreted as the result of a 'natural' lower demand for money (provided the supply did not rise), monetary policy takes a harder line and becomes a depressive force.

Thus, despite the fact that the two theoretical approaches share the same objectives in the field of macroeconomic governance (that is, full employment, price stability, sound public finance), the type of governance which has been designed by the NCM may be singularly inappropriate in a Keynesian monetary union.

Keynesian Macroeconomic Governance

Controlling inflation

Even though inflation always comes from a gap between the money supply and the demand for money expressed at current prices, it is instructive to consider the causes of the gap. For example, according to the real balance effect, a decrease in effective demand may produce inflation, insofar as it reduces the demand for money. This is quite different from surprise inflation or seigniorage; it takes part in the adjustment process towards equilibrium. It develops especially when wages rigidity impedes the adjustment of real wages. It would be strange if monetary policy aimed to fight inflation after a demand depression when wages are rigid. Central banks rather tend to decrease interest rates in such cases, so as to facilitate the adjustment. New and old Keynesians could agree on this, although the former consider the effective demand failures as shocks with temporary effects.

The conflict on income distribution is a different source of inflation. The mainstream economics interprets distributive tensions in terms of stochastic supply shocks or in terms of structural change (if they are recurrent), never as a moving compromise which interacts with other economic decisions. In this perspective, insofar as economic agents may, by assumption, freely adjust their plan to the perceived market real prices, a disagreement about nominal earnings, given expected future prices, takes the form of a supply cut at current prices. That comes to an increase in the natural rate of unemployment. If the central bank aims to smooth the depressive effects on output, it can be driven to create money temporarily, so as to compensate the supplementary need for transaction money which is induced by (temporary) tensions. But, in the long run, monetary policy cannot avoid the depressive effects of the negative supply shocks. Indeed, in case of recurrent (then foreseeable) pressures, the central bank could not repetitively smooth the negative effects on the supply side, because recurrent inflationary measures would be expected, and therefore would not deliver real effects.

The Keynesian point of view about this question is quite different, even though the results are comparable. First, we have seen that in the presence of recurrent distributive tensions, low inflation targeting may introduce a deflationary bias in monetary policy, which contrasts sharply with the neutrality of money in the NCM's 'long run'. In addition, when strong tensions compel the central bank to implement a restrictive monetary policy, high unemployment may drive the governments to accept high deficits in a context of high interest rates. On the contrary, safe distributive conditions help monetary policy to contain interest rates and to contribute, thereby, to the policy mix effectiveness (see below).

Hence, monetary policy is not always the unique way, nor is it the best, to control inflation; legal and institutional rules concerning the distribution of income play a crucial role as well. Actually, these two aspects should not be considered separately.

Inflation control raises additional problems in monetary unions, for the same monetary policy applies in all member countries, regardless of where inflationary pressures started. Furthermore, interest rate interactions with national fiscal policies have to be taken into account. The following section discusses this point.

Governing according to the context

In non-ergodic systems, the macroeconomic governance should not hinge on mechanic rules whose consequences are supposed being well known and able to reach predefined targets. It is always possible to have ideal objectives, but it is not always reasonable to make these the short-run target of a policy mix, because economic policy may spark changes in expectations and private economic decisions, which may in turn make the policy inappropriate (as popularized in the Lucas critique).[16] Keynesian contexts require a pragmatic governance, which goes through intermediate targets in order to avoid jolts which could destabilize expectations and private decisions.

Formally, such an approach suggests replacing equation (4.7), that is, the government objective in the NCM model, by a condition of the type:

$$n_i = \mu_i q_i, \quad 0 < \mu_i \leq 1 \tag{4.8}$$

where μ_i is a coefficient the government chooses in accordance with the confidence it has in the success of operations. It is important to bear in mind that this equation, like most equations of Keynesian models, does not pretend to the stability that is usually assumed. Indeed μ_i is subject to various changing factors. Some of them concern the effective demand expected sensitivity to the policy instruments; others depend on financial constraints which may limit the governments' room for manoeuvre; others may add political considerations (for example public opinion). In this perspective, economic policy design hinges as much on the selection of the objective (value of μ_i) as on the adjustment of instruments (value of g_i or $\hat{t}_i$ which solves equation 4.8, given equations 4.1', 4.2_k, 4.3 and 4.4).

Nevertheless, since the budget balances depend on the short-run employment objectives, governments may have to limit the increase in public expenditures, unless they are able to adjust taxes. Consequently, employment and budget balance objectives, as well as the concerned instruments, turn out to be interdependent, and therefore must be simultaneously chosen within a country. Hence, let us suppose that the budget-balance target depends more or less on the magnitude of unemployment (according to the room for manoeuvre of the period and to the relative importance the governments give to employment):

$$b_i = -\psi_{ki}(q_i - n_i) + z_i \tag{4.9}$$

where $\psi_{ki} \geq 0$ represents the 'fiscal flexibility' in country i (the higher ψ_{ki} is, the less the government adjusts taxes, and the higher the deficit is), and z_i represents other factors which may interfere in the short run, like deliberate structural deficit due to long-run public investments or debt management considerations. Once again, the problem as much concerns the objective selection (value of ψ_{ki}) as the instruments adjustment (value of $\hat{t}_i$ or g_i which solves equation 4.9).

It is then possible to determine the pairs (g_i, $\hat{t}_i$) which solve (4.8) and (4.9), given equations (4.1'), (4.2_k), (4.3) and (4.4). As can be seen from the solutions (Appendix 4.C), the instruments of country i are not only moved when it has been hit by a shock, but also when the partner has been hit. The reason is of course that shocks transmit across countries, as well as policies.

Economic policies often carry positive or negative externalities, depending on the type of spillover and depending on the macroeconomic context abroad. For example, in the system formed by equations (4.1'), (4.2_k), (4.3) and (4.4), an increase in expenditure of country i has positive externalities when $q_1 < 0$ and $q_2 < 0$ (because $\partial n_i / \partial g_j \neq 0$), and negative ones when $q_2 = 0$. Many configurations are possible, according to the initial situation, the type of the shock, the transmission of shocks and policies. No general rule can be drawn, in contrast to the NCM world, where the system always tends to a 'natural' anchorage, where, given the shock, the transmission always has the same sign (as long as the 'structural' parameters do not change), and where shocks do not prevent the predictability of the long-run trajectory. In Keynesian economics, each configuration has to be examined according to the context.

One of the important elements of the context is the central bank behaviour. Let us suppose, for example, that it pursues the objective described in equation (4.6). It can be shown that the system formed by equations (4.1'), (4.2_k), (4.3), (4.4) and (4.6) then exhibits negative international transmission of expenditure variations.[17] More generally, because of the effective demand and employment sensitivity to the interest rate, the moves of the fiscal policies instruments required by conditions (4.8) and (4.9) depend on the monetary policy decisions (see Appendix 4.C). Of course, interest rates also matter for the choice of objectives (μ_i,ψ_{ki}). For example, if the governments think that the central bank will accommodate, they can adopt more ambitious plans in terms of employment, or limit the cost of a given increase in employment in terms of deficits, taxes and/or expenditure adjustment. Thus, the monetary policy can make it more or less difficult for the governments to reach their objectives.

Notice that the central bank participation to the economic recovery does not absolutely necessitate lower interest rates. Remember that $\hat{\imath} = 0$, for example, means that the banks adjust the supply of money to the demand expressed at the initial rate of interest. Thus, even when the central bank cannot significantly reduce the interest rates (if, for example, they are already very low), it can help in a decisive way by controlling the monetary tensions that economic recovery usually provokes.

CONCLUSION

Our discussion of the macroeconomic governance of a monetary union shows that, whereas the NCM principles exhibit a kind of symbiosis between monetary and decentralized fiscal policies in ergodic regimes, this causes severe dysfunctions in Keynesian regimes. Indeed, as far as unemployment does not tend to be spontaneously corrected by the market forces, contrary to what authorities believe, both the central bank and the national governments 'symbiotically' activate their policy so as to maintain the current rate of unemployment. Hence, the unemployment trap mechanisms identified in Asensio (2006, 2007) generalize to monetary unions, and offer new arguments regarding the failure of the European macroeconomic governance.

On the other hand, the Keynesian approach pleads in favour of important changes in the current principles of the eurozone governance.

First, since the European Central Bank cannot repress recurrent distributive inflationary pressures without having non-temporary depressive effects on aggregate demand and employment, authorities should recognize that another way for fighting this kind of inflation rests on the continuous pursuit of a consensual income distribution.

Second, authorities should no longer refer to the fictitious 'natural' rate of (un)employment and derivative concepts which do not apply to non-ergodic systems. If there is no long-run predictable trajectory, the ordinary conduct of monetary and fiscal policies cannot be guided by any systematic 'optimal rule' designed in order to stabilize the economy near from a predetermined trajectory. Instead, uncertainty imposes a gradual and pragmatic approach, closely linked to the context. Our modelling of such an approach suggests that the European Monetary Union could take advantage of the complementarity between the European Central Bank interest rate decisions and the national fiscal instruments. That certainly would help the governments to fight unemployment without denying their financial constraints. The Stability and Growth Pact constraints should not hide the dissuasive impact of the expected liquidity constraint that may result from a reputed non-accommodating monetary policy. Accommodating actually does not necessarily require an interest rate reduction; it may simply hinge on avoiding interest rate increases when governments aim to reflate their economy. Of course such a policy mix could produce some rise in the price indexes, but this is a necessary condition for economic recovery when nominal wages are sticky and productivity is constant. Even in the NCM, relative price adjustments are quite different from inflation.

APPENDIX 4.A

Let begin with the national aggregate-demand functions:

$$Y_{di} = \upsilon_i (Y_i - t_i Y_i) - \beta_i (i - p^a_{+1i}) + \left(\frac{P_j}{P_i}\right)^{\varsigma} + G_i + A_i,\ i = 1,2,\ i \neq j$$

where Y_i represents the output volume in country i, t_i the tax rate (taxes/output), υ the propensity to consume, G_i the government's expenditure, A_i an autonomous component, P_i the price level of goods, p^a_{+1i}, the expected variation of P_i till the next period, $i - p^a_{+1i}$ the real rate of interest.

Through differentiation (assuming $d\upsilon = d\beta = 0$ and $dp^a_{+1i} = 0$), and dividing by Y_0, we get:

$$\frac{dY_i}{Y_{i0}} = \upsilon_i \frac{dY_i}{Y_{i0}} - \upsilon_i t_{i0} \frac{dY_i}{Y_{i0}} - \upsilon_i dt_i - \frac{\beta_i}{Y_{i0}} di + \frac{\varsigma}{Y_{i0}} \left(\frac{P_{j0}}{P_{i0}}\right)^{\varsigma} \frac{dP_j}{P_{j0}} - \frac{\varsigma}{Y_{i0}} \left(\frac{P_{j0}}{P_{i0}}\right)^{\varsigma} \frac{dP_i}{P_{i0}} + \frac{dG_i}{Y_{i0}} + \frac{dA_i}{Y_{i0}}$$

Since $t_{i0} = T_{i0}/Y_{i0}$, the equality $dG/Y_{i0} = t_{i0}\, dG/G_{i0}$ holds when the budget is balanced ($T_{i0} = G_{i0}$). Writing relative deviation rates with small letters ($x_i = dX_i/X_{i0}$, excepting $a_i = dA_i/Y_{i0}$), we have:

$$y_{di} = \upsilon_i (1 - t_{i0}) y_i - \upsilon_i dt_i - \frac{\beta_i}{Y_{i0}} di + \frac{\varsigma}{Y_{i0}} \left(\frac{P_{i0}}{P_{j0}}\right)^{\varsigma} (p_j - p_i) + t_{i0} g_i + a_i$$

The market equilibrium requires $y_i = y_{di}$, hence:

$$y_i = -\gamma_i \hat{t}_i - \sigma_i \hat{i} + \kappa_i (p_j - p_i) + \lambda_i (\varphi g_i + a_i),\ i = 1,2,\ j = 1,2,\ i \neq j$$

where $\hat{\imath} = di$, $\hat{t}_i = dt_i$, $\varphi_i = t_{i0}$, $\gamma_i = \dfrac{\upsilon_i}{1 - \upsilon_i (1 - \varphi_i)}$, $\lambda_i = \dfrac{1}{1 - \upsilon_i (1 - \varphi_i)}$,

$$\sigma_i = \frac{1}{1 - \upsilon_i (1 - \varphi_i)} \frac{\beta}{Y_{i0}},\ \kappa_i = \frac{1}{1 - \upsilon_i (1 - \varphi_i)} \frac{\varsigma}{Y_{i0}} \left(\frac{P_{i0}}{P_{j0}}\right)^{\varsigma}$$

As a matter of simplicity, the same set of parameters is supposed to hold in both countries (γ, υ, σ, κ, φ).

APPENDIX 4.B

The budget balance (B) is defined as:

$$B = tPY - PG$$

Differentiating around a solution indexed by 0 yields:

$$dB = t_0P_0dY + P_0Y_0dt + t_0Y_0dP - P_0dG - G_0dP$$

and dividing by the initial value of output:

$$dB/(P_0Y_0) = t_0dY/Y_0 + dt + t_0dP/P_0 - dG/Y_0 - (G_0/Y_0)(dP/P_0)$$

Hence, around a situation of balanced budget where $t_0 = G_0/Y_0$ (remember

$$g = dG/G_0):$$

$$b = t_0(y - g) + dt$$

and, with the same notation as in Appendix 4.A:

$$b = \varphi(y - g) + \hat{t}$$

APPENDIX 4.C

$$\begin{aligned}
g_1 = {} & \frac{\sigma}{\varphi(\lambda-\gamma)} i + \frac{\kappa}{\varphi((\lambda-\gamma)-2\kappa\xi)}(\bar{w}_1 - \dot{\alpha}_1 - \bar{w}_2 + \dot{\alpha}_2) + \\
& \frac{(\xi\alpha(\lambda\varphi-1)-(\lambda-\gamma)(1-\alpha+\theta_k))\mu_2 + \lambda\xi\psi_{k2}(1-\mu_2)}{\varphi((\lambda-\gamma)-2\kappa\xi)(\lambda-\gamma)} \kappa q_2 + \\
& \frac{((\lambda-\gamma)((1+\theta_k)\kappa+(1-\gamma\varphi-\kappa)\alpha)+((2\gamma-\lambda)\varphi-1)\xi\alpha\kappa)\mu_1 + (\kappa\xi(2\gamma-\lambda)-\gamma(\lambda-\gamma))(1-\mu_1)\psi_{k1}}{\varphi((\lambda-\gamma)-2\kappa\xi)(\lambda-\gamma)} q_1 + \\
& \frac{((\lambda\varphi-1)\xi+\lambda-\gamma)\kappa}{\varphi((\lambda-\gamma)-2\kappa\xi)(\lambda-\gamma)} c_2 + \frac{(\xi((2\gamma-\lambda)\varphi-1)-(\lambda-\gamma))\kappa+(1-\gamma\varphi)(\lambda-\gamma)}{\varphi((\lambda-\gamma)-2\kappa\xi)(\lambda-\gamma)} c_1 + \\
& \frac{\lambda\kappa\xi}{\varphi((\lambda-\gamma)-2\kappa\xi)(\lambda-\gamma)}(a_2 - z_2) + \frac{\lambda(\kappa\xi-(\lambda-\gamma))}{\varphi((\lambda-\gamma)-2\kappa\xi)(\lambda-\gamma)} a_1 + \frac{\gamma(\lambda-\gamma)+\kappa\xi(\lambda-2\gamma)}{\varphi((\lambda-\gamma)-2\kappa\xi)(\lambda-\gamma)} z_1
\end{aligned}$$

$$
\begin{aligned}
\hat{\imath}_1 = {} & \frac{\sigma}{(\lambda-\gamma)} i + \frac{\kappa}{((\lambda-\gamma)-2\kappa\xi)} (\overline{w}_1 - \dot{\alpha}_1 - \overline{w}_2 + \dot{\alpha}_2) + \\
& \frac{(\xi\alpha(\lambda\varphi-1)-(\lambda-\gamma)(1-\alpha+\theta_k))\mu_2 + \lambda\xi\psi_{k2}(1-\mu_2)}{((\lambda-\gamma)-2\kappa\xi)(\lambda-\gamma)} \kappa q_2 + \\
& \frac{((\lambda-\gamma)((1+\theta_k)\kappa+(1-\gamma\varphi-\kappa)\alpha)-(1-\varphi\lambda)\xi\alpha\kappa)\mu_1 - (\lambda-\gamma-\kappa\xi)\lambda(1-\mu_1)\psi_{k1}}{((\lambda-\gamma)-2\kappa\xi)(\lambda-\gamma)} q_1 + \\
& \frac{((\lambda\varphi-1)\xi+\lambda-\gamma)\kappa}{((\lambda-\gamma)-2\kappa\xi)(\lambda-\gamma)} c_2 + \frac{((\lambda\varphi-1)\xi-(\lambda-\gamma))\kappa+(1-\lambda\varphi)(\lambda-\gamma)}{((\lambda-\gamma)-2\kappa\xi)(\lambda-\gamma)} c_1 + \\
& \frac{\lambda\kappa\xi}{((\lambda-\gamma)-2\kappa\xi)(\lambda-\gamma)} (a_2 - z_2) + \frac{\lambda(\gamma-\lambda+\kappa\xi)}{((\lambda-\gamma)-2\kappa\xi)(\lambda-\gamma)} (a_1 - z_1)
\end{aligned}
$$

NB: g_2 and t_2 can easily be deduced by permutation of the variable coefficients: ψ_{k1} and ψ_{k2}, μ_1 and μ_2.

Since at equilibrium: $n_i = \mu_i q_i$ (equation 4.8), then we have $y_i = \alpha\mu_i q_i + c_i$ and $b_i = z_i - \psi_{ki} q_i (1-\mu_i)$.

NOTES

1. It is of interest to note that the two leading countries in the achievement of the European Union were among the first to test the excessive deficit procedure. Actually, considering the depressive context of 2003, the decision they made could have been a better way to protect the stability pact than the one recommended by the Commission: restrictive fiscal policies in two major economies of the Union could have harmed the situation and triggered a string of excessive deficits in other countries.
2. The reader will find more details upon the methodological aspects of our modelling in Asensio (2006, 2007).
3. Ergodicity supposes that competitive mechanisms anchor the system in a predetermined trajectory. It has been identified as the dynamic stability of a stochastic process. See Vercelli (1991, pp. 40, 154), Davidson (2002, pp. 39, 69).
4. See Appendix 4.A.
5. Following Tobin (1958), money helps to diversify portfolios in order to optimize the return – risk ratio (the higher the rate of interest, the more one is encouraged to increase the proportion of risked assets, and to reduce the proportion of money).
6. As Palley (2006) stated, this assessment of endogenous money substantially differs from the post-Keynesian one.
7. Theoretically, it is possible that flexible nominal wages reach this solution without any variation in the rate of interest (but it is not certain; see *The General Theory*, Chapter 19): through positive effects on the marginal efficiency of capital and effective demand, wage flexibility may produce inflation, reduce real wages and raise production. If on the other hand nominal wages are sticky, the role of the interest rate becomes crucial.
8. It could solve the problem in an open union, but that would suppose that other countries support the negative consequences. Hence it seems reasonable to work with an autarkic union, in order to force the partners to deal with their own externalities.

9. See Tobin (1975) and Palley (2005) about this kind of instability.
10. It is not essential to make imperfect competition assumptions in order to obtain a mark-up relation. For example, starting from the production function $Y = CN^{\alpha}$, $\alpha < 1$, competitive pricing requires the marginal productivity to be equal to the real cost of labour: $\partial Y/\partial N = W(1+\xi t)/P \Rightarrow P = W(1+\xi t)/(C\alpha N^{\alpha-1}) = (WN(1+\xi t)/Y)/\alpha$; hence, by differentiation of the associated logarithmic expression (for small values of $\hat{t}$), we have $p = w + n - y - \dot{\alpha} + \xi\hat{t}$, where $\dot{\alpha}$ is the rate of variation in α (exogenous). Notice that an increasing mark-up on unit labour cost expresses in this case a declining wages–output ratio ($\dot{\alpha} < 0$) and/or increasing fiscal taxes ($\hat{t} = dt > 0$).
11. From equation (4.3), we have: $y - n = (\alpha - 1)n + c$. Hence, an increase in effective demand and employment reduces the productivity of labour in the absence of technological change (that is, c constant), and rises the unit cost of production. This shows that cost-pushed inflation and demand-led inflation may express the same reality. In fact, whatever apparent causes it has, inflation always requires an increase in demand (see the next subsection).
12. According to the no-inflation-bias hypothesis we should have in general $p_i^a = 0$, but it may be useful nevertheless to conserve this variable as an exogenous temporary shock on expected inflation.
13. These policy rules could be derived by minimization of a loss function. For example, starting from $L = (1/2)(\varsigma n^2 + b^2)$, the first-order condition requires $\varsigma n(\partial n/\partial g) + b(\partial b/\partial g) = 0$, which is equivalent to $b = \psi n$ provided that $\psi = -\varsigma(\partial n/\partial g)/(\partial b/\partial g)$. This approach sometimes raises difficulties that will not be considered here.
14. In Dixit and Lambertini (2001, 2003), if monetary and fiscal policy-makers agree about the ideal levels of output and inflation, the responses to the shocks are spontaneously driven to this ideal.
15. See the Minisymposium on hysteresis in the *Journal of Post Keynesian Economics*, **15**(3), Spring 1993.
16. Keynes actually raised the question in *The General Theory* (Chapter 15, see the last third of section II). Of course, the meaning and implications of the argument differ considerably owing to the methodological opposition (see Vercelli, 1991).
17. Since an increase in g_i reduces the average level of unemployment below the natural rate, the central bank increases the rate of interest in order to stabilize the whole economy, which finally involves a depressive effect in country j.
18. Notice that this requires notably $T_{i0} = T_{i0}^*$ and $Y_{i0} = Y_{i0}^*$, a hypothesis we make in order to simplify algebra at a rather high level of abstraction, but which should be abandoned in more sophisticated models.

REFERENCES

Arestis, P. and M. Sawyer (2003), 'Reinventing fiscal policy', *Journal of Post Keynesian Economics*, **26** (1), 3–26.

Asensio, A. (2006), 'New-Consensus macroeconomic governance in a Keynesian world, and the Keynesian alternative', *Brazilian Journal of Political Economy*, **26** (4), 537–51.

Asensio, A. (2007), 'Monetary and budgetary–fiscal policy interactions in a Keynesian context: revisiting macroeconomic governance', in Arestis, P., E. Hein and E. Le Heron (eds), *Aspects of Modern Macroeconomic and Monetary Policies*, London: Palgrave Macmillan, 80–105.

Davidson, P. (2002), *Financial Markets, Money and the Real World,* Cheltenham, UK and Northampton, MA, USA: Edward Elgar.

Dixit, A. and L. Lambertini (2001) 'Monetary–fiscal policy interactions and commitment versus discretion in a monetary union', *European Economic Review*, **45**, 977–87.

Dixit, A. and L. Lambertini (2003), 'Symbiosis of monetary and fiscal policies in a monetary union', *Journal of International Economics*, **60**, 235–47.

Lavoie, M. (2006), 'A post-Keynesian amendment to the New Consensus on monetary policy', *Metroeconomica*, **57** (2), 165–92.

Palley, T.I. (2005), 'Keynesian models of recession and depression', unpublished manuscript, www.thomaspalley.com, November.

Palley, T.I. (2006), 'A post Keynesian framework for monetary policy: why interest rate operating procedures are not enough', in Gnos, C. and L.-P. Rochon (eds), *Post Keynesian Principles of Economic Policy*, Cheltenham, UK and Northampton, MA, USA: Edward Elgar, 81–101.

Romer, D. (2000), 'Keynesian macroeconomics without the LM curve', *Journal of Economic Perspectives*, **14** (2), 149–69.

Sargent, T. and N. Wallace (1981), 'Some unpleasant monetarist arithmetic', *Federal Reserve Bank of Minneapolis Quarterly Review*, Fall, 1–17.

Tobin, J. (1958), 'Liquidity preference as behaviour towards risk', *Review of Economic Studies*, **25**, 65–86.

Tobin, J. (1975), 'Keynesian models of recession and depression', *American Economic Review*, **65**, 195–202.

Vercelli, A. (1991), *Methodological Foundations of Macroeconomics: Keynes and Lucas*, Cambridge: Cambridge University Press.

5. Inflation targeting and monetary policy governance: the case of the European Central Bank

Sergio Rossi

INTRODUCTION

Monetary policy governance is a form of public governance, to wit, state intervention in establishing a legal and institutional environment in which any kinds of economic activities may flourish thanks to economic stability, in particular price stability over the long run. Indeed, the content of monetary policy decisions is led today by a less dogmatically constrained debate than used to be the case in the second half of the twentieth century. In particular, it has become increasingly evident that there is no single, and unambiguously 'correct', form of 'good governance' for monetary policy in the modern world economy, where globalization seems to be pervasive, and shapes the reaction that nation-states put into practice in engaging with a globalized world by pursuing cooperative strategies between countries and constructing international regulatory regimes in order for them to manage cross-border issues (Held et al., 1999, pp. 7–9).

Owing to an increasing number of international agreements and increasingly important international financial flows, traditional policy tools such as exchange rate adjustments and changes in the money supply have completely lost their effectiveness (Organisation for Economic Co-operation and Development, 2001, pp. 25–6). On the other hand, as pointed out by Weiss (1998), among others, financial markets might be the only economic sector that has become truly globalized. As a result, the state has to ensure financial stability, to elicit sufficiently stable expectations and moderate real interest rates, if there is to be economic growth over the long run. In this regard, states need to reduce uncertainty, set new rules of the game, and negotiate them at the world level (Boyer and Drache, 1996, p. 3).

As a matter of fact, a number of monetary authorities have modified their policy rules as well as their strategies over the last 15 years. In light of the poor results in terms of price stability and macroeconomic stabilization that monetary targeting strategies led to up to the 1980s, several central banks have explicitly adopted an inflation target, following the example of the Reserve Bank of New Zealand in 1990 (Dalziel, 1998). In a move to increase transparency and hence foster credibility and policy efficiency, central banks have been implementing a monetary policy framework whose centrepiece is some numerical definition of price stability, as measured by a price index, around which the measured inflation rate has to remain in order for monetary authorities to control the business cycle in the short run without affecting price stability in the long run (Bernanke et al., 1999).

Together with this change in strategy, many central banks have been made independent (at least to some extent) of the government and political parties. A central bank's independence is indeed considered as an efficient means to guarantee the attainment of price stability, as it disposes of the inflation bias that the politically dependent central banks are prone to as a result of the so-called dynamic inconsistency problem pointed out by Rogoff (1985). This is so much so that independent central banks are associated with lower inflation rates but not slower economic growth than politically dependent central banks in monetary policy literature (see, for instance, Alesina and Summers, 1993; Persson and Tabellini, 1993).

In fact, empirical evidence shows that independent central banks do not provide a 'free lunch', that is to say, costless low inflation rates, always and everywhere. In a number of cases of disinflation processes carried out by politically independent monetary authorities in advanced countries – to date, transition and emerging market economies have not been sufficiently investigated in this respect – the reduction in inflation rates has been noticed alongside of some recession, notably in terms of output and employment losses (see, for example, Debelle and Fischer, 1994; Walsh, 1995b; Fischer, 1996; Gärtner, 1997; Jordan, 1997, 1999; Posen, 1998; Down, 2004). This literature coined the expression of 'sacrifice ratio' as an operational measure of the economic costs of disinflation in terms of output and/or employment losses (see Ball, 1994).

Now, very few studies examine whether central banks with inflation targeting strategies induce low sacrifice ratios (see Bernanke et al., 1999; Corbo et al., 2002). In addition, to our knowledge, no study in this area has been carried out on the European Central Bank (ECB), to investigate whether a sharp regime shift – such as creation of the European Monetary Union and the euro changeover – produces credibility and makes expectations to adjust quickly, making disinflation costless, as argued by Sargent (1983) and recent monetary policy literature (see Clarida et al., 1999; Diana and Sidiropoulos, 2004). The purpose of this chapter is to address this issue from a political-economy stance. We will argue that in the European Union (EU), with a fully independent central bank pursuing the single objective of price level stability in the euro area, the single monetary policy does not live up to its goal(s), as enshrined in the Treaty on the European Union. As a matter of fact, the monetary policy of the ECB has not been interested in economic stabilization so far, but merely concentrated on the stability of the targeted price index, without being able to meet it, however, even though this may seem surprising in light of the ECB resolute attachment to price stability over the medium to long run.

To guarantee financial stability and enhance economic performance, this chapter proposes to strengthen the incentives of monetary policy decision-makers to care for long-run macroeconomic stability. In this respect, the chapter proposes to allow non-EU-nationals also to run for office as ECB Governing Council members. Further, beyond individuals, also political parties, businesses and organizations should be allowed to take executive positions at the ECB. This new form of monetary policy governance is likely to increase the incentives for central bankers to pursue stabilization-oriented policies in order for them to stay in office, so that they are led to care more for the long-term interests of the citizens, and hence ignore well-organized pressure groups and their own short-term particular goals. To reinforce these incentives, it would be possible, and desirable from a political-economy viewpoint, to let the citizens choose, by direct election, their monetary policy-makers. Indeed, democracy would further strengthen the incentives for any monetary policy suppliers to care for the long-term interests of the citizens and to offer therefore a stabilization-oriented monetary policy more conducive to real growth and employment than is the case today in several countries, as the euro-area situation shows well.

The structure of this chapter is as follows. The next section discusses the pros and cons of inflation targeting strategies, in light of recent monetary policy literature on central bank independence. The third section focuses on the European Central Bank, to point out that the monetary policy strategy of one among the world's most independent central banks could, in fact, improve if account is taken of the merits of inflation targeting. The fourth section puts forward a proposal for reforming the governance of ECB monetary policy, to make it more democratic and conducive to economic stability than has been the case up to date. The fifth section concludes.

A COSTS–BENEFITS ANALYSIS OF INFLATION TARGETING AND CENTRAL BANK INDEPENDENCE

According to Svensson (1999, p. 279), the monetary policy strategy of inflation targeting consists of an explicit target for the rate of inflation and an implicit employment target, with an implicit relative weight on employment stabilization. An explicit inflation target is a targeted rate of inflation publicly announced by the government or the central bank (or both), indicating that the monetary authority will be obliged to attain and keep the stated inflation rate over some time horizon, to be specified *ex ante* (Bernanke and Mishkin, 1997, pp. 97–8). As a result, a low and stable rate of inflation is the final monetary policy goal under an inflation targeting strategy. This amounts to a higher weight given to price-level stability in the central bank's loss, or policy reaction, function with respect to other macroeconomic goals, such as output stabilization or full employment.

As Bernanke et al. (1999, pp. 299–301) note with respect to the old 'rules-versus-discretion debate' à la Kydland and Prescott (1977), inflation targeting may be viewed as a halfway station between a rules-based and a fully discretionary monetary policy. As a matter of fact, this regime gives rise to a discretionary monetary policy under constraint: those central banks that target inflation explicitly are in a position to take advantage of some flexibility in policy-making, in order for them to affect the business cycle in the short run, insofar as their actions do not jeopardize price stability in the long run. Thus the inflation targeting strategy is neither as rigid as a policy rule, as it does not imply a mechanical monetary policy action, nor as fully flexible as the notional case for absolute discretion, since the central bank is obliged to announce the rate(s) of inflation that it targets over time. Owing to this public announcement, the central bank is accountable for the effects of its monetary policy interventions, both in the short and long run, for instance as regards the actual rates of inflation and real GDP growth. This is likely to affect its credibility, thereby agents' expectations, with important implications for both the time lags and the effects of monetary policy on the country's economic performance.

Recent inflation targeting literature points out that targeting an inflation rate instead of some growth rate of a monetary aggregate like M0, M1 or M3 increases a central bank's transparency, discipline and accountability, and improves communication with financial markets and the general public (Mishkin and Schmidt-Hebbel, 2002). Indeed, a number of inflation targeters, such as the Bank of England, publish periodically both inflation reports and inflation forecasts by means of which they implement a backward-looking as well as a forward-looking monetary policy communication strategy with the public at large. This compels the monetary authority to inform also on the policy it aims to carry out in order for the measured inflation rate to be on track with the stated target. By this information campaign, central banks hope to affect the agents' expectations with respect to future inflation, providing transparency on many important features such as:

- the goals and scope of monetary policy interventions;
- the rationale for the numerical value of the inflation targets over different horizons;
- the targeted price index (for instance, a consumer price index or a core inflation index);
- the policy tools that the central bank will put to practical use to meet its targets;
- the reasons explaining possible deviations from the targeted inflation rates.

As a matter of fact, monetary policy transparency is important for a number of reasons, all of which are crucial for policy performance. First, it improves private sector decision-making in the long run, since it decreases uncertainty as regards monetary policy goals, inflation and interest rates, provided that the central bank is credible. Secondly, it avoids that in pre-election periods the government and/or political parties put the central bank under pressure to carry out an expansionary monetary policy that contrasts with current and prospective economic performance – just for election purposes. Thirdly, it allows a more flexible monetary policy over time, because a transparent central bank can address unforeseen economic shocks by deviating from the preannounced target without fearing that this will affect agents' expectations negatively. If a central bank's interventions are credible and both the public and the financial markets support them, then the monetary authority will benefit from greater flexibility in its actions, since it will be able to justify deviating from the targeted inflation rate with no loss of credibility. This flexibility is an important factor of good economic performance.

Now, the question arises as to the choice between a point target and a target band for the policy-desired rate of inflation, granted that the latter is stable and positive.[1] This choice affects monetary policy flexibility to a significant extent. The *sine qua non* condition for adopting a precise inflation target (say, 2 per cent per annum) without putting monetary policy at stake is that the central bank is able to persuade the general public as well as financial markets that its policy tools remain highly volatile to meet the target, and that unforeseen shocks (on either aggregate demand or aggregate supply) may be the cause for a target over- or undershooting (Bernanke et al., 1999, pp. 294–5). Only in this case will the economic agents be prone to accept a deviation from the inflation target without losing confidence in the central bank's credibility, which is necessary for a point target strategy to influence the agents' expectations closely. By contrast, a target band for the price stability goal offers more flexibility to monetary policy-makers, and conveys to the general public the idea that a central bank cannot control the inflation rate independently of the economic situation. In this case, however, markets will react more strongly – and the central bank's credibility will be much more at issue – if the observed inflation rate lies outside the targeted band than if it does not correspond to the point target. As a result, agents' expectations would be more volatile and uncertain.

In this respect, a central bank should carefully assess the width of its target band: if this band is too large (to meet it more easily), it may jeopardize the central bank's credibility and ability to implement a disinflation policy effectively (that is, with low costs in terms of output and employment). If the band is too narrow, by way of contrast, the likelihood that the central bank does not meet it rises, which might give rise to credibility problems, too (see Mishkin, 2000; Jonas and Mishkin, 2005).

In fact, the choice of a target band instead of a point target might also be an indication that the central bank weighs, at least to some extent, real variables in its loss, or policy-reaction, function. The monetary authority might in particular consider macroeconomic stabilization, that is to say, full employment, among its goals in the short run. If it chooses a point target, this would then imply that it can do nothing to stabilize the real economy, if this makes it deviate from its inflation target. This issue raises the question of the sacrifice in terms of output and employment losses that a central bank elicits in pursuing an anti-inflation policy (captured by the so-called sacrifice ratio).[2]

On the ground of the credibility hypothesis, that is, the proposition that a more credible central bank is able to reduce inflation at lower costs with respect to sacrificed output (Blinder, 2000, p. 1425), several studies have shown that there exists a positive correlation between a country's sacrifice ratio and the extent of its central bank's independence (see Down, 2004, for a recent survey). This result seems surprising, and has been debated for at least ten years (see Diana and Sidiropoulos, 2004, for a restatement of that debate). It seems indeed surprising that central bank independence is linked to high sacrifice ratios. According to the credibility hypothesis, an independent central bank's monetary policy should be more conducive to low and stable rates of inflation, in line with the agents' expectations, so that output (as well as employment) losses during disinflation periods should be smaller than with a politically dependent central bank.

As suggested by Debelle and Fischer (1994) and Walsh (1995b), among others, a likely explanation for the positive correlation between central bank independence and sacrifice ratios in a number of Organisation for Economic Co-operation and Development (OECD) countries observed over many disinflation periods relies on the slope of the Phillips curve upon which central bank independence is supposed to act. The empirical evidence provided by Alesina and Summers (1993) shows indeed a lower and less volatile inflation rate as a result of central bank independence. This, in turn, is likely to lead to less frequent wage and price adjustments, which explains a flatter short-run Phillips curve and, therefore, higher disinflation costs in terms of unemployment on account of sluggish wages (Lucas, 1973; Ball et al., 1988; Diana and Sidiropoulos, 2004).

Now, the speed of the disinflation process seems to be an important element to consider in order to estimate the sacrifice ratio in terms of both output and employment losses.[3] In this respect, two alternatives exist: either gradualism or what Ball (1994) dubs 'cold turkey', that is, quick disinflation. According to Taylor (1983), if nominal wages adjust slowly, a quick disinflation reduces output, while a slow disinflation does not, owing to the real costs of production. This argument is, however, in sharp contrast with a number of empirical studies, which point out that the length of a disinflation period is positively related to output losses (see Ball, 1994; Posen, 1998; Diana and Sidiropoulos, 2004). In addition, these losses are related to the inflation rate at the beginning of the period: the sacrifice ratio is higher when the initial inflation rate is low (as measured with quarterly data). If initial inflation is considered as a proxy for average inflation, then this finding supports the argument put forward by Ball et al. (1988), who explain that a higher rate of average inflation reduces nominal rigidities, makes the short-run Phillips curve steeper, and thereby brings the sacrifice ratio down.

A further point worth considering in this respect is the actual extent of labour and goods markets rigidities. 'If a country's labor market is more rigid than its goods market, the inflation–unemployment sacrifice ratio ought to be higher than the inflation–output ratio and vice versa' (Down 2004, p. 405). As Down (2004) notes, however, the kind of policy that the government puts into practice may also have a strong bearing on these two ratios and their relative dynamics as regards employment losses during a disinflation period. A government may indeed react in two fashions in order to counteract rising unemployment: it may just deregulate the labour market, or promote employment in a variety of forms. While deregulation can elicit some reduction in unemployment insofar as it disposes of labour market regulations that limit the employers' incentives to hire, it can also lead to an increase in unemployment, since it removes workers' protection against firing, which is particularly important during disinflation periods.

If a restrictive monetary policy – to limit inflation – is carried out together with some forms of public promotion of employment,[4] by way of contrast, then the unemployment costs that result from disinflation can be reduced, although this intervention cannot have the same effects on sacrificed output, which might therefore be higher than employment losses. As the partisan hypothesis suggests, however, the problem in this respect is that left and right governments do not have the same political preferences over inflation and unemployment. Governments on the right of the political spectrum are more inclined to support the interests of capitalists rather than those of wage earners, and therefore to care more about inflation than about unemployment, whilst governments on the left are more representative of workers and, hence, should actually care more about employment losses than inflation (see Alesina and Roubini, 1997).

Needless to say, all governments may be willing to reduce inflation when the latter is at too high a level, because of the detrimental effects of high inflation on economic growth and international competitiveness. The partisan hypothesis, however, suggests that right- and left-wing governments may differ in their propensities to disinflate, on the extent of their disinflation policies, and on the costs they are willing to impose on the whole economy to reduce the inflation rate. As Down points out in this regard: 'if disinflation is a higher priority for right governments than for left governments, right governments should (a) endure higher unemployment costs than left governments to reduce inflation, (b) engage in disinflations at lower levels of inflation than left governments, and (c) reduce inflation to lower levels than left governments' (Down, 2004, p. 407).[5]

This left–right distinction is a thread running through the creation and functioning of the European Economic and Monetary Union (EMU). Generally speaking, the parties on the left of the political spectrum have been critical about the EMU, because the latter is likely to increase unemployment levels as a result of the loss in monetary sovereignty encountered by its member countries. By contrast, right-wing political parties have been in favour of the single European currency and the resulting 'one size fits all' monetary policy of the ECB, preferring low and stable rates of inflation rather than low rates of unemployment (see Jespersen, 2002). Let us investigate this question more closely.

THE EUROPEAN CENTRAL BANK'S POLICY STANCE: A POLITICAL-ECONOMY ASSESSMENT

The primary objective of the ECB is to maintain price stability in the whole euro area. According to the Treaty on the European Union agreed in Maastricht in 1992, however, the single monetary policy of the ECB should also support the general economic policy goals of the European Union – including economic growth and a high employment level – without prejudice to the objective of price stability (Article 105.1 of the Treaty on the European Union as agreed by the European Council meeting in Amsterdam on 2 October 1997, which entered into force on 1 May 1999).

In light of the prevailing economic conditions in the EU countries prior to the EMU's launch and the ensuing adoption of the single currency,[6] many EU officials and central bankers prescribed a sharp reduction of budget deficits in respect of gross domestic product (GDP), labour market deregulation and reform of welfare systems, in order not to jeopardize the credibility of the newly created ECB and of its monetary policy oriented to price stability. The results of this policy stance are illustrated in Figure 5.1.

After a period of growth in domestic demand in the late 1990s, euro area countries have entered a period of marked and protracted deceleration of consumption and investment in the private sector since 2000. The slight increase in public sector spending in 2001–02 did not suffice to avoid a negative growth rate of domestic demand in those years, despite a positive contribution to growth by exports as long as the exchange rate of the euro against the US dollar did not begin to soar in spring 2002 (Figure 5.2).

According to the ECB assessment published in its June 2001 *Bulletin*, the deceleration of euro area growth in 2001 was due to external factors – mainly, the US slowdown – but was expected to be boosted by Euroland's fiscal and monetary policies conducive to sound public finances and price-level stability with very favourable financing conditions (European Central Bank, 2001, p. 5). As Bibow (2004, p. 13) points out, at that time the ECB 'seemed either unaware of the slump in domestic demand that had started in mid-2000, or at least never took seriously the possibility that decisive interest rate cuts might be warranted to bolster demand, judging its monetary stance as conducive to growth anyway'. In fact, this monetary policy stance continued well after the economy of the euro area entered into a marked recession, which the euro's sharp appreciation against the US dollar as from April 2002 contributed to aggravate, with the ECB complacency for its expected disinflationary effects.

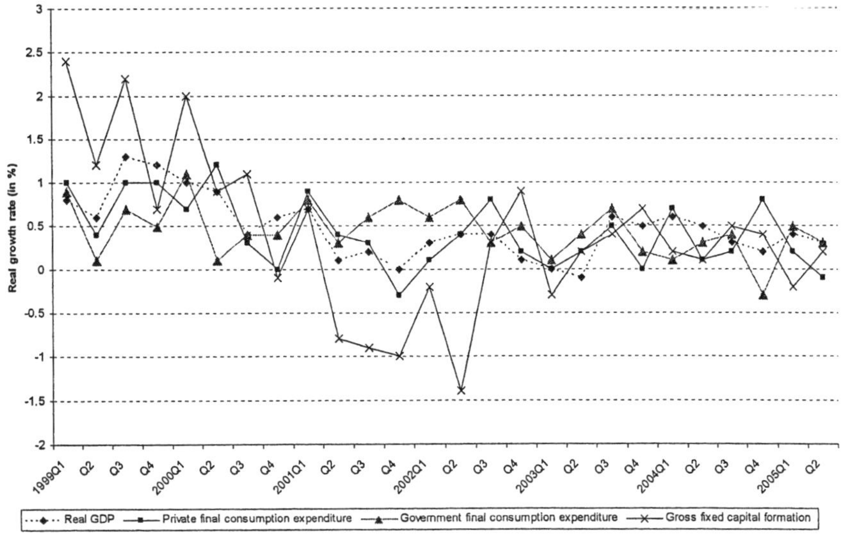

Source: Eurostat (Statistical Office of the European Communities), author's elaboration. The growth rate with respect to the previous quarter (*t*/*t*–1) is calculated from seasonally adjusted figures.

Figure 5.1 Some indicators of economic performance in the euro area (1999–2005)

In 2002–03, ignoring the warnings issued by the International Monetary Fund about the risks of a recession in Euroland and its recommendation to implement an expansionary monetary policy to the benefit of growth and with no prejudice to price level stability, the ECB did not cut its policy rates of interest below the level it decided on 5 June 2003,[7] arguing that 'with interest rates at historical lows, monetary policy has made a significant contribution to improving the conditions for a recovery in economic growth. Now, other policy-makers also have to make their contributions' (European Central Bank, 2003b, p. 6). In the ECB view, this means fiscal and structural reforms to improve further the conditions for investment and employment, a strong commitment to the Stability and Growth Pact, and well-designed fiscal consolidation strategies.

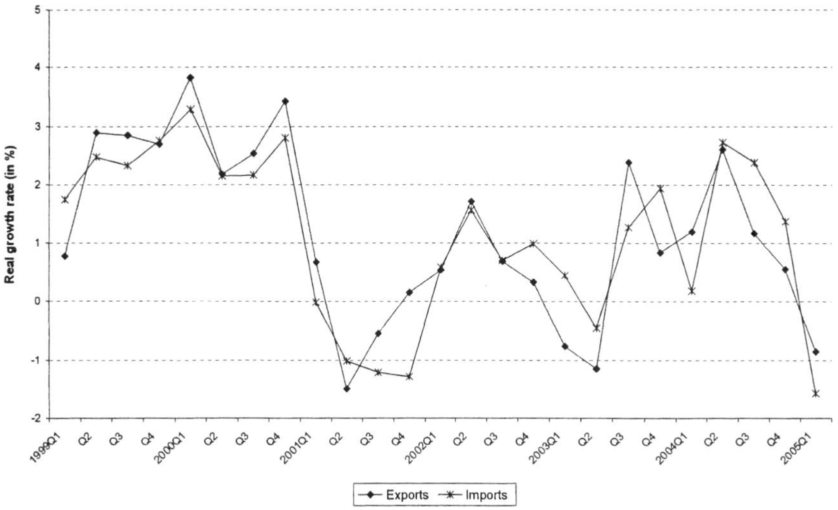

Source: Organisation for Economic Co-operation and Development (2005).

Figure 5.2 Euro area imports and exports of goods and services (1999–2005)

The monetary policy stance of the ECB did not change in 2004, although the bank noted that economic growth had slowed down in the second half of 2004 to only 0.3 per cent (quarter on quarter), after a 0.7 per cent and a 0.5 per cent increase of real GDP in the two previous quarters. The note that the ECB published in its December 2004 *Bulletin* states that: '[t]he short-term outlook for inflation remains worrisome' (European Central Bank, 2004, p. 5). The ECB wants it for proof the development of oil prices, which 'are having a sizeable impact on consumer prices in the euro area' (p. 5). It substantiates its view on the euro area further, notably by arguing that:

> [T]he conditions remain in place for economic growth to proceed. Euro area exports should continue to benefit from global demand conditions. On the domestic side, investment should be supported further by the very favourable financing conditions in

> the euro area … Finally, scope exists for private consumption to strengthen, particularly if a strong commitment is made to fiscal consolidation and structural reforms, thereby reducing uncertainty surrounding the extent and pace of progress in these fields. (p. 5)

This same (self complimentary) view was taken by the ECB in 2005 and, at the time of writing, its own assessment is that 'careful monitoring of upside risks to price stability continues to be necessary, notably in connection with persistently high oil prices. Cross-checking with the monetary analysis confirms the need for ongoing vigilance in order to maintain inflation expectations in line with price stability' (European Central Bank, 2005, pp. 5–6).

Now, the fact that the ECB failed to meet its price stability goal over the last six years (2000–05) should have worried its Governing Council and led it to reconsider afresh its monetary policy strategy, which many consider as inspired by inflation targeting. In fact, as Bibow (2004, p. 27) explains, 'the ECB is not at all engaged in what is generally understood as inflation targeting … The roots of its thinking which guides its conduct lie in German economic thought and received Bundesbank wisdom.' What a proper inflation targeting regime implies, as noted earlier on, is a discretionary monetary policy under constraint. Within this framework, flexibility means that the central bank does not always try to stabilize forecasted inflation at its target rate, if this involves a high degree of output fluctuation, particularly in the case of output losses and with an ensuing high rate of unemployment (see Svensson, 1997; King, 2002).

Conceptually, inflation targeting may be considered as fine-tuning the economy with the flexibility that this strategy provides to monetary policy, particularly in case of demand shocks, which move output and prices in the same direction, and hence do not represent a problem for inflation targeters (see Clarida et al., 1999; Cecchetti, 2000). In this regard, inflation targeting 'is all about optimally adjusting the policy instrument (that is, interest rate) so as to stabilize the economy through deliberate demand management, with continuously updated and published inflation forecasts providing the key input for aiming at some desired mix between inflation and output volatilities' (Bibow, 2004, p. 29). This is neither what the ECB claims to do, nor what it does in point of fact. As the ECB President declared at the Press Conference on 1 April 2004: 'We do not fine-tune the economy. We do not reason as though we would like to speed up any part of the economy with a view to monitoring the output. We have a magnetic north, which is price stability. We believe that through price stability we can help to considerably improve the situation, the economic situation of Europe' (Trichet, 2004, p. 1).

Many ECB watchers and financial media have raised concern about the monetary policy that the ECB has been implementing so far, which is indeed a 'stability policy' rather than a 'stabilization policy'. The legal obligation to support the EU's general economic policies that the Treaty mentions with respect to the ECB seems to be largely ignored by the latter bank, which up to date has shown that it does not go beyond its unconditional support 'through' price stability in any case. As Begg et al. (2002, p. 12) observed: '[I]n this remarkable interpretation of the Treaty, the ECB fulfils its double mandate by reducing it to a single responsibility, a focus solely on price stability. All other objectives are then realized automatically. In this view the ECB cannot be held responsible for what happens in the real economy. We consider that this view is not just narrow, but mistaken.'

This severe assessment of the ECB monetary policy echoes the critiques that a number of authors address to those inflation targeting advocates who consider this regime as a monetary policy rule in the sense of Friedman (1968). As Bernanke and Mishkin (1997) and Bernanke et al. (1999) noticed, a monetary policy whose sole objective is long-run price stability suffers from many drawbacks and shortcomings:

- it has few supporters among the whole set of agents and policy-makers;
- it gives rise to unsatisfactory results in terms of real magnitudes; and
- it can address neither supply shocks nor demand shocks effectively.

In a nutshell, this kind of monetary policy affects both the credibility of the central bank and its support by the general public and the financial markets. As a result, the central bank's actions do not provide the desired outcomes in terms of economic performance. In the case of the ECB, these problems are further aggravated by the set of considerations developed with respect to the sacrifice ratio (see above):

- The losses in output and employment are more important because initial inflation in the euro area is low (slightly above 2 per cent on a year-to-year average).
- The losses in employment are higher than the losses in output because of structural rigidities in European labour markets (Euroland is not an optimum currency area).
- The deregulation of European labour markets is likely to bring about an increase in unemployment in the euro area, owing to the strong anti-inflation

monetary policy of the ECB (which is, let us recall, one of the most independent central banks in the world).

Last but not least, the case of the ECB also shows a regular asymmetry between policy interventions that aim at tightening monetary conditions in view of foreseen inflationary risks, and policy responses to actual rather than expected declines in inflation below the targeted rate (Bibow, 2004, pp. 35–6).[8] In fact, 'avoidance of potential disinflation costs by pre-emptively engineering a recession because of perceived inflation risks does not at all avoid those real costs from arising. Quite the opposite. *A central bank obsessed with the idea of taking no risks with inflation and, as a corollary, disinclined to give growth a chance will be the very mechanism that enforces an anti-growth bias upon the system*' (p. 40).

REFORMING MONETARY POLICY GOVERNANCE TO MAKE IT DEMOCRATIC AND ACCOUNTABLE

The monetary policy of the ECB so far is systematically biased against output stabilization and lacks the flexibility that an inflation targeting strategy grants. In the low-inflation framework of the euro area (with measured inflation rates around 2 per cent year-to-year), where average unemployment rates fluctuate around 9 per cent annually and real growth rates are currently below 1 per cent, a symmetric monetary policy would be very helpful and provide the support to the EU's economic policy objectives that the Treaty on the EU compels the ECB to give, as long as the price stability goal is not at stake. It would also be consistent with both the theory and practice of inflation targeting all around the world.

In fact, being independent of a democratically elected body, the ECB's decision-makers are in a position to care for their own preferences as well as for the interests of special pressure groups, particularly the banking community and financial markets, which have a clear and strong preference for low inflation rates and high interest rates. This leads to the macroeconomic costs discussed earlier on and threatens ECB credibility, with all its negative consequences for economic stabilization in terms of output and employment. Further, in spite of the ECB's political independence, European monetary policy-makers might tend to consider the interests of their country's government, because they are at least informally close to government officials and/or members of parliament. To be sure, all central bank executives owe their appointment to the parliament and/or government. As a matter of fact, all the governors of those national central banks that participate in the meetings of the ECB's Governing Council are still organically integrated into their home institution, and thus remain an integral part of the national administration (Ripoll, 2002, p. 11). Hence, the domestic interests of a particular member of the ECB's executive board might influence the monetary policy decisions of the ECB, which then apply at the level of the whole euro area, with possibly a number of asymmetric effects across that (still heterogeneous) area.

To be true, Article 108 of the EU Treaty states that the members of the ECB Governing Council should decide without either taking instructions from or being influenced by national central banks or other national and European institutions. In its statements, the ECB has been claiming the same point time and again: '[W]hen taking monetary policy decisions, the members of the Governing Council of the ECB do not act as national representatives, but in a fully independent personal capacity' (European Central Bank, 1999, p. 55). As Dornbusch et al. (1998, p. 15) noted, however, this kind of moral agreement is not enough to make the ECB really independent of national interests: '[T]he issue is not that bank presidents take or solicit direct instructions from their patrons, but whether they are cloned and then sent on their mission. When an issue of difference arises, a French appointee would vote in the style of France, and a German, as predictably, in the way of the Bundesbank.' An interesting work by Meade and Sheets (2002, p. 15) seems to confirm this prediction: as they show in their simulation inspired by the results obtained in their investigation of the US Federal Open Market Committee's (FOMC) decisions, 'the majority of ECB Council members typically voted on monetary policy changes in a manner that can be justified by the differential between their national inflation rate and the EMU average'.[9] Although the ECB does not publish the minutes of its Governing Council's meetings, and no formal vote is said to occur during these meetings, national economic performance of euro-area member countries seems therefore to play a role in the decision-making behaviour of the current members of the ECB Governing Council. This issue might become even more worrying when the new EU countries become full EMU members, namely, once they respect all the nominal convergence criteria set out in Maastricht to adopt the euro (see Rossi, 2005).

To eradicate the home-country bias that seems to exist in the present decision-making process of the ECB, a reform of monetary policy governance has to occur. The principle of an open market for monetary policy suppliers should be put into practice, with a view to improving the contribution of monetary policy to the euro-area economic performance, with respect to price stability as well as to output and employment stabilization. In particular, any nationality requirements for central bank governors have to be abolished. This increases competition for being appointed to an executive position at the ECB, that is, on its Governing Council board. Indeed, the set of candidates has to increase in order to drive incumbent central bankers to implementing stabilization-oriented policies and to keeping their campaign promises – because otherwise they risk being removed from office, which is a sanction strong enough to deter them from following the interests of special pressure groups. Generally speaking, in fact, in today's nationally segmented markets for monetary policy suppliers, central bankers have only few incentives not to adhere to the short-term interests of the government and the well-organized pressure groups. In a deregulated market for monetary policy suppliers, by way of contrast, central bankers have a much stronger incentive to pursue stabilization policies: if they carry out their mandate in the long-run interests of the citizens (and the government) of a country, their chances to stay in office will increase. For their own interest it is thus worth building up a reputation for pursuing stabilization-oriented monetary policies, notably with respect to local unemployment rates (see Eichenberger and Rossi, 2004, for elaboration on this point).

With an open market for 'good' monetary policy suppliers, there would be no need any more to restrict eligibility to the ECB Governing Council to EU nationals, which further implies negotiations and logrolling at the level of the EU countries' heads of government to reach a political agreement on the name and nationality of the ECB President or of a leading economist in the ECB research unit.[10] In fact, a monetary authority's executive board composed of members selected (by the market mechanism) on the ground of their own reputation for pursuing stabilization-oriented policies, without caring for their passport, is immune from the diverging national interests and economic performances that might exist within the same currency area. As such, the euro area will be in a position to take advantage of monetary policy-making in order to create the macroeconomic conditions for financial stability and real economic growth, to the benefit of employment and wage earners that is, European households and consumers.

This reform of monetary policy governance can be further enhanced if political parties, monetary policy businesses and other organizations are allowed to run for office without nominating a particular individual. This would be even more profitable to economic stabilization if the decision-makers were elected by the population, which is not yet the case today (see Walsh, 1995a, p. 150). When a political party or firm is chosen, it can delegate whomsoever it likes to carry out the tasks related to its mandate. It might also substitute new delegates for hitherto active ones, and thereby bring in specialists for the specific problems to be solved by monetary policy. In such a framework, the success of a firm, organization or political party depends on the professional skills of the whole institution involved, rather than on the individual performance of its members. The direct election of monetary policy-makers by the population would bring about at least two important advantages: the central bank would become truly independent of the short-term interests of the government and the pressure groups, but nevertheless would be democratically accountable – two important features that the ECB has been lacking since its creation in 1999, which might in fact explain the poor economic performance of the euro area after the currency changeover took place.

CONCLUSION

Over the last 15 years, academics have proposed and policy-makers have put into practice a change in monetary policy strategies around the world. The current regime of inflation targeting represents an improvement in terms of efficiency, credibility, transparency and communication with both the public and the financial markets, with respect to monetary targeting regimes. This change in strategy has been accompanied by the general move to make the central banks independent of governments and political parties, with a view to increase further their ability in meeting the inflation targets over the long run. The ECB is among the most independent central banks in the world. It is therefore legitimate to expect that its ultimate monetary policy goal, that is, price stability in the euro area, is met consistently and at a low cost in terms of output and employment losses – as argued by proponents of central bank independence. Empirical evidence stemming from recent studies that attempt to measure these losses as a result of disinflation policies points out, however, many structural elements that positively relate central bank independence and the so-called 'sacrifice ratio'. This chapter investigates that subject matter with regard to monetary policy governance. It shows that, to date, the ECB monetary policy has been systematically biased against output stabilization and growth, and lacks the flexibility that an inflation targeting strategy would indeed grant it. A process-oriented reform of monetary policy governance is therefore required, if a central bank's decisions are to have some effects on real growth and employment that can be measured positively. This chapter proposes to open up the market for monetary policy services internationally, by: (1) disposing of the legal constraint that imposes that the central bank's executive board members have to be nationals; (2) allowing private institutions such as monetary policy firms and organizations to run for office at the central bank's board (beyond individuals, who will still be in a position to candidate); and (3) choosing executive board members by direct election, instead of by political appointment, so that the population may decide to whom to delegate monetary policy decision-making according to the voters' preferences in regard of output and inflation stabilization and may sanction monetary policy-makers (by dismissing them or, more simply, by not renewing their mandate) if the latter do not attain the stated objectives in the interests of the citizens. The major result of this new form of central bank governance will be a monetary policy more conducive to macroeconomic stabilization and output growth than is presently the case with the highly independent, but poorly accountable, central banks in the world – in the European Union as well as elsewhere.

ACKNOWLEDGEMENTS

This chapter is the result of research work presented at the conference on Developments in Economic Theory and Policy in Bilbao, Spain, on 7–8 July 2005, at the conference on European Macroeconomics and Macroeconomic Policies in Berlin, Germany, on 28–29 October 2005, and at the conference on The Political Economy of Governance in Dijon, France, on 2–3 December 2005. The author would like to thank Jörg Bibow, Xavier Bradley, Luiz Bresser-Pereira, Laurent Cordonnier, Giuseppe Fontana, James Galbraith, Claude Gnos, Jochen Hartwig, Eckhard Hein, Jörg Huffschmid, Jesper Jespersen, Nistha Khurana, Eric Mayer, Thomas Palley, Alain Parguez, Louis-Philippe Rochon, Achim Truger, and Larry Randall Wray for their helpful comments. Valuable research assistance provided by Nadège Bochud, Grégoire Cantin, Dante Caprara, Mathieu Grobéty, and Szymon Klimaszewski is also gratefully acknowledged. The usual disclaimer applies.

NOTES

1. All countries with an inflation targeting strategy define price-level stability as a measured inflation rate above zero. In fact, analogously to a price-level targeting strategy, targeting zero inflation is more easily conducive to deflation, owing to the measurement biases in price index analysis that overestimate actual inflation (see Rossi, 2001 [2003], pp. 31–41). See also Mishkin and Schmidt-Hebbel (2002).
2. 'The sacrifice ratio (SR) is the cumulative increase in the yearly rate of unemployment that is due to the disinflation effort divided by the total decrease in the rate of inflation' (Cukierman, 2002, p. 1).
3. A number of additional factors such as the labour market characteristics or the openness of an economy have been put forward in the literature (see Ball, 1994; Temple, 2002).
4. The state might decide to increase transfers or tax incentives to firms in order to support employment, or it might strengthen employment protection to compel businesses to internalize some of the costs of the economic downturn resulting from disinflation. Alternatively, the state may subsidize job creation in the private sector, and/or increase taxes on business dislocation. Other forms of intervention can be found in practice. For instance, the Italian government in the 1980s cut employer social security contributions to encourage the retention of workers (Andersen, 1992).
5. As Down notes, in fact: '[I]t might well be argued that right governments should conduct more credible disinflations than left governments because of their stronger anti-inflation reputation. However, if the results for central bank independence are indicative of the relationship between policy makers' inflation aversion and the costs of disinflation, right governments should also be associated with higher disinflation costs. Moreover, a positive relationship between right governance and the unemployment costs of disinflation would reinforce the argument that it is the higher degree of inflation aversion associated with independent central banks that causes the positive relationship between central bank independence and the cost of a disinflation' (Down, 2004, pp. 407–8, fn. 9).
6. In 1990, that is, the year before the Maastricht Treaty was discussed, 'the annual inflation rate exceeded 10 percent in two EU countries and exceeded 5 percent in three others. No country had an inflation rate lower than 2.5 percent. Furthermore, five countries had budget deficits larger than 5 percent of GDP, while four had stocks of public debt larger than 90 percent of GDP, and these conditions were deemed to pose a serious threat to the future functioning of the monetary union' (Kenen and Meade, 2003, p. 3).
7. On 5 June 2003, the Governing Council of the ECB decided to lower the minimum bid rate on its main refinancing operations by 0.5 percentage points to 2 percent. It also decided to lower the interest rates on both its marginal lending facility and its deposit facility by 0.5 percentage points, to 3 percent and 1 percent respectively. These rates were not changed in the course of 2004, and remained at these levels up to 1 December 2005, when the ECB Governing Council decided to increase all of them by 25 basis points (that is, 0.25 percentage points).
8. In its May 2003 evaluation of its monetary policy strategy, the Governing Council of the ECB 'clarified the focus of its monetary policy within the definition by stating that in the pursuit of price stability the ECB aims to maintain the inflation rate below, but close to, 2 percent over the medium term' (European Central Bank, 2003a, p. 79). As the then ECB President explained a few months earlier, at the Monetary Dialogue on 17 February 2003, 'this basically implies that, in practice, we are more inclined to act when inflation *falls below* 1 percent and we are also inclined to act when inflation *threatens to exceed* 2 percent in the medium term' (Duisenberg, 2003, p. 10, emphasis added).

9. As regards regional influences in the actual monetary policy decisions of the FOMC, Meade and Sheets (2002) convincingly show that in the period 1978–2000 an increase by one percentage point in a region's unemployment rate (for a given national rate) reduced by around 2 percentage points the probability that this region's FOMC member dissented from the majority vote to lower the bank rate of interest. In the case of Germany, Berger and de Haan (2002) also present evidence that regional differences in inflation and real GDP growth rates had an important influence on the actual voting behaviour of the members of the Bundesbank's Zentralbankrat.
10. The next deadline in this respect will be the spring 2006 appointment of the chief economist at the ECB who will succeed to Otmar Issing, the 'mastermind behind the bank's strategy and interest rate decisions' (Bibow, 2005, p. 5).

REFERENCES

Alesina, A. and N. Roubini (1997), *Political Cycles and the Macroeconomy*, Cambridge, MA: MIT Press.

Alesina, A. and L.H. Summers (1993), 'Central bank independence and macroeconomic performance: some comparative evidence', *Journal of Money, Credit, and Banking*, **25** (2), 151–62.

Andersen, P.S. (1992), 'OECD country experiences with disinflation', in A. Blundell-Wignell (ed.), *Inflation, Disinflation and Monetary Policy*, Sydney: Reserve Bank of Australia, 104–80.

Ball, L. (1994), 'What determines the sacrifice ratio?' in N.G. Mankiw (ed.), *Monetary Policy*, Chicago, IL: University of Chicago Press, 155–82.

Ball, L., N.G. Mankiw and D. Romer (1988), 'The new Keynesian economics and the output–inflation trade-off', *Brookings Papers on Economic Activity*, **19** (1), 1–65.

Begg, D., F. Canova, P. De Grauwe, A. Fatás and P. Lane (2002), 'Surviving the slowdown', *Centre for Economic Policy Research Monitoring the European Central Bank*, no. 4 (April), London.

Berger, H. and J. de Haan (2002), 'Are small countries too powerful within the ECB?' *Atlantic Economic Journal*, **30** (3), 1–20.

Bernanke, B.S., T. Laubach, F.S. Mishkin and A.S. Posen (1999), *Inflation Targeting: Lessons from the International Experience*, Princeton, NJ: Princeton University Press.

Bernanke, B.S. and F.S. Mishkin (1997), 'Inflation targeting: a new framework for monetary policy', *Journal of Economic Perspectives*, **11** (2), 97–116.

Bibow, J. (2004), 'Assessing the ECB's performance since the global slowdown: a structural policy bias coming home to roost?' The Levy Economics Institute Working Paper, no. 409 (July), New York.

Bibow, J. (2005), 'Refocusing the ECB on output stabilization and growth through inflation targeting?' The Levy Economics Institute Working Paper, no. 425 (July), New York.

Blinder, A.S. (2000), 'Central bank credibility: why do we care? How do we build it?' *American Economic Review*, **90** (5), 1421–31.

Boyer, R. and D. Drache (1996), *States Against Markets: The Limits of Globalization*, London and New York: Routledge.

Cecchetti, S.G. (2000), 'Making monetary policy: objectives and rules', *Oxford Review of Economic Policy*, **16** (4), 43–59.

Clarida, R., J. Galí and M. Gertler (1999), 'The science of monetary policy: a new Keynesian perspective', *Journal of Economic Literature*, **37** (4), 1661–707.

Corbo, V., Ó. Landerretche and K. Schmidt-Hebbel (2002), 'Does inflation targeting make a difference?' in Loayza, N. and R. Soto (eds), *Inflation Targeting: Design, Performance, Challenges*, Santiago: Central Bank of Chile, 221–69.

Cukierman, A. (2002), 'Does a higher sacrifice ratio mean that central bank independence is excessive?' *Annals of Economics and Finance*, **3** (1), 1–25.

Dalziel, P. (1998), 'New Zealand's experience with an independent central bank since 1989', in Arestis, P. and M. Sawyer (eds), *The Political Economy of Central Banking*, Cheltenham, UK and Northampton, MA, USA: Edward Elgar, 199–216.

Debelle, G. and S. Fischer (1994), 'How independent should a central bank be?' in J.C. Fuhrer (ed.), *Goals, Guidelines and Constraints Facing Monetary Policymakers*, Boston, MA: Federal Reserve Bank of Boston, 195–221.

Diana, G. and M. Sidiropoulos (2004), 'Central bank independence, speed of disinflation and the sacrifice ratio', *Open Economies Review*, **15** (4), 385–402.

Dornbusch, R., C. Favero and F. Giavazzi (1998), 'Immediate challenges for the European Central Bank', *Economic Policy*, **13** (26), 15–64.

Down, I. (2004), 'Central bank independence, disinflations, and the sacrifice ratio', *Comparative Political Studies*, **37** (4), 399–434.

Duisenberg, W. (2003), 'Monetary dialogue with Wim Duisenberg, president of the ECB', EU Economic and Monetary Committee, Brussels, 17 February, http://www.europarl.eu.int/comparl/econ/pdf/emu/speeches/20030217/ft_en.pdf.

Eichenberger, R. and S. Rossi (2004), 'Die deregulierung der zentralbanken: auf zu einem internationalen markt für gute geldpolitik!' *Swiss Journal of Economics and Statistics*, **140** (3), 327–53.

European Central Bank (1999), 'The institutional framework of the European system of central banks', *Monthly Bulletin*, **1** (7), 55–63.

European Central Bank (2001), 'Editorial', *Monthly Bulletin*, **3** (6), 5–6.

European Central Bank (2003a), 'The outcome of the ECB's evaluation of its monetary policy strategy', *Monthly Bulletin*, **5** (6), 79–92.

European Central Bank (2003b), 'Editorial', *Monthly Bulletin*, **5** (7), 5–6.

European Central Bank (2004), 'Editorial', *Monthly Bulletin*, **6** (12), 5–7.

European Central Bank (2005), 'Editorial', *Monthly Bulletin*, **7** (8), 5–6.

Fischer, A.M. (1996), 'Central bank independence and sacrifice ratios', *Open Economies Review*, **7** (1), 5–18.

Friedman, M. (1968), 'The role of monetary policy', *American Economic Review*, **58** (1), 1–17.

Gärtner, M. (1997), 'Central bank independence and the sacrifice ratio: the dark side of the force', *Swiss Journal of Economics and Statistics*, **133** (3), 513–38.

Held, D., A. McGrew, D. Goldblatt and J. Perraton (1999), *Global Transformations: Politics, Economics and Culture*, Cambridge: Polity Press.

Jespersen, J. (2002), 'Why do macroeconomists disagree on the consequences of the Euro?' in Arestis, P., M. Desai and S. Dow (eds), *Money, Macroeconomics and Keynes*, Vol. 2, London and New York: Routledge, 193–204.

Jonas, J. and F.S. Mishkin (2005), 'Inflation targeting in transition economies: experience and prospects', in Bernanke, B.S. and M. Woodford (eds), *The Inflation-Targeting Debate*, Chicago, IL and London: University of Chicago Press, 353–413.

Jordan, T.J. (1997), 'Disinflation costs, accelerating inflation gains, and central bank independence', *Weltwirtschaftliches Archiv*, **133** (1), 1–21.

Jordan, T.J. (1999), 'Central bank independence and the sacrifice ratio', *European Journal of Political Economy*, **15** (2), 229–55.

Kenen, P.B. and E.M. Meade (2003), 'EU accession and the euro: close together or far apart?' Institute for International Economics Policy Brief, no. PB03-9 (October), Washington, DC.

King, M.A. (2002), 'The inflation target ten years on', *Bank of England Quarterly Bulletin*, **42** (4), 459–74.

Kydland, F.W. and E.C. Prescott (1977), 'Rules rather than discretion: the inconsistency of optimal plans', *Journal of Political Economy*, **85** (3), 473–91.

Lucas, R.E., Jr. (1973), 'Some international evidence on output–inflation tradeoffs', *American Economic Review*, **63** (3), 326–34.

Meade, E.E. and D.N. Sheets (2002), 'Regional influences on US monetary policy: some implications for Europe', *International Finance Discussion Paper*, no. 721 (February), Washington, DC.

Mishkin, F.S. (2000), 'Inflation targeting in emerging-market countries', *American Economic Review*, **90** (2), 105–109.

Mishkin, F.S. and K. Schmidt-Hebbel (2002), 'A decade of inflation targeting in the world: what do we know and what do we need to know?' in Loayza, N. and R. Soto (eds), *Inflation Targeting: Design, Performance, Challenges*, Santiago: Central Bank of Chile, 171–219.

Organisation for Economic Co-operation and Development (2001), *Devolution and Globalisation: Implications for Local Decision-Makers*, Paris: Organisation for Economic Co-operation and Development.

Persson, T. and G. Tabellini (1993), 'Designing institutions for monetary stability', *Carnegie–Rochester Conference Series on Public Policy*, **39**, 53–84.

Posen, A. (1998) 'Central bank independence and disinflationary credibility: a missing link?' *Oxford Economic Papers*, **50** (3), 335–59.

Ripoll, J. (2002), 'National appointments to multinational monetary policymaking: a role conflict?' University of Geneva, unpublished.

Rogoff, K. (1985), 'The optimal degree of commitment to an intermediate monetary target', *Quarterly Journal of Economics*, **100** (4), 1169–89.

Rossi, S. (2001), *Money and Inflation: A New Macroeconomic Analysis*, Cheltenham, UK and Northampton, MA, USA: Edward Elgar (reprint 2003).

Rossi, S. (2005), 'European monetary integration: convergence, divergence, or exclusion?' paper presented at the Italian Geographical Society annual conference on European Territorial Cohesion and Sustainable Development: Convergence and Competitiveness, University of Sannio, Benevento, 7 October.

Sargent, T.J. (1983) 'Stopping moderate inflations: the methods of Poincaré and Thatcher', in Dornbusch, R. and M.H. Simonsen (eds), *Inflation, Debt, and Indexation*, Cambridge, MA: MIT Press, 54–96.

Svensson, L.E.O. (1997), 'Inflation forecast targeting: implementing and monitoring inflation targets', *European Economic Review*, **41** (6), 1111–46.
Svensson, L.E.O. (1999), 'Price-level targeting versus inflation targeting: a free lunch?' *Journal of Money, Credit, and Banking*, **31** (3), 277–95.
Taylor, J.B. (1983), 'Union wage settlements during a disinflation', *American Economic Review*, **73** (5), 981–93.
Temple, J. (2002), 'Openness, inflation, and the Phillips curve: a puzzle', *Journal of Money, Credit, and Banking*, **34** (2), 450–68.
Trichet, J.-C. (2004), 'Introductory statement to the press conference on April 1, 2004', http://www.ecb.int/press/pressconf/2004/html/is040401.en.html.
Walsh, C.E. (1995a), 'Optimal contracts for central bankers', *American Economic Review*, **85** (1), 150–67.
Walsh, C.E. (1995b), 'Central bank independence and the cost of disinflation in the EC', in Eichengreen, B., J. Frieden and J. von Hagen (eds), *Monetary and Fiscal Policy in an Integrated Europe*, New York: Springer, 12–37.
Weiss, L. (1998), *The Myth of the Powerless State: Governing the Economy in a Global Era*, Cambridge: Polity Press.

PART TWO

Macroeconomic Policy and the Global Economy

6. Enforcing the IMF in the global economy: an institutional analysis[1]

Jean-Pierre Allegret and Philippe Dulbecco

INTRODUCTION

The increasing number of financial crises involving particularly emerging markets has led international financial institutions (IFIs) to focus their attention on the reform of the international financial architecture. This new architecture has focused mainly on the scope of IFIs activities, on the adoption of sound macroeconomic policies in domestic economies and on ways of stabilizing international capital flows.[2] Particular attention is placed on the question of governance in domestic economies. Indeed, considering the positive link between good governance practices and economic performance, governance represents nowadays one of the main themes according to which the international institutions' policies are structured. The International Monetary Fund's (IMF) involvement in governance derives from its mandate to promote macroeconomic stability and sustained non-inflationary growth (IMF, 2001). According to the IFIs, among the causes of the financial crises during the 1990s, we have the inefficiencies of governance in emerging markets; that is, the weak protection of property rights, the lack of bankruptcy laws, few or weak contract enforcement mechanisms, the low quality of public policies due to corruption, and bad private-sector incentives explained by distortions due to state interventions in market mechanisms. As a consequence, IFIs became the main advocates for the adoption at a worldwide scale of 'good practices' of governance. For example, the IMF imposed on countries under IMF programs specific measures dedicated to governance issues such as the design and adoption of standards in banking, the harmonization of domestic bankruptcy laws and the implementation of codes of good practice in fiscal, monetary and financial areas (Fischer, 1999). According to IFIs, good governance implies that governments become more accountable and more representative of the civil society in order to strengthen their legitimacy and their degree of democracy.

Nevertheless international institutions, especially the IMF, have recently been severely criticized for their lack of both accountability and democracy, which questions their political, as well as economic, legitimacy. Put in other words, it appears that the IFIs themselves do not respect the good governance principles required from countries under their programs (Woods, 2000). According to Stiglitz, the IMF 'has pursued the collective interests of a subset of the international community, rather than serving the broader collective interests for which it was originally created' (Stiglitz, 2002, p. 243).[3] Helleiner (2002) considers, in a close perspective, that the agenda of international financial liberalization resulted from the disproportionate influence of stronger countries and private interests.

Consequently the IMF has to face two closely interlinked challenges: on the one hand, it needs to improve the domestic governance of economies connected to the global capital market and, on the other hand, it needs to follow their own advice with respect to governance standards given to member countries.

These two challenges refer to the institutional dimension of the IMF, which is surprisingly often omitted debating the governance of international institutions. The aim of this chapter is to propose an analysis of these two institutional challenges which are at the center of the debates on the IFM reforms.

Focusing on the institutional dimension of the IMF means that the analysis should allow for the understanding of the role played by the international institution in the market economy. When it is costly to transact and coordinate, then institutions matter (North, 1994). Institutions represent 'orientation points' which have the authority to render both actions and individual expectations compatible. Like any other institution, the main role of the IMF is then to facilitate coordination between decentralized agents or countries, which are ignorant of each other's actions and expectations. But for such a role to be fulfilled, we require that two institutional conditions be satisfied, which refer to the enforcement property of the international institution of the IMF, that is, to its capacity to influence durably agents' expectations and behaviors in a stabilizing manner.

The first condition deals with the IMF governance structure, its capacity to promote higher legitimacy, accountability, transparency and democracy. One can find here the necessary condition for the IMF playing its coordination function.

The second one refers to the compatibility between the standard institutional reforms promoted by the IMF and the specific domestic institutional arrangement in each country in the program. Indeed a relevant criticism is the IMF's lack of adaptability when implementing institutional reforms in developing countries (Rodrik, 1999). Indeed one has to take into account that market institutions are specific to each domestic economy and are subject to path-dependency constraints. Moreover the institutions of a domestic economy are mutually compatible and complementary (Aoki, 2001). That is why, in our view, the main challenge of the IMF is to promote reforms dedicated to strengthen domestic economies in the new global environment together with warranting the coherence of institutional order in each country under IMF program.

But again, the necessary condition in order for such a challenge to be met makes reference to the IMF governance structure.

The remainder of the chapter is structured as follows. The next section analyses the necessary condition of the enforcement of the international institution of the IMF; measures in order to promote the IMF's legitimacy are proposed, while the section after that puts forward an analytical framework to evaluate the ability of the IMF to render compatible institutional reforms with the coherence of the institutional order in each domestic economy; this is our way of highlighting the issue of the enforcement of the IMF. The last section concludes.

THE IMF LACK OF LEGITIMACY

Institutions are often conceptualized as the rules of the games in a society (North, 1990). We were told that there are two types of game rules: formal ones and informal ones. The necessary condition for the formal institution to fulfill its coordination function is that it must be accepted as an orientation point by economic agents. As a result a formal institution must be not only functional but also enforceable (Aoki, 2001). And the main concern becomes to inquire into the possibility of designing an institution that can implement a given social goal in a way that is compatible with the incentives of the players for a certain class of environment (Hurwicz, 1996).

In the case of the IMF, the necessary condition of enforcement is directly connected with the IMF legitimacy issue. Indeed the capacity for the IMF to organize a coordination process well matched with the countries' objectives requires a strong acceptance of the IMF rules of the game by the numerous countries. However the difficulty lies in the fact that the IMF exhibits some important 'institutional failures' which undermine its legitimacy. Indeed two critical issues concerning IMF governance have to be highlighted: (1) the weight of developing countries in a changing world economy; and (2) the ownership of reforms.

Weight of Developing Countries in the IMF Structure of Governance

IMF legitimacy is undermined by the asymmetry between industrialized and developing countries as the majority of the world's population are weakly represented within the Fund.[4] Industrialized countries remain the main shareholders, and hence the main initiators of reforms, in the Bretton Woods institution.

The cornerstone of this governance structure is quotas. The slow adjustment of quota shares is in contradiction with the rapid transformation of the world economy. There is now a large gap between the structure of the world economy and the repartition of quotas between member countries.

The legitimacy problem is the following: minor shareholders, that is the developing countries, have become the main 'client' of the IMF. When they borrow from the IMF, they must apply corrective macroeconomic measures which exert a determinant influence on the domestic structures of these countries. For most developing countries, this influence appears non-legitimate because they do not significantly participate in the decision-making procedure of the IMF. They consider that corrective measures are imposed by the most powerful industrialized countries.[5]

At the same time, IMF legitimacy is questioned by the influence exerted by stronger states. Barro and Lee (2005) find that political connections to the IMF are a significant explanatory variable of the probability and size of IMF loans.[6] Thacker (1999) studies the underlying causes of the IMF's behavior concerning lending decisions and sanctions if borrower compliance with IMF conditionality is weak. Decisions to lend are analyzed over the period 1985–94 for 87 developing countries. This analysis clearly highlights that politics matters in the IMF and that the governance of international institutions becomes a major preoccupation once we take into account the influence of political factors. The necessity to ensure that the decisions of international institutions result from the general interest and not from the strategy of powerful states in the world economy becomes more and more obvious.

One can find here the first institutional failure of the IMF as an orientation point which should render both actions and expectations compatible. Indeed, a necessary condition for an institution effectively to play the role of an orientation point is that it must be accepted by every player. But such an acceptance first requires a better representation of the developing countries in the decision-making procedure and/or less influence for political factors. It is otherwise difficult, if not impossible, for decisions taken by the IMF to be accepted and efficaciously implemented by non-represented countries or regions. The risk, again, is that the IMF objectives might be seen as being in contradiction with domestic ones.

Ownership of Reforms

In his study on adjustment programs, Killick (1995) identifies two major trends. On the one hand, programs exhibit high mortality or interruption rates.[7] On the other hand, the connection between structural adjustment programs and the implementation of policy reforms is weak, more particularly for institutional reforms. These weak results can be explained by the lack of ownership of reforms initiated by the IMF. Ownership refers to the extent to which the initiative for reforms planned in programs is local or external.

Traditionally, member countries borrow from the IMF in crisis circumstances. Under these circumstances, structural adjustment programs raise two major problems. First, in a context of imperfect knowledge about local particularities, the IMF cannot render domestic and global objectives compatible. The IMF does not take the time to invest in institutional knowledge. Second, the adoption of IMF programs does not result from consensus building. Not only do the IMF staff not devote enough time to ensuring that the government is fully involved in reforms, but also the government rarely consults the civil society. The letter of intent – in which the borrowing country formally presents the policies it will undertake to meet program objectives and conditions – is drafted in Washington. From this point of view, IMF reforms appear coercive and thus undermine ownership.

One can find here the second institutional failure of IMF. Lack of ownership also means that the risk exists that agents follow behaviors which may enter into contradiction with the rules of the game imposed by what could be seen as an external *deus ex machina*; the possibility also exists that agents try to break these rules. Again the global logic appears to be in contradiction with the domestic objectives.

To sum up, lack of ownership and the low weight attributed to developing countries in the IMF governance structure constitute the two main institutional failures of the international institution of the IMF which undermine its legitimacy and hence its enforcement. As the enforcement property represents one of the necessary conditions for an economic institution to play its role and fulfill its function successfully, the question now is to examine the circumstances under which the enforceability of IMF rules of the game should be enhanced.

Strengthening IMF Political Legitimacy

As previously explained the IMF's design confronts to the legitimacy challenge as well as the accountability and democracy one. Each of these challenges results from the deep difference between domestic and international institutions. The former are embedded in a coherent political sphere where citizens belong to the same political identity. The latter are embedded in international relations based on unequal partners. As a result, rules of the game are asymmetric not only in terms of construct, but also in terms of implementation and modification. The most powerful states exert a decisive influence in this area.

Accountability refers to the ability of people to exert control over governments or institutions. The latter are delegated to fulfil missions in the interest of the former. In a democratic system, a government is accountable to the majority of the citizens in a specific jurisdiction. For example, the government presents its program in front of the parliament which is the democratic representation of citizens. The main pillar of this electoral accountability is the existence of a political community whose citizens are members. In the international sphere, there is no comparable political identity because there is no world government and no world identity. As a result, at a global level, electoral accountability cannot become a realistic system to control international institutions.[8]

Taking into account these difficulties, a more legitimate IMF rests on both an increase in the influence of developing countries in its structure of governance and the creation of a political body susceptible to influence the behavior of member countries. However, it is important to highlight that the inequality between states which characterizes international relations implies that a strict application of democratic rules – largely founded on the principle 'one citizen, one voice' – is inapplicable. Indeed, it should be contrary to a democratic principle to consider that a large country – Brazil for example – could have the same voting power than small countries such as Panama.

The voice of developing countries could increase by using two non-mutually exclusive mechanisms: reviewing the quota formula and modifying voting rules.

Quota formula review

Quota formula review is a major stake for the Bretton Woods institution. In 1999, the Managing Director requested a group of external experts who published a report (Cooper, 2000). The Board's mandate was clear: reviewing the quota formula with respect to

> their adequacy to help determine members' calculated quotas ... in a manner that reasonably reflects members' relative position in the world economy as well as their relative need for and contributions to the IMF's financial resources, taking into account changes in the functioning of the world economy and the international financial system and in light of the increase globalisation of markets (Cooper, 2000, p. 3).

The review group has proposed a simplification of the current system based on one formula containing two variables, one representing a country's ability to contribute to the IMF's resources[9] and the other its external vulnerability.[10] Such a formula has not been applicable because it exacerbated the decline of developing countries' quota shares. The failures of the Cooper Group have two main origins. First, the current formula runs into the 'assignment problem': one instrument is dedicated to several objectives. As stressed by Kelkar et al. (2004), it is necessary to assign a specific instrument to a particular objective. Second, the political dimension of any revision of quota formula has been underestimated. On the one hand, a quota formula respecting economic criteria – such as capacity for contribution to the IMF's resources – seems contradictory with a political formula implying a new repartition of quota shares in favour of developing countries. Any new repartition should not be based exclusively on economic reasons, but mainly on political factors linked to IMF governance. On the other hand, a greater weight to developing countries should lead to more diverse coalitions, implying a shift in the balance of power. From this perspective, a more legitimate IMF must both maintain the confidence of creditor countries (otherwise the financial integrity of the IMF could be undermined) and give to developing countries a more participatory decision-making process.[11]

A practical and realistic solution to balancingeconomic (financial integrity) and political (legitimacy) constraints is to restore the original share of basic votes in total votes. Basic votes determine voting rights of member countries without reference to economic criteria. In 1945, they constituted 11.3 per cent of total votes, but with regular quota increases, their share has declined to 2.1 per cent at present. Basic votes remain very important for countries with small quotas. For instance, out of 1983 members there are 25 countries for whom basic votes represent more than half of their individual voting rights. A restoration of the initial share of basic votes would significantly increase the voting power of these countries without contradicting the necessity to preserve the creditors' confidence: for the previous 25 countries, a return to the original ratio would increase the share of their basic votes from 0.406 percent to 1.651 percent.[12]

Voting majority rules

A second way to improve the position of developing countries in the IMF structure is to modify voting majorities. Decisions within the Fund are adopted on the basis of weighted voting power of the members. Ordinarily, a simple majority rule is required. But for sensible decisions – as a new SDRs allocation – special majorities are needed. Currently, there are two special majority rules: 70 percent and 85 percent. The second rule allows the United States to exert a decisive influence on the main IMF decisions. Indeed, it can exert its veto power with its 17.5 percent voting share. In addition, industrialized countries – through the Group of Eight – have a powerful position within the Fund. It is more difficult for developing countries to exert a veto power because of their limited capacity to coordinate between them. The number of decisions requiring special majorities has increased from nine categories originally to more than 50 at present. There is thus a strong relationship between the increasing role of special majority votes and the expanded responsibilities of the IMF. This trend has created inequalities within the Board and more widely within the IMF governance structure. An increasing part of major IMF decisions – those relating to the IMF governance structure – are under the control of major countries. Such evolution undermines the legitimacy of the IMF. As suggested by the Overseas Development Council (2000), a solution to strengthen the IMF's legitimacy is to set special majorities below the voting share of its Board's main shareholder.

Woods and Lombardi (2005) propose a more radical reform: to extend within the IMF the double majority voting requirement. Indeed, under such a system, it is necessary to obtain a majority both in terms of votes and in terms of members. As a result, a more 'contestable veto power market' could be emerging in promoting more diverse coalitions – including both developing and developed countries to fulfil the majority members rules – between IMF members. Consequently the influence of developing countries in the Bretton Woods institution, and the IMF's legitimacy, should be strengthened.

Improving the political legitimacy of the IMF

The political legitimacy of the IMF could be improved by creating a more effective political oversight on the part of the IMF. At present, the IMF as a political body is weak in terms of both legitimacy and effectiveness. Legitimacy is undermined by frequent political pressure from the governments of the major industrial countries within the Executive Board. IMF lending to Russia is a striking illustration of such pressures. Effectiveness is undermined by a fragile balance within the Fund between its shareholders and its management. On the one hand, governors of the IMF – who are already ministers in their country with full agendas – do not devote enough time to controlling IMF activities effectively. They tend to delegate their functions to lower-level staff in their ministries or to the Executive Board. On the other hand, executive directors rarely spend more than three years in the Board. Unlike the staff, they cannot develop their expertise while there is a growing complexity and diversity of the IMF's agenda. In general, contrary to the principle of good IMF governance, there is neither effective political leadership nor a strong Executive Board.

In order to meet these two objectives, it seems to us necessary to promote both a more political body within the IMF and at the same time a less political decision-making process in the Board.

One way is to transform the International Monetary and Financial Committee (IMFC) (the former Interim Committee) into a body possessing real decision-making power. At present, this committee, which stems from the Committee of the Twenty which dates back to the early 1970s, is composed of 24 members: IMF governors, ministers or officials of similar rank. The IMFC meets only twice a year. Notwithstanding its ministerial level and thus its political character, the IMFC has no formal decision-making power, being merely consultative. In addition, the frequency of its meetings is too low to permit it to exert a real impact on the management of the world economy.

An additional method could be to constitute the IMF's Executive Board at ministerial level.[13] The Executive Board is the IMF's true, permanent, decision-making authority. However, as presently constituted, the Executive Board does not have the political power that would enable it to discuss with member states at the same level of political competence and responsibility. Such a transformation of the Executive Board into a ministerial decision-making body, called 'Council', was provided for in the second amendment of the Bretton Woods Agreement (in 1978). But it is necessary to find a balance between the current absence of a political body within the IMF and the risk of excessive politicization. In order to avoid a problem of excessive politicization of the Board, different measures, more complementary than mutually exclusive, can be envisaged.

First, with respect to central banks, the independence of the Executive Board should allow it to take decisions without political influence from its main shareholders.[14] Taking into account the strong influence of the Board on the agendas of national governments, this is a crucial measure. So, its decisions should be better accepted by members.

Second, the Executive Board must be accountable for its actions to a political body which represents the international community. Under the condition that the IMFC becomes the effective political body of the IMF, the Executive Board could regularly present its results and projections to the IMFC. Members of the IMFC could be composed of non-resident personalities (as suggested by Keynes in 1944) and in charge of broad oversight of the IMF and not directly implicated in specific decisions by it (Cottarelli, 2005).

Third, the office term of the Managing Director could be limited to six or seven years in order to decrease the influence of major shareholders. Indeed 'the power of the major shareholders increases as the term of the chief executive begins to reach the current five-year limit and his eagerness to be re-elected becomes a factor in his willingness to bend to their wishes' (Kapur and Naim, 2005, p. 13).

Overall, if the main objective of any IMF reform is to increase its capacity to organize the coordination process worldwide, its political legitimacy must be strengthened by two main categories of reforms. First, the influence of developing countries – the main clients to the IMF – should be significantly increased by restoring the initial share of basic votes in total votes and by introducing a double majority rule. Secondly, the reduction of the political influence of the major shareholders of the IMF implies the creation of an independent decision-making process in the Board. At the same time, in promoting reforms in member countries, the IMF must take into account the domestic institutional constraints.

FINDING A COMPLEMENTARITY BETWEEN THE GLOBAL SOCIAL GOAL AND THE DOMESTIC INSTITUTIONAL CONSTRAINTS

As noticed by Kapur and Webb (2000), both the IMF and the World Bank are introducing more and more governance-related conditionalities in their programs. This new form of conditionality implies institutional changes in countries following IMF programs or benefiting from World Bank loans. Not only do international formal institutions exert an influence on countries' behaviors, but they also impose institutional changes in formal domestic institutions compromising the coherence of the domestic institutional structure.

Finding a Coherence for the International Institutional Order

As previously explained, the two main institutional failures met when analyzing the legitimacy issue each refer to the same fundamental question: that of the articulation between global objectives and domestic ones. Such articulation is at the cornerstone of the enforcement issue of the IMF. Indeed even if the rules of the game promoted by the IMF appear to be good formal rules, tension may be created since domestic rules of the game, that is, domestic institutions are inert and difficult to change. As a result the formal global rules of the game, that is, the IMF as an international institution, may be neither enforceable nor functional. But if an institution, in our case the IMF, that was designed with the purpose of achieving a prescribed global social goal[15] is not self-enforceable, then it needs to be supplemented by an enforcement mechanism. However this creates a dilemma for the institution designer. To make the enforcement mechanism effective, appropriate incentives may be needed for the enforcers to perform their mission properly (Aoki, 2001). Further, the operation of the enforcement mechanism may require the use of resources that have to be diverted away from activities directly contributing to the prescribed social goal. As a result, the achievement of the original social goal will need to be compromised. Another much more satisfactory solution should be for the IMF to pursue a social global goal which takes into account the institutional constraints accumulated at the domestic level.

Any analysis of the governance of international institutions then requires that we specify the conditions for the coherence of the international institutional order, because the systems components evolve at different speeds. More precisely, such analysis must allow two types of problems to be solved.

Firstly, the issue of the institutional order and its unity is formulated: if the complementarity of domestic and global institutions builds the institutional order of a society – in our case the 'international society' – the purpose is then to identify integration forces as well as circumstances under which these forces cease to work. This first problem is, as we have explained in the previous section, worsened by the fact that it associates two specific spheres: the domestic one and the international one, each of them following specific objectives.

Secondly, there is the problem of the institutional change, more precisely of an imposed institutional change (Lin, 1989), initiated and executed by IMF fiat. Contrary to the induced institutional change driven by countries who expect a change in rules to yield net benefit, the institutional change imposed by the IMF is often seen as providing benefits to a specific group of countries at the expense of others.[16]

Solving these two kinds of problems comes down to providing a solution to what we have agreed to call the permanency-flexibility dilemma.[17] On the one hand, if institutions are to remove uncertainty, they must be permanent, but on the other hand if they are to be shaped by global market forces they must be flexible. How, within the institutional order of modern market society, is this problem resolved?

The solution to cope with this problem consists in setting up internationally designed institutions which allow change to be integrated without altering the institutional structure as a whole. Then the IMF represents one of the main designed institutions which permit – or do not – the complementary articulation of both domestic and international objectives.

The question of governance arises when players adopt behaviors which jeopardize the coherence of the international order and/or when the IMF is submitted to structural changes which affect its own design. The design of the IMF is consequently closely linked to its evolution; that is, to its capacity to articulate in time domestic and global objectives. In other words, the design of the IMF should be analyzed as a potential of change which authorizes the co-evolution of both international and domestic objectives over time.

Structural Reforms and Institutional Order: How to Find a Coherence Between Them?

If it is always possible, both in theory and in practice, to imagine a situation in which an economic or political authority decides to implement new institutions – for example a new system of property rights – where the benefits expected from this type of measure are a controversial issue. The reason is that, insofar as such a policy is, by definition, limited to formal institutions, its success depends on the capacity of these new elements to meet the demand for change in institutions not yet designed. The difficulty lies in the fact that, although the transformation of formal institutions is, in general, both radical and fast, that of informal institutions is of an incremental nature, and is necessarily subject to path-dependence constraints.[18]

Financial reforms in emerging economies are a striking example of such challenge (Allegret et al, 2003). In these economies, the degree of asymmetric information is high for two reasons: on the one hand, financial markets are less sophisticated than in developed countries; on the other hand, economic relations are traditionally based on bilateral relationships and then information is not publicized. As a result, the implantation of Western standards in such economies does not necessarily lead to the emergence of institutions. Indeed, not only must such new laws be coherent with the basic properties of the financial system, but they must also be adopted by private agents.

In other words, in our view promoting banking reforms whose main objective is to bring banking practices in emerging economies to converge towards practices adopted in numerous mature markets, is not necessarily the most efficient way to favor economic growth. Interpersonal relationships are less prominent in developed countries because of the presence of liquid financial markets with strong legal rules and contract enforcement mechanisms.

Numerous authorities in emerging markets have implemented reforms in which the role of banks was reduced in order to promote the financial markets. South Korea is a striking example. If the role of the state limited the capacity of banks to monitor and exercise a credible threat over non-financial firms, it does not imply that the relationship banking system was inefficient per se. The main response of the Korean government to these inefficiencies has not been to implement a reform in which banks could stay at the heart of the system but effectively monitor non-financial firms. On the contrary, the government followed the advice of the international financial institutions and introduced principles of corporate governance originating from the Western experience. Such a strategy could be dangerous in the longer term: let us recall that in numerous emerging economies, and particularly in South Korea, banks are the main institutions which allow the development of the contractual sphere.

From this perspective, the role of the Fund staff could be that of external advisors or consultants in order to take into account the specificities of each country in a global context. By 'global context', we refer to the new constraints implied by the globalization process which tend to impose a standardization of behavior. For each country, with the advice of the IMF, it is necessary to find the right trade-off between the specificity of the domestic institutional order and the global market. This is the main challenge of the coherence between global governance and domestic objectives. A limited, although very important, reform from this viewpoint could be to give a new role to resident experts in member countries. Not only are these experts able to learn during the time the main institutional characteristics of each country, but they are at the same time able to build trust relations between the IMF and the domestic stakeholders.

CONCLUSION

This chapter has studied the enforcement of the IMF in the global economy from an institutional perspective. Considering that the main challenges of the IMF are to promote reforms in developing countries without destroying their domestic institutional order on the one hand; and to increase its political legitimacy on the other hand, we consider that two main trends of reforms are particularly critical. First, the IMF must promote an increasing role of developing countries in its current functioning. The revisions of the quota formula and majority rules are particularly important. At the same time, it seems necessary to create a political body within the IMF in order to strengthen its legitimacy. Second, in promoting institutional reforms in developing countries, the IMF must improve its knowledge about countries' specificities in order to favor successful institutional reforms. Globalization does not imply that institutional order must be identical in all countries. As a consequence, it seems to us that the current IMF strategy based on the implantation of Western practices in developing countries is not the right strategy.

Overall, our analysis leads us to propose an intermediate approach between an independent and specialized IMF on the one hand, and the constitution of a political IMF with a large but imprecise mandate on the other.

NOTES

1. A previous version of this chapter was presented at the conference Economics for the Future, Celebrating 100 years of Cambridge Economics, Cambridge (UK) 17–19 September 2003. We would like to thank P. Davidson, J. Kregel, E. Le Heron, J. Miller, J.F. Ponsot, A. Suarez and J. Williamson and for their remarks and suggestions. Usual caveats apply.

2. A comprehensive analysis of the new international financial architecture is beyond the scope of this chapter. For an overview, see, for instance: Eichengreen (1999), Williamson (2000), Vines and Gilbert (2004), Lane (2005), Ranis et al.(2006).
3. The main interlocutors of the IMF are financial ministries and central banks which have close connections to the financial community. Consequently, it seems natural that IMF remedies tend to reflect the interests of that community. These close connections between the IMF and the finance ministry exert a decisive influence on the conduct of IMF program negotiations
4. 'Whereas developed countries ... accounted for only 17 percent of voting strength in the United Nations ..., 24 percent in the WTO, and 34 percent in the International Fund for Agricultural Development, they account for 61–62 percent in the World Bank and IMF' (Helleiner, 2002, p. 312).
5. The increasing influence of the IMF in domestic affairs is clear if we consider the distinction made by Gould (2003) between targets conditionality and procedures conditionality. Targets refer to measures – like a fiscal deficit limit – that can be met by borrowing countries whatever way they choose. Procedures specify both ends and means by requiring countries to implement a single one-time action – for example a change in exchange rate regime and the adoption of new corporate governance principles. As a result, procedures more directly dictate borrowing country policies. After 1982, we observe a steadily increase of procedures conditionality.
6. The determinants of the political connections are the following: country quota, national participation in the IMF staff, and member country's political and economic proximity to the IMF's major shareholding countries. Each of these determinants exerts a positive influence on IMF loans.
7. From 1991 to 1993, 61 percent of IMF programs were stopped before the end of their intended life.
8. A deeper analysis of this question is beyond the scope of this chapter. For a comprehensive analysis, see Woods and Narlikar (2001) and Keohane and Nye (2002).
9. Estimated by the gross domestic product (GDP) converted into a common currency at market exchange rates.
10. Estimated by the variability of current receipts including the variability of net long-term capital flows.
11. In this chapter, we focus of the structure of voting rights. Evans and Finnemore (2001) propose a complementary approach based on the increasing voice of developing countries within the IMF. For instance, they consider the influence of developing countries in the department research and policy formulation.
12. Source: Kelkar et al. (2004, p. 740).
13. Williamson and Henning (1994) adopt a similar point of view.
14. We follow here De Gregorio et al. (1999). See also 6(2005).
15. In that sense the IMF may be seen as producing a global public good.
16. An induced institutional change refers to the modification or replacement of an existing institution or the emergence of a new one that is voluntarily initiated and executed by an individual or a group of individuals in response to profitable opportunities. An imposed change, in contrast, is introduced and executed by an authority following its own rationality.
17. Our analysis is inspired by Lachmann's work (1970).
18. This point is underlined in several other studies dedicated to reforms in developing countries. See, for instance: Ahrens (2002), Berkowitz et al. (2003), Teunissen and Akkerman (2004) and Rodrik (1999).

REFERENCES

Ahrens, J. (2002), *Governance and Economic Development: A Comparative Institutional Approach*, Cheltenham, UK and Northampton, MA, USA: Edward Elgar.

Allegret, J.P., B. Courbis and Ph. Dulbecco (2003), 'Financial liberalization and stability of the financial system in emerging markets: the institutional dimension of financial crises', *Review of International and Political Economy*, **10** (1), February, 73–92.

Aoki, M. (2001), *Toward a Comparative Institutional Analysis*, Cambridge, MA: MIT Press.

Barro, R.J. and J.W. Lee (2005), 'IMF programs: who is chosen and what are the effects?' *Journal of Monetary Economics*, **52** (7), 1245–69.

Berkowitz, D., K. Pistor and J.F. Richard (2003), 'Economic development, legality, and the transplant effect', *European Economic Review*, **47** (1), February, 165–95.

Cottarelli, C. (2005), 'Efficiency and legitimacy: trade-offs in IMF governance', IMF Working Paper, WP/05/107, June.

Cooper, R.N. (2000), *Report to the IMF Executive Board of the Quota Formula Review Group*, April, Washington, DC: IMF.

De Gregorio, J., B. Eichengreen, T. Ito and C. Wyplosz (1999), 'An independent and accountable IMF', *International Centre For Monetary and Banking Studies, CEPR, Geneva Reports on the World Economy*, **1**, Oxford: Oxford University Press.

Eichengreen, B. (1999), *Toward a New International Financial Architecture: a Practical Post-Asia Agenda*, Washington, DC: Institute for International Economics.

Evans, P. and M. Finnemore (2001), 'Organizational reform and the expansion of the South's voice at the fund', G-24 Discussion Paper Series, 15, December.

Fischer, S. (1999), 'Reforming the international finance system', *Economic Journal*, **109**, November, 557–76.

Gould, E.R. (2003), 'Money talks: the role of external financiers in influencing IMF conditionality', *International Organization*, **57** (3), 551–86.

Helleiner, G.K. (2002), 'Developing countries in global economic governance and negotiation processes', in Nayyar, D. (ed), *Governing Globalization, Issues and Institutions*, Oxford: Oxford University Press, 308–33.

Hurwicz, L. (1993), 'Institutions as families of game forms', *Japanese Economic Review*, **47**, 13–132.

International Monetary Fund (IMF) (2001), *Review of the Fund's Experience in Governance Issues*, http//:www.imf.org.

Kahler, M. (2006), 'International governance and the IMF performances', in Truman, E.M. (ed.), *Reforming the IMF for the 21st Century*, Peterson Institute for International Economics, Special Report no. 19, April, 257–70.

Kapur, D. and M. Naim (2005), 'The IMF and democratic governance', *Journal of Democracy*, **16** (1), 89–102.

Kapur, D. and R. Webb (2000), 'Governance-related conditionalities of the international financial institutions', *G24 Discussion Paper Series*, 6, August.

Kelkar, V., V. Yadav and P. Chaudhry (2004), 'Reforming the governance of the International Monetary Fund', *World Economy*, **27** (5), May, 727–43.

Keohane, R.O. and J.S. Nye Jr. (2002), 'The club model of multilateral cooperation and the World Trade Organization: problems of democratic legitimacy', The J.F. Kennedy School of Government, Visions of Governance in the 21st Century, Working Paper 4.

Killick, T. (1995), 'Adjustment and economic growth', in Boughton, J.M. and K.S. Lateef (eds), *Fifty Years After Bretton Woods, the Future of the IMF and the World Bank*, Washington, DC: IMF and World Bank, 139–59.

Lachmann, L. (1970), *The Legacy of Max Weber*, London: Heinemann.

Lane, T. (2005), 'Tensions in the role of the IMF and directions for reform', *World Economics*, **6** (2), 47–66.

Lin, J.Y. (1989), 'An economic theory of institutional change: induced and imposed change', *Cato Journal*, **9** (1), 1–33.

North, D. (1990), 'A transaction cost theory of politics', *Journal of Theoretical Politics*, **2** (4), 355–67.

North, D. (1994), 'Economic performance through time', *American Economic Review*, **84** (3), 359–68.

Overseas Development Council (2000), *The Future of the IMF in Development*, ODC Task Force Report, Washington DC, April.

Ranis, G., J.R. Vreeland and S. Kosack (eds) (2006), *Globalization and the Nation State: The Impact of the IMF And the World Bank*, Oxford: Routledge.

Rodrik, D. (1999), 'Institutions for high-quality growth: what they are and how to acquire them', *IMF Conference on Second Generation Reforms*, November, Washington, DC: IMF.

Stiglitz, J.E. (2002), 'Globalization and the logic of international collective action: re-examining the Bretton Woods institutions', in Nayyar, D. (ed), *Governing Globalization, Issues and Institutions*, Oxford: Oxford University Press, 238–53.

Teunissen, J.J. and A. Akkerman (eds) (2004), *Diversity in Development: Reconsidering the Washington Consensus*, The Hague: FONDAD.

Thacker, S.C. (1999), 'The high politics of IMF lending', *World Politics*, **52** (1), 38–75.

Vines, D. and C.L. Gilbert (eds), (2004), *The IMF and its Critics, Reform of the Global Financial Architecture*, Cambridge: Cambridge University Press.

Williamson, J. (2000), 'The role of the IMF: a guide to the reports', International Economics Policy Briefs, 00-5, May, Washington, DC: Institute for International Economics.

Williamson, J. and C.R. Henning (1994), 'Managing the monetary system', in Kenen, P.B. (ed.), *Managing The World Economy: Fifty Years After Bretton Woods*, Washington, DC: Institute for International Economics, 83–111.

Woods, N. (2000), 'The challenge of good governance for the IMF and the World Bank themselves', *World Development*, **28**, (5), 823–41.

Woods, N. and D. Lombardi (2005), 'Effective representation and the role of coalitions within the IMF', Global Economic Governance Programme, Working Paper, February.

Woods, N. and A. Narlikar (2001), 'Governance and the limits of accountability: the WTO, the IMF and the World Bank', *International Social Science Journal*, **53** (170), 569–83.

7. Too much Consensus could be harmful: assessing the degree of implementation of stabilization and structural policies and their impact on growth

Eric Berr, François Combarnous and Eric Rougier

INTRODUCTION

The International Monetary Fund's (IMF) and the World Bank's approach of tying aid to the implementation of stabilization and structural policies (SSPs) has been a reality for numerous developing countries since the early 1980s. Such policy programs are designed as a 'one size fits all' strategy (Rodrik, 2003) and they generally conform to the 'three-pronged approach' (Knight and Santaella, 1997; Mussa and Savastano, 2000; Krueger, 2003; Butkiewicz and Yanikkaya, 2005): firstly, inflows of multilateral loans[1] or aid compensate for the lack of external sources of lending during a monetary or a financial crisis; secondly, macroeconomic stabilization policies such as fiscal adjustment or monetary restriction are carried out to reduce domestic absorption and to restore external equilibrium; thirdly, structural reforms towards liberalization and market regulation are undertaken in order to cement the stabilization policies and to increase the potential of economic expansion.

Even if it proceeds from what Williamson (1990) has called the Washington Consensus, the policy program that developing countries have actually implemented is quite different from the former version that Williamson coined when he listed at the end of the 1980s the ten central areas of policy reform that most people in Washington thought were needed in Latin American countries.[2]

The differences occur mainly in the definition of a competitive exchange rate and in the desired degree of capital account liberalization. Thus, Williamson (2004a, p. 200) claims that a competitive exchange rate 'necessarily implies an intermediate regime, because either fixed or floating rates can easily become over-valued', while on the contrary, 'the Bretton Woods institutions increasingly came to espouse the so-called bipolar doctrine toward exchange rate ... according to which countries should either float their exchange rate "cleanly", or else fix it firmly by adopting some institutional device such as a currency board'. Moreover, he observes that 'the Bretton Woods institutions, or at least the IMF, came in the mid-1990s to urge countries to liberalize their capital accounts, whereas ... [my] version had deliberately limited the call for liberalization of capital flows to FDI'. Bresser-Pereira and Varela (2004) think the capital account liberalization to be the starting point of a 'second' Washington Consensus.

Subject to numerous critiques since the second half of the 1990s (Gore, 2000; Davidson, 2004; Rodrik, 2003, 2004; Stiglitz, 1998, 1999, 2002; Birdsall and de la Torre, 2001; Easterly, 2001, 2005), international financial institutions (IFIs), and notably the World Bank,[3] have also reorientated their position so as to promote equity and pro-poor growth. They propose to enhance the Washington consensus with a 'human face' program involving policies designed to better income distribution. Such a Post-Washington Consensus is requested by Stiglitz (1998, 1999, 2002) or Rodrik (2003, 2004) while Kuczynski and Williamson (2003) define a set of 'second generation' policies in such a way. On the contrary, post-Keynesianism and Neostructuralism claim for a program emphasizing domestic demand as promoting investment and income distribution and reducing uncertainty and macroeconomic instability (Davidson, 2004; Gnos and Rochon, 2004; Taylor, 1983, 1988).

Whatever their names and the goals they are attached to, the design of these policy sets has been rather stable from the former Washington Consensus to the post-Consensus contemporaneous era. They include various policies, among them trade liberalization, price liberalization, privatization, the introduction of indirect means of monetary control, foreign exchange market liberalization, banking system restructuring, fiscal reform, taxes and subsidies cuts, and change in the structure of government spending (Fischer, 1997). Consequently, we will refer to as SSP those policies which are in the purview of the international financial institutions (IFIs), mainly the IMF and the World Bank, with whom coordination and cooperation is essential.

If numerous studies estimate the impact of one or another measure of these SSPs, very few attempts have been made to assess the whole impact of the entire policy set advocated by IFIs. Thus, two questions have not been correctly addressed yet. Firstly, how have developing countries implemented such 'necessary' reforms towards higher growth? Secondly, do these policies work for growth whatever way they are implemented?

In this chapter, we suggest that the extent to which such policies affect long-run income growth depends on both the degree and the pace of reform implementation. We also argue that the relationship between policy implementation and growth is non-linear. With these intentions, we propose an index measuring the degree of implementation of the IFI program called the Washington Consensus Index (WCI) that can be easily processed into growth equations. Thus, we suppose that IFI policies act as a factor of increased economic efficiency in the extended neoclassical growth model.

The following section examines the relevant literature on the effects of IFI policies on economic growth. Section 7.3 proposes a measure of the IFI program degree of implementation by the way of our Washington Consensus Index (WCI). Section 7.4 presents our methodology and model. Section 7.5 presents the empirical models testing the impact of WCI on economic growth and their results, followed by a discussion of said results. Section 7.6 concludes.

THE EFFECTS OF IFI PROGRAMS ON GROWTH IN EMPIRICAL LITERATURE

Do these SSPs, advocated by IFIs as necessary reforms towards higher growth and development, work or not, and do they work whatever the degree the policies are implemented at by developing countries? The evidence is quite unclear as regards both the measure of the degree of implementation of the SSPs and the assessment of their effect on growth.

Empirical literature on the macroeconomic effects of IFI programs can be divided into at least three approaches. The first one is to assess the effects of stabilization programs on macroeconomic outcomes through case studies. Country studies by Taylor (1988) or more recently by Zaki (2001) show that IMF policies can actually have an adverse impact on growth in some specific contexts. Even if a well-documented country study can give a balanced and complete picture of how IFI programs work in a specific context, it cannot be generalized and give any assessment of the average effectiveness of such policies, which is what we are looking for. The second approach consists in counterfactual analysis or develops specific methodologies such as generalized estimator evaluation

(GEE) or simulation models. Former studies by Killick (1995), Schadler et al. (1993), Goldstein and Montiel (1986) or Khan (1990) focus on the early 1980s and do not find any significant relationship[4] or any adverse significant relationship between stabilization programs and growth, whereas more recent studies including data for the end of the 1980s and the beginning of the 1990s are more conclusive, even if their results are mixed. Conway (1994), Bagci and Perraudin (1997) and Dicks-Mireaux et al. (2000) find that IMF programs have a significant positive impact on growth, and though Bird (2001) Bird and Rowlands (2003) show that they have a significant adverse effect on growth.[5] But there are crucial differences between the short-run and long-run estimated effects on growth and investment too. Conway (1994), Hutchinson (2001) and Killick (1995) find that the short run effect on growth is adverse or neutral while it is positive in the long run, although Prezkowics and Vreeland (2000) report a sustained adverse effect on growth of IMF programs, even in the long run as IMF program participation lowers growth rates for as long as countries remain under a program, and post-program growth is lower than it would have been without participation. Despite their methodological shortcomings[6] these studies give a rather general picture of the way stabilization and structural reforms do, on average, impact on growth and show that even if during the reform process growth rates tend to be depressed in the short run and to be triggered in the medium or long-run, the overall effects of such programs are rather limited.

The last approach estimates, in a cross-section of countries, the way policy changes explain variations in gross domestic product (GDP) while controlling for other factors of growth. Cross-sectional studies can be differentiated by the way they introduce IFI policies in growth regressions. Many studies try to appraise the growth effects of specific stabilization outcomes or adjustment policies, but only a few have tried to evaluate the effects of the entire policy set promoted by IFIs. Economic growth has been regressed on fiscal and monetary targets such as the public consumption share of GDP, exchange rate distortions or inflation rates, but also on policy variables like financial liberalization or trade openness[7] in order to assess the impact of these policies on income expansion, but generally without any attempt to measure the global effect of the policy set underlying IFI programs. Thus, they provide only partial appraisals of the growth effects of IFI programs because they only address specific policies instead of a set of policies implemented together, and because they do not draw on measures of the actual implementation of that policy set.

Nevertheless, partial cross-country studies have produced several results. Large government deficits and public consumption have been found to be negatively associated with growth (Levine and Renelt, 1992; Barro, 1991, 1997; Barro and Sala-i-Martin, 1995; Sala-i-Martin et al., 2004) but fiscal deficit is generally captured by the average ratio of government consumption on GDP and it often excludes public investments and focuses on non-productive public spending. Barro (1991) finds on the contrary that public investment significantly fosters GDP expansion, while Caselli et al. (1996) find the coefficient of the ratio of government consumption to GDP is positive. Inflation is detrimental to growth according to Barro (1991), De Gregorio (1992), Levine and Renelt (1992), Fischer (1993) and Bruno and Easterly (1998), but at rates above about 40 percent per annum for the last study, whereas for Barro (1991) the threshold is around 15 percent per annum. As regards structural reforms, higher financial integration[8] was found to be associated with higher growth rates in earlier works of King and Levine (1993) and Easterly (1993) and forward in the work of Levine et al. (2000), which accounts for the effects of institutional control variables on that positive relationship. But recent studies produce more heterogeneous results. While Rodrik (1998b), Klein and Olivei (1999), Arteta et al. (2001) and Edison et al. (2002) find no evidence of such a positive link for developing countries, Edwards (2001) and Klein (2003) find a negative relationship for poorer developing countries and Stiglitz (2000) claims that capital market liberalization provokes increasing economic instability and adverse effects on growth.[9] Trade reform and the related liberalization of the balance of payments are often measured by the average trade share of GDP and by the average black market premium. While the latter is usually significantly and negatively associated with growth, as in Easterly (1993), Levine and Renelt (1992), Barro and Sala-i-Martin (1995) and Sala-i-Martin (1997), measures of trade openness are more ambiguously related to growth as argued in Rodriguez and Rodrik (2001).[10] Yanikkaya (2003) among other studies has then recently shown that openness has only a limited direct effect on growth, and that trade liberalization does not have the positive effect expected by the previous Consensus. Finally, as regards other structural reforms, Barro (1997) and Sala-i-Martin (1997) show that the rule of law, including secured property rights, fosters growth.[11]

Thus, 'partial' correlation studies are a first step on the way to assessing the effects of IFI programs, but they fail to deliver a clear overall picture of the effects of a set of policies implemented together by countries under reforms. Another problem with using a limited series of macroeconomic outcomes as a measure of policy reform is that priorities differ across countries so that stabilized inflation or financial liberalization are not necessarily the more relevant reforms everywhere and in any conditions.[12] Moreover, partial correlation studies are often badly specified because they do not control for all the other structural reforms associated with the fiscal or stabilization policy explicitly specified in growth equations. Then, the bias due to this misspecification is likely to overweight the fiscal factor if they do not control for the other policies simultaneously implemented. Our methodology address both the previous caveats as it measures the actual implementation of each of the policies in the SSP set, and as it associates them in a unique index in regressions.

Despite the limits of 'partial regressions', only a few cross-country studies have attempted to appraise the joint effect of an extended set of the policies implied by conditionality. Moreno-Brid et al. (2004) use the five-dimensions index of reforms developed by Lora (2001), and show that there is no clear association between the depth of macroeconomic reform and economic growth performance in Latin America. Easterly et al. (1997) and Fernandez-Arias and Montiel (2001) introduce several policy variables as additional explaining factors in a basic growth regression and argue that growth could even have been higher if reforms had been deepened or broadened. But they add that post-reform growth impetus has not been disappointing, given the depth of the reforms and the unfavorable external environment, since Latin America's growth rates rose relative to East Asia's during the period because it reformed more (Easterly et al., 1997). However, the set of indicators they use can be seriously misleading. For example, they measure structural reforms such as the privatization of public firms, the resolution of debt-overhang problems or the liberalization of the foreign direct investment (FDI) regime, by the log of the average ratio of investment to GDP. Yet, such a rough proxy gives a poor measure of the underlying outcomes it is assumed to account for. Indeed, the average ratio of investment to GDP could rise for purely cyclical reasons, or because of the expansion of a capital-intensive sector, without any influence of structural reforms on that increase. It could also be explained by the importance of public investments in a low-income and unattractive country where private investments are shrinking. Moreover, Easterly et al. (1997) remark that the coefficient estimates are very sensitive to estimation procedures and to time period because of the difficulty in separating out effects of different policies.

An alternative approach by Svensson (2003), Dollar and Svensson (1998) and Mercer-Blackman and Unigovskaya (2004) is to use information from the World Bank or the IMF reflecting the failure or success of supported programs, but such measures are subjective and often consist in binary variables that cannot assess the degree or the pace of implementation. They are also poor proxies of policies in order to measure the growth effect from different degrees of reform implementation. Then, biased or inefficient empirical methods can fail to assess an effect that actually can exist.

Implementations of the SSPs can also fail to deliver any significant growth impetus because they are inadequately designed to address the problems of the countries that implement them. Fischer (1997), Mussa (1997) and Mussa and Savastano (2000) have questioned the 'rightness' of the policy set under Consensus, and Rodrik (2003) claims that 'one size fits all' policy sets are inadequately designed to foster growth and sustained macroeconomic performance every time. But Killick (1995), Bordo and Schwartz (2000) and Krueger (2003) have claimed that policies also fail to spur sustainable growth because they are generally too poorly implemented to raise sufficiently positive outcomes. Incompletion problems are rather well documented and Mussa and Savastano (2000) and Bird (2001) report that more than two-thirds of programs are poorly implemented and finally break down. But empirical evidence of the adverse effect on growth of incompletion actually relies on a very short series of subjective or indirect indicators. The most commonly used approach in the literature is based on alternative measures of the degree of commitment of loans or of their repetition. Many studies regress growth rates on measures of the extent to which the agreed loan is drawn down by the end date of the program. Some of them have also tried to assess the growth effects of the duration and of the repetition of IMF programs by using alternative measures of loans as an explaining variable.[13] But the survey by Killick et al. (1998) shows that evidence of the effects of adjustment lending on growth is mixed with positive, zero or negative effects. More recently, Barro and Lee (2003) show that a higher IMF loan-participation rate reduces economic growth in the subsequent five years, while Butkiewicz and Yanikkaya (2005) show that IMF lending is either neutral or detrimental to growth through a negative impact on public and private investment. Easterly (2003, 2005) finds no systematic effect of adjustment lending on growth and on policies, and shows that neither did the prevalence of macroeconomic distortions in inflation rates, black market premium, real exchange rate overvaluation, interest rates, fiscal and current account deficits diminish with intensity and repetition of structural adjustment lending, nor did per capita growth rates improve. These results are consistent with results showing that foreign aid does not on average increase growth (World Bank, 1998; Burnside and Dollar, 2000).

The 'loan approach' supposes that conditionality works and that agreed-upon policies are actually implemented by receivers. But they are sometimes poorly implemented either because governments do not want to complete the reforms, or because they cannot do so due to the internal uneffectiveness of the whole core policy set. Easterly (2005) shows that conditionality does not significantly affect domestic policies on average. Moreover, Rodrik (1996) finds that lagged IMF lending is negatively related to growth and suggests that IFIs do not actually have the informational advantage that their familiarity with government policies could have produced. More recently, Svensson (2003) and Easterly (2005) confirm such a failure of the monitoring of programs implementation by IFIs when they show that successive loans do not respond to significant policy changes or growth accelerations. Svensson (2003) finally explains that conditionality associated with aid does not work because of the lack of incentives for the donor to control for and to reward good policies.

Another caveat is that a given shortfall in the use of IMF credits can correspond not only to a failure of the implementation of the policy reforms, but also to a success, especially when the signaling effect of the policy reform program eases the substitution of sustainable external private capital inflows for multilateral lending. Such a shortfall could also be the result of macroeconomic external shocks breaking down the policy program.

The many aspects of the policy program related to IFIs' conditionality make arduous any appraisal of the economic effects of its implementation. Svensson (2003) claims systematic quantitative studies of aid and reform policies are so rare because it is hard to find the convenient data. He also remarks that the instability of estimated aggregate effects of policy packages is lower than the estimated effect of each separate policy. Moreover, each of the policies can be loosely or fully implemented, making any picture more blurred and any appraisal more dubious. Thus, we have built an index measuring the extent to which each policy aspect has been implemented and combining these measures into a unique and synthetic figure.

The WCI can be described by ten variables standing for the ten policy instruments featured both in Williamson's (1990) former approach and in latter versions of structural adjustment or conditionality. The choice of these variables requires very detailed attention in order to avoid any confusion between the measurement of objectives and means of such a policy set. As we want to assess the actual degree of application of the set of policies, we opt only for variables measuring the level of completion of the so-called objectives.[14] We further present the indicators standing for stabilization and structural measures.[15] A country's overall budget balance, expressed as a percentage of GDP, accounts for fiscal deficits (FD). As a balanced budget should be a minimal medium-run norm according to IMF programs, the highest values of balance stand for countries in better positions. The public expenditure priorities indicator (*PE*) – that is, cutting down of subsidies and reorientation towards education, health and infrastructure (Williamson, 1990) – is proxied by a composite variable mixing the share of public consumption in overall consumption and the share of transfers and subsidies in GDP. The highest values are for countries having the lowest shares of public consumption and subsidies.[16] The action on interest rates by the mean of monetary orthodoxy (*IR*) is estimated by a composite indicator of the interest rates determination mode, the monetary policy orientation and the level of real interest rates. The lowest values of this variable are for countries with state-fixed interest rates, durably negative real interest rates and/or very loose monetary policies leading to hyperinflation. Highest values stand for countries where interest rates are market-determined, real interest rates are positive and/or an orthodox monetary policy is implemented. The indicator of competitive exchange rates (*ER*) is also proxied by a composite variable summarizing the annual growth of exports of goods and services and the external balance on goods and services expressed as a percentage of GDP. The higher this indicator, the higher are the country's growth of exports and external balance.[17]

Regarding structural measures, the indicator of trade policy (*TP*) is measured by a hybrid variable including the extent of trade liberalization (level of tariff and non-tariff barriers) and capital liberalization (degree of control over access to international capital markets). The highest values are attributed to countries with weak tariff and non-tariff barriers and with free access to international capital markets. While Williamson did not include capital account liberalization in his Washington Consensus (Williamson, 1990, 2000, 2004a), the IMF did in the 1990s. A country's competitiveness regarding FDI (*FI*) is accounted for by another composite variable combining net FDI flows, expressed as a percentage of GDP, and a measure of capital market regulation. This variable is higher as the country receives significant FDI flows and/or has a more deregulated capital market. The indicator of privatization (*PI*) assesses the public sector share in the economy and is computed by using data on the number of public companies, their share in total output and the share of the public sector in total investment. The lowest values are for economies that are dominated by publicly owned firms and/or where public investment represents more than 50 percent of total investment. Highest values are for countries with few publicly owned firms and/or where public investment is less than 15 percent of total investment.[18] The indicator of deregulation (*DE*) is a composite variable accounting for the degree of regulation of credit and labor markets and for the degree of business regulation. This indicator has the highest values for countries with low regulations over business and/or markets. Tax reform (*TR*) is estimated by a composite variable accounting for taxes on income, profits and capital gains as a share of total taxes and for highest marginal tax rates. The highest values are attributed to countries with the lowest direct taxes share and/or the weakest marginal tax rates. Finally, a composite variable summarizing the existence of a legal framework allowing the defense of private interests and the protection of intellectual property will stand for the property rights indicator (PR). The highest values are for countries where the legal system totally secures property rights.

These explanatory variables have been reduced by factor analysis into one single indicator called the WCI. The methodology of principal components analysis (PCA) is used because it is well suited for our purpose.[19] The PCA says the correlation between several variables is to be that of 'measuring the same thing', here the degree of implementation of SSP. It authorizes the building of indicators from weighted linear combinations of the independent variables principal components (PCs). For the year 2000, the ten previous indicators of implementation of the policy set are available for 98 developing countries.[20] Simple correlations between these variables are reported in Table 7.1.

They show that most of the independent variables are more or less positively correlated. However, we notice an adverse correlation of *PE* with other variables like *IR*, *TP*, *DE* and *PR* which reveals a particularly interesting phenomenon. Whereas we expected developing countries to implement, more or less intensively, the entire set of measures advocated by the Consensus, it appears that the restriction of public expenditure and subsidies is adversely correlated with several other measures, such as monetary orthodoxy, liberalization, deregulation or property rights. Thus, countries with high levels of deregulation and liberalization, with guaranteed property rights and monetary orthodoxy, are also those where the public sector keeps a significant weight and where transfers and subsidies remain high. This observation suggests that most of the countries implementing IFIs' recommendations do it while keeping a relatively high degree of state involvement, consequent public expenditure and sectored subsidies. Thus, in observed countries, the Washington Consensus has not been applied in the whole of its ten dimensions. Rodrik (1998a) has previously shown that bigger states are associated with more openness, while Williamson (2004b) confirms that reforming public expenditure priorities has been widely neglected.

Anyway, such a significant amount of cross-correlation suggests that these variables effectively account for various aspects of the same object, that is, implementation of the policy set. Principal components estimation proves that most of the previous independent variables do load adequately onto the first PC extracted from the data, as reported in the first column of Table 7.2. That result corroborates our hypothesis that the degree of implementation of IMF programs can be treated as a one-dimensional concept.

The percentage of the variation in the data captured by the first PC, almost 30 percent, is also satisfactory for our purpose. The higher the contribution of a variable, the more that variable contributes to the variation accounted for by the particular PC. We can see that the first PC is heavily determined by variables accounting for structural measures, with little contribution of variables accounting for stabilization measures (except for *IR*). This suggests that in year 2000, the basic stabilization measures have already been implemented among countries to an almost similar extent, while structural measures have been carried out in a much more dissimilar way. Then, what discriminates values of the WCI for different countries is mainly the degree of implementation of the structural dimension of the IFI policy set.

The WCI is a linear combination of the initial variables so that:

$$WCI_{ij} = \Sigma\, a_k\, x_{kij}$$

where WCI_{ij} is the composite indicator of the degree of Washington Consensus implementation in the *i*th country in *j*th time, a_k is the weight of the *k*th variable (first principal component loading of the *k*th variable), and x_{kij} is the standardized value of the *k*th variable for the *i*th country in *j*th time. For the year 2000, the WCI attributes its highest values to the most advanced countries in the implementation of all the measures recommended by IFI programs, that is, Singapore, Chile, Botswana, Panama or Argentina. Conversely, it assigns its lowest values to countries that did not come up to Consensus expectations: the Syrian Arab Republic, Democratic Republic of Congo, Sierra Leone, Central African Republic, and Islamic Republic of Iran.

As such, this indicator does not address our question adequately because it is not relevant to confront countries' growth over 1980–2000 with the degree of implementation of a given number of Consensus objectives for the final year 2000.[21] What we need is to regress countries' growth rates over 1980–2000 on the changes of WCI during the same period. To compute the WCI values for the year 1980, we use additional case technique which simply weights the value for the year 1980 of the ten initial indicators with the a_k coefficients produced by the first PC executed on data for the year 2000.

Table 7.1 Simple correlations between WCI variables

	Fiscal deficit	Public expenditure	Interest rates	Exchange rate	Trade policy	Foreign investment	Privatization	Deregulation	Tax reform	Property rights
FD	1.000	0.018	-0.120	0.048	0.098	0.198**	0.020	0.034	-0.092	-0.116
PE		1.000	-0.218**	-0.081	-0.254**	-0.107	-0.004	-0.204**	-0.149	-0.389***
IR			1.000	0.081	0.221**	0.255**	0.388***	0.632***	0.280***	0.415***
ER				1.000	0.095	-0.228**	0.026	0.023	-0.014	0.186*
TP					1.000	0.429***	0.313***	0.384***	0.062	0.291***
FI						1.000	0.311***	0.491***	0.295***	0.103
PI							1.000	0.469***	0.100	0.173*
DE								1.000	0.215**	0.424***
TR									1.000	-0.034
PR										1.000

Note: *** denotes a significant correlation at the 1% level (2-tailed), ** at the 5% level and * at the 10% level.

The variations (ΔWCI) of the WCI over the 1980–2000 time period then measure the extent of implementation of IFI programs during this period.[22] They are normally distributed with Venezuela, Togo and Guatemala getting the weakest values and Nicaragua, Ghana and the Syrian Arab Republic the highest values.

If the design of conditionality is right, the degree of completion of programs might then matter and the depth and the breadth of such reforms should be associated with higher growth over a sufficiently long period. Our intention is to test such a proposal on a sample of developing countries having more or less completed the IFI policy set and over a 20 year time span. Therefore, we use the WCI composite variable, which is a quantitative measure of the degree of implementation of the policy reforms as they are designed by IFIs for developing countries, with or without IMF agreement.[23]This index appraises the extent to which each given country has implemented every aspect of the stabilization and adjustment program. Hence, WCI variations measure the depth and the pace of the reforms undertaken.

METHODOLOGY AND MODEL

Relationships between the degree of implementation of the IFIs' programs and growth are now investigated by explicitly including the WCI as an explaining variable into the standard growth model by Mankiw et al. (1992) (MRW). There are two ways of proceeding in the empirical literature. Either the WCI is added to the macroeconomic production function as a 'policy' factor of production associated with the traditional economic factors or it is introduced as a factor of the dynamics of technological efficiency $G(X)_t$.[24] We follow this last method because of its consistency both with theory and with our purposes. Stabilization programs and structural reforms are aimed at making the price right and at getting the allocation of resources better through more effective factor markets or more macroeconomic stability, and at opening the economy more widely to trade and to FDI. The potential effects on economic efficiency, and especially on technological efficiency, of such outcomes cannot be denied. Introducing the WCI into the augmented model of growth is therefore preferable in order to interpret the results within an economic model and to compare them with usual results in literature.

We follow Mankiw et al. (1992) who derivate from a Cobb–Douglas production function with constant returns to scale:

Table 7.2 Principal components loadings

	PC1	PC2	PC3	PC4	PC5	PC6	PC7	PC8	PC9	PC10
FD	0.011	0.191	**0.672**	**0.360**	-0.105	**-0.526**	0.048	0.169	-0.253	0.008
PE	-0.218	**0.462**	-0.237	**0.385**	0.301	0.091	**0.635**	-0.145	-0.034	-0.102
IR	**0.430**	-0.063	**-0.332**	0.039	0.050	**-0.372**	-0.112	**-0.371**	**-0.391**	**-0.506**
ER	0.044	**-0.421**	-0.033	**0.773**	-0.197	0.149	-0.118	-0.150	**0.343**	-0.087
TP	**0.360**	-0.017	**0.349**	0.031	-0.109	**0.676**	0.142	-0.175	**-0.476**	0.039
FI	**0.359**	**0.416**	0.254	-0.175	-0.200	0.082	0.049	-0.089	**0.606**	**-0.422**
PI	**0.351**	0.157	-0.026	0.219	**0.655**	0.150	**-0.364**	**0.466**	0.036	-0.023
DE	**0.490**	0.058	-0.054	0.016	0.106	-0.235	0.123	**-0.356**	0.197	**0.711**
TR	0.172	**0.403**	**-0.433**	0.180	**-0.603**	0.037	-0.117	**0.390**	-0.162	0.174
PR	**0.339**	**-0.452**	-0.062	-0.102	-0.038	-0.111	**0.620**	**0.505**	0.062	-0.101
Eigen values	2.992	1.508	1.243	1.022	0.843	0.732	0.546	0.428	0.401	0.284
% of variance	29.91 6	15.076	12.433	10.219	8.432	7.324	5.461	4.285	4.015	2.840
Cumulative %	29.91 6	44.992	57.425	67.644	76.076	83.400	88.860	93.145	97.160	100.000

Note: Bold values heavily contribute to principal components (PCs) variation.

$$Y = K^{\alpha} H^{\beta} (AL)^{1-\alpha-\beta} \tag{7.1}$$

the following expression of the growth of income around the steady state:

$$\ln\frac{Y(t)}{L(t)} - \ln\frac{Y(0)}{L(0)} = \theta \ln A(0) + G(X) + \theta\frac{\alpha}{1-\alpha-\beta}\ln(s_k)$$
$$+\,\theta\frac{\beta}{1-\alpha-\beta}\ln(s_h) - \theta\frac{\alpha+\beta}{1-\alpha-\beta}\ln(n+g+\delta) - \theta\ln\frac{Y(0)}{L(0)} \tag{7.2}$$

where $\theta = 1 - e^{-\lambda t}$ and λ is the rate of convergence to a country's steady state, $Y(t)/L(t)$ is per capita income at time t, K and H are physical and human capital, s_k and s_h are the rates of physical and human capital accumulation, α and β are technology parameters, n is the labor force growth, $A(t)$ is the level of efficiency at time t and $G(X)$ is the rate of efficiency growth depending on the vector of variables X. As usual and to avoid further methodological problems, we suppose that g in the fifth term of (7.2) is a constant exogenous growth rate of efficiency. We make the standard assumption that g is 0.02 and the rate of capital depreciation δ is assumed equal to 0.03. Hence $G(X)$ is a term measuring increase in efficiency and it is proxied here by the degree of implementation of the previous policy set of stabilization and structural reforms: ΔWCI.

So as to assess fully the effects of IFI programs on growth, we add a discrete choice model to the usual growth regression one. Both models are successively estimated in a cross-section by averaging over 20 years and in a panel framework. The results are then discussed in the next section.

We first estimate the equation (7.3) by ordinary least squares:

$$\Delta y_{i,t} = \alpha y_{i,t-1} + \beta x_{i,t} + \varepsilon_{i,t} \tag{7.3}$$

and then the corresponding equation (7.4) including fixed time and country effects by partitioned OLS and generalized least squares:[25]

$$\Delta y_{i,t} = \alpha y_{i,t-1} + \beta x_{i,t} + \lambda_t + \mu_i + \varepsilon_{i,t} \tag{7.4}$$

where y is the natural logarithm of per capita GDP, x is the set of explanatory variables including changes in the WCI and initial levels of the WCI, and the time subscript t refers to the four sub-periods of five years.

We consider that there are significant gains attached to the greater relevance of long time spans regarding growth analysis as the elimination of business cycle effects that likely affect the results of regression computed over shorter time periods.[26] But we also address the costs of not controlling for individual unobserved fixed effects and not removing the unobservable country-level heterogeneity underpinning the $A(0)$ term in (7.2) and the constant term in regressions. We first introduce dichotomized terms that control for the likely country heterogeneity in the initial conditions of economic and technological efficiency. Hence countries with higher initial market efficiency (right prices, effective capital and labor markets), with higher macroeconomic stability (lower inflation and black market premium) and with larger openness (high trade share and high level of received FDI) will probably have higher global efficiency, but especially higher technological efficiency thanks to the higher incentives to innovate or to imitate, to invest in training and owing to the technological spillover of trade and FDI. Thus, the need to control for the initial heterogeneity in efficiency is partially addressed in the cross-sectional pattern of long-run changes. But we simultaneously compute similar regressions on the corresponding panel of data in order to obtain estimates while controlling for unobserved effects.

Moreover, we introduce that policy set index in a long-term panel framework with time-specific effects over four periods of five years so as to overcome the difficulties associated with exogenous shocks and with lags between policies and effective results underlined by Svensson (2003).

Finally, the composite indicator *WCI*, that includes one measure for each respect of the policy set designed by IFIs, puts together measures of the achievement of policies objectives instead of the proximate outcomes usually chosen for proxies, and it reduces the risk of collinearity between a growing numbers of policy indicators used as explaining variables. Thereupon, we are able to measure the growth effect of this set of policies while controlling both for the degree of completion of each part of the program and for the pace of their implementation. Hence, variety in the implementation process as regards the pace and the depth of reforms can be controlled for.

RESULTS AND DISCUSSION

Using a methodology based on the Solow augmented model, we test the impact of ΔWCI on economic growth in growth regressions and in a discrete choice model. Both models are successively estimated in a cross-section and in a panel framework. The results are then discussed.

Growth Regressions of the Impact of the Washington Consensus Implementation

What we are interested in is the effect of the implementation of a set of policies on increase of GDP controlling for traditional factors of growth. Table 7.3 shows the OLS regressions results for the log difference of real GDP per capita between 1980 and 2000 and for 63 developing countries[27] in columns (1) to (4), and the corresponding results for the panel of four sub-periods in columns (5) to (8).

Models (1) and (5) are the basic MRW growth model. The estimated coefficients have the expected signs and almost all are statistically significant. The adverse association between changes in the (log) GDP per capita and the (log) levels of the initial GDP suggests that conditional convergence occurs. The (log) level of investment has a significant positive effect on growth, whereas the (log) level of demographic growth significantly reduces growth. The (log) level of schooling is not statistically significant.[28]

The impact of SSP is estimated in models (2) to (4) and (6) to (8). Firstly, ΔWCI is included in model (2) and (6) as an additional explanatory variable for growth and is not significant at conventional levels, but it is so close to significance in (2) and significant at 10 percent level in (6) that it suggests that the relationship between GDP growth and IFI programs implementation could be non-linear. In model (3) and (7) ΔWCI squared is henceforth included as an additional variable, but without significance and the coefficient of ΔWCI is unaffected.

Models (4) and (8) control for initial levels of WCI in model (3) and (7).[29] This initial level of WCI matters in at least two respects. Firstly, it may have a direct effect on growth if stabilization and structural reforms are about to be prerequisites for higher growth. But it can also act as a control for the effects of ΔWCI on growth. A given absolute variation of WCI from 1980 to 2000 can actually account for very different policy 'efforts' depending on whether they set off from a high or low level of reform implementation. They show that even if ΔWCI has no significant impact on growth, a high initial WCI level has a significantly positive effect on it. Countries that had already set up stabilization policies and/or structural reforms before 1980 and were not driven to do so, experience a subsequent stronger growth.

A Probit Estimation of Higher Growth Probability: The Non-Linear Effect on Growth

The probit framework is used to catch the likely non-linear relationship between IFI policies' implementation and growth. Thereupon, we go further in our analysis by shifting the emphasis from the impact of Washington Consensus implementation on growth to its impact on improving the probability for a given country to experience a growth rate higher than that of other countries. Such a shift in analysis is supposed to be fertile as we can expect Bretton Woods institutions programs to improve the proximate conditions of growth impetus more than to foster growth directly. In order to test this hypothesis, we transform the endogenous variable into a dichotomous one, with value 1 if the country did experience a stronger growth than the median during 1980–2000, and 0 otherwise. Table 7.4 shows that probit regressions of the same model specifications as in Table 7.3 produce very interesting results for cross-country estimates (1) to (4) and that panel estimates (5) to (8) are less relevant. That can reveal the difficulty of short-period regressions to catch the effects of long-run structural policies on the probability to benefit from a higher growth.

The basic growth model remains stable within this new framework whatever the specification that is chosen.[30] While model (2) shows that ΔWCI has no linear impact on higher growth probability, model (3) shows a significant quadratic impact of ΔWCI on higher growth probability. This quadratic association between IMF programs implementation and higher growth probability is strengthened by controlling for initial WCI levels, as shown in model (4). The results thus suggest that implementing such programs increases the probability to experience higher growth rates, but that there is a turning point above which furthering such policies can be harmful to growth. Once such a threshold has been gauged over which the relationship between ΔWCI and higher growth probability becomes negative,[31] it appears that many countries may have respectively gone 'too fast' or 'too far' in the implementation of IFI programs. Among those which experience the highest values of ΔWCI in the sample, ten countries could have gone 'too fast': the Syrian Arab Republic, Central African Republic, Islamic Republic of Iran, Burundi, Nigeria, Indonesia, Bangladesh, Ghana and the Arab Republic of Egypt. Although they do not really come up to IFIs' expectations, as their WCI value remained weak in 2000, they have strongly implemented IFI programs during the 1980–2000 period. The others, Nicaragua, Bolivia, Peru, Guyana, Argentina and Turkey, could have gone 'too far'. Their

Table 7.3 Estimates of MRW growth model with IFI programs impact (standard errors)

	Dependent variable: log difference of real GDP per capita 1980–2000							
	Cross-country regressions (OLS)				Panel regressions (partitioned OLS, fixed effects)			
Models	*(1)*	*(2)*	*(3)*	*(4)*	*(5)*	*(6)*	*(7)*	*(8)*
Observations	63	63	63	63	234	234	234	234
Constant	2.896*** (1.074)	2.805** (1.061)	2.772** (1.090)	3.139*** (1.072)	0.548** (0.240)	0.644*** (0.247)	0.647*** (0.248)	0.638*** (0.245)
ln (GDPini) [a]	-0.152** (0.074)	-0.160** (0.073)	-0.158** (0.074)	-0.202*** (0.075)	-0.041** (0.018)	-0.042** (0.018)	-0.043** (0.018)	-0.051*** (0.018)
ln (I / GDP)	0.673*** (0.104)	0.660*** (0.103)	0.659*** (0.104)	0.638*** (0.101)	0.174*** (0.021)	0.159*** (0.021)	0.157*** (0.022)	0.155*** (0.021)
ln (SCHOOL)	-0.123 (0.170)	-0.096 (0.168)	-0.096 (0.170)	-0.105 (0.165)	-0.025 (0.037)	-0.034 (0.040)	-0.032 (0.040)	-0.029 (0.040)
ln (n + g + □)	-1.135*** (0.365)	-1.073*** (0.362)	-1.066*** (0.368)	-1.111*** (0.358)	-0.189** (0.081)	-0.197** (0.083)	-0.197** (0.083)	-0.171** (0.083)
□WCI	-	-0.081 (0.050)	-0.062 (0.133)	0.113 (0.154)	-	0.041* (0.024)	0.055* (0.031)	0.042 (0.031)
□WCI square	-	-	-0.005 (0.032)	-0.038 (0.034)	-	-	-0.011 (0.016)	-0.007 (0.016)
High initial WCI	-	-	-	0.228** (0.108)	-	-	-	0.060* (0.023)
Ajusted R^2	0.508	0.522	0.514	0.542	0.224	0.192	0.191	0.210
Breusch-Pagan Chi^2 [b]	4.333	6.817	7.239	12.275				

Notes: *** Significant at 1% level, ** Significant at 5% level, * Significant at 10% level.
(a) Initial value of ln(GDP): ln(GDP) in 1980 for cross-country regressions and ln(GDP) at the beginning of each period *t* for panel regressions.
(b) None of the values of the Breusch-Pagan test rejects the null hypothesis of residuals homoscedasticity.

Table 7.4 Probit estimates of MRW growth model with IFI programs impact (standard errors)

Dependent variable: log difference of real GDP per capita 1980-2000 > median = 1; 0 otherwise								
	Cross-country regressions				Panel regressions[a]			
Models	*(1)*	*(2)*	*(3)*	*(4)*	*(5)*	*(6)*	*(7)*	*(8)*
Observations	63	63	63	63	234	234	234	234
Constant	13.193*	22.417*	11.745	12.936	4.430**	4.877**	4.901**	5.254**
	(6.888)	(12.283)	(7.432)	(8.137)	(2.050)	(2.102)	(2.108)	(2.138)
ln (GDPini) [b]	-0.892*	-1.541*	-0.862*	-1.221**	-0.167	-0.143	-0.146	-0.277
	(0.480)	(0.825)	(0.518)	(0.619)	(0.153)	(0.155)	(0.156)	(0.166)
ln (I / GDP)	3.081***	5.577***	3.022***	3.054***	0.686***	0.723***	0.718***	0.713***
	(0.854)	(1.713)	(0.902)	(0.939)	(0.188)	(0.192)	(0.192)	(0.195)
ln (SCHOOL)	0.273	0.247	0.676	0.926	-0.255	-0.310	-0.302	-0.277
	(1.043)	(1.796)	(1.188)	(1.251)	(2.058)	(0.341)	(0.343)	(0.344)
ln (n + g + □)	-7.742***	-12.932***	-8.107***	-8.286***	-1.917***	-2.210***	-2.219***	-2.207***
	(2.571)	(4.645)	(2.881)	(3.155)	(0.693)	(0.715)	(0.718)	(0.721)
□WCI	-	-0.643	4.112*	5.869**	-	0.589**	0.642**	0.700**
		(0.902)	(2.228)	(2.636)		(0.234)	(0.294)	(0.302)
□WCI square	-	-	-3.838**	-4.761**	-	-	-0.054	-0.059
			(1.927)	(2.111)			(0.176)	(0.181)
High initial WCI	-	-	-	1.177	-	-	-	0.273
				(0.752)				(0.213)
R^2 (Efron)	0.541	0.546	0.593	0.617	0.091	0.111	0.111	0.113

Notes: *** Significant at the 1% level, ** Significant at the 5% level, * Significant at the 10% level.
(a) Likelihood ratio tests (chi squared) reject random effects.
(b) Initial value of ln(GDP): ln(GDP) in 1980 for cross-country regressions and ln(GDP) at the beginning of each period *t* for panel regressions.

strong implementation of IFI programs ranks them among the countries with the highest WCI values in 2000.

Panel estimates do not catch the quadratic association between IFI programs implementation and higher growth probability. Short-run estimates only measure the positive effect of ΔWCI, in models (6) to (8), without being able to assess for the alleged effect of implementations gone 'too fast' or 'too far'. Five-year periods are not long enough to capture the entire magnitude of the 'extreme' implementations of the programs that are about to produce growth reversals in the medium or long run.

Discussion

The results reported above show that IFI programs do not necessary produce the growth pay-off they are expected to do. The depth and the pace of the reforms are critical factors of the effectiveness of programs. In section 7.2 we underlined that some studies have tried to show that reforms do not foster growth because they are not sufficiently deepened or broadened. We now argue that such ineffectiveness is rather the consequence of reforms that have gone too far or too fast.

As expected, we find that lower growth is associated with poor implementation of the reforms. But we also show that further implementation can be associated either with higher or lower growth depending on the depth and pace of the reforms. Countries going fast and far in reforms can be divided in two sub-groups according to their position relative to the turning point we identify for the relation between implementation and growth. If the set of reforms is driven too far or too hastily, it can hamper growth. This is an interesting result but it gives little information about what has been too far. Actually, those countries do not only contrast by their absolute degree of implementation of SSPs. The comparison of their average commitment to the ten measures standing for the Consensus shows that the 'form' of their implementation significantly differs. The t-test for equality of means for all the constitutive variables of ΔWCI between the two sub-groups of countries shows that IMF programs become harmful for countries which have gone much further in monetary orthodoxy and deregulation (*IR* and *DE* variables).[32] How can we interpret such results?

Countries that have deregulated too far or too fast may have betrayed Williamson's approach of 'market-oriented' reforms and have chosen a 'market-fundamentalism' version of them. However, too much deregulation can finally fail to deliver the pro-competitive and pro-growth effects expected from unfettered markets, if the institutional context is not sufficiently developed: poor social rules and weak regulation of competitive activities, low public interventions regarding activities producing externalities. The reorientation of IFIs' concerns towards institutions and good governance may corroborate the hypothesis that there are institutional thresholds beyond which deregulation can have poor or even adverse effects on growth.

But, the increased instability provoked by deregulation reforms in a developing economy can be decisive in understanding our results in several respects. Firstly, the deregulation process includes business reforms aimed at easing market access and efficiency – such as FDI regimes – but also some form of financial liberalization. A number of studies have shown that capital account liberalization results in an increased volatility of financial flows that finally reduces investment and growth (Stiglitz, 2000; Bordo and Eichengreen, 2002). Moreover, capital flows are even more sensitive to macroeconomic outcomes for a country which is recovering from crisis and whose policies are scrutinized by close monitoring. Secondly, if the degree of deregulation is higher because of substantial capital account liberalization, such countries can excessively rely on high interest rates to prevent outward capital flight (Stiglitz, 2000; Bresser-Pereira and Varela, 2004). In this context of openness, inflation targeting remains a central objective, and it generally results in orthodox monetary policies likely to be too restrictive. Even if inflation targeting can be overemphasized as regards the potential adverse effects on growth of increasing prices,[33] countries are more or less compelled to do it for financial reasons. Thirdly, such high interest rates will deter investment and therefore growth. This adverse effect of deregulation and of orthodox monetary policies on growth through interest rates can be amplified by the effects on interest rates of the increase in public consumption observed in countries implementing the reforms further and faster. Thus, one can conceive that self-reinforcing adverse effects on growth could result from the mutual strengthening of deregulation reforms and of monetary orthodoxy.

Finally, if public and private investments are complements, the decrease in public investments following the cuts of government spending required by IFI stabilization programs will finally affect private investments too. Butkiewicz and Yanikkaya (2005) show that IMF lending – and consequently the IMF-supported policy set – has such significant negative effects on both private and public investments. Our data show that countries implementing further reforms simultaneously increase their public consumption share, and shall then necessarily reduce public investment to limit deficits. This overall decrease in domestic investment can be balanced by inflows of FDI when business reforms are able to create adequate incentives for foreign firms. However, FDI inflows partially depend on the growth rate and on the pace of productivity increase of host economies. Hence, the mutual depressing effect of deregulation reforms 'gone too far' and of monetary orthodoxy on domestic investment and on domestic growth could significantly impede such FDI inflows. Such a drop in overall capital formation is likely to deter subsequent growth and can feed inflation pressures from the supply side as argued by the Neostructuralists.

CONCLUSION

One of the major contributions of this chapter has been to compute a multidimensional index of IFI programs implementation, which provides a useful complement to usual investigative techniques. As PCA offers a unique quantitative measure of the depth and pace of all aspects of the IFI policy set, we have been able to investigate its whole impact on economic growth, within the well-known MRW growth model, and to show that the impact on growth is non-linear.

What then have we learned? Concerning the construction of our index, an important implication should be noted. The adverse correlation of public expenditure priorities with other variables like monetary orthodoxy, commercial openness and deregulation discloses an interesting phenomenon. Among observed countries, those who come up to Consensus expectations do not implement the entire set of measures advocated by IFIs. These countries adopt IFI recommendations while maintaining a relatively high degree of government involvement. But the key finding of this chapter is that, when combined with usual explanatory variables, our index is relevant in predicting long-term growth in developing countries. Although IFI programs implementation seems to have a doubtful impact on growth rate itself, it presents a significant non-linear relationship with the probability of getting a higher growth than in other countries. To a certain degree, the Consensus implementation increases the probability of benefiting from a higher economic growth. However, there could be a limit beyond which a further implementing of IFI programs becomes harmful. Indeed, it seems that a too abrupt, unprepared ('too fast') and/or intense ('too far') implementation of IFI programs can harm growth in developing countries.

APPENDIX 7.A DATA SOURCES FOR WCI CONSTITUTIVE VARIABLES

Fiscal deficit – Overall budget balance (World Bank, 2003).

Public expenditure – Mean of variables 1A and 1B (Gwartney et al. 2003).

Interest rates – Variable 5Aiv (Gwartney et al. 2003).

Exchange rate – Hybrid variable of annual growth of exports of goods and services and external balance on goods and services as a percentage of GDP (World Bank, 2003).

Trade policy – Mean of variables 4A, 4B and 4Ei (Gwartney et al. 2003).

Foreign investment – Hybrid variable of net FDI flows as a percentage of GDP and variable 4Eii (see respectively World Bank, 2003; and Gwartney et al. 2003).

Privatization – Variable 1C (Gwartney et al. 2003).
Deregulation – Variable 5, except 5Bv (Gwartney et al. 2003).

Tax reform – Hybrid variable of taxes on income, profits and capital gains as a share of total taxes and variable 1Dii (see respectively World Bank, 2003; and Gwartney et al. 2003).
Property rights – Mean of variables 2B and 2C (Gwartney et al. 2003).

APPENDIX 7.B LIST OF COUNTRIES

Argentina	Dominican Republic	Korea, Rep.	Senegal
Bangladesh	Ecuador	Malawi	Sierra Leone
Barbados	Egypt, Arab Rep.	Malaysia	Singapore
Benin	Fiji	Mali	South Africa
Bolivia	Gabon	Mauritius	Sri Lanka
Botswana	Ghana	Mexico	Syrian Arab Rep.
Brazil	Guatemala	Morocco	Thailand
Burundi	Guyana	Nicaragua	Togo
Cameroon	Honduras	Niger	Trinidad and Tobago
Central African Rep.	Hungary	Nigeria	Tunisia
Chile	India	Pakistan	Turkey
Colombia	Indonesia	Panama	Uruguay
Congo, Dem. Rep.	Iran, Islamic Rep.	Paraguay	Venezuela, RB
Congo, Rep.	Jamaica	Peru	Zambia
Costa Rica	Jordan	Philippines	Zimbabwe
Ivory Coast	Kenya	Rwanda	

APPENDIX 7.C DATA SOURCES FOR GROWTH MODELS

Real GDP per capita – (Summers et al. 2002).

Investment share of real GDP – (Summers et al. 2002).

School: average combined gross enrolment ratio (primary + secondary + tertiary) from 1980 to 2000 (Unesco, Institute for statistics – http://www.uis.unesco.org/en/stats/centre.htm).

Population – (Summers et al. 2002).

APPENDIX 7.D DATA SUMMARY STATISTICS

Variables	All	Low income	Middle income	Severely indebted	Moderately or less indebted	Low HDI	Middle or high HDI
				Averages for 63 developing countries			
Δ ln (GDP per capita)	0.712	0.488	0.849	0.451	0.883	0.373	0.837
Initial GDP (1980)	2346	865	3258	2004	2571	810	2914
I / GDP	13.451	8.723	16.361	11.149	14.966	7.714	15.572
School	58.190	43.252	67.382	54.422	60.669	38.300	65.540
$n + g + \delta$	7.170	7.684	6.853	7.457	6.981	7.787	6.941
ΔWCI	1.554	1.565	1.547	1.847	1.361	1.108	1.719
High initial WCI	0.333	0.083	0.487	0.160	0.447	0.059	0.434
Low initial WCI	0.333	0.500	0.231	0.520	0.210	0.471	0.282

NOTES

1. The short-run standby arrangements (SBA) and medium-run extended fund facilities (EFF).
2. For Davidson (2004, p.210), 'the only analytical difference between Williamson and ideological market fundamentalists is the question of the length of time required for a free market to achieve a social optimum'. Then 'all ten reform of the Washington Consensus are founded on classical economic theory that supports the laissez-faire doctrine as necessary to solve all our economic problems – at least in the long run'.
3. See for instance World Bank (1997) in its annual report where 'good governance' was supposed to ensure market efficiency. In the same way, Manuel (2003, pp.19–20) asserts that, in the case of sub-Saharan Africa, the problem is 'that most states are weak and limited, not that states try to do everything and account for 50 percent or so of national income ... Most African states need to expand, not contract, their public sector – and dramatically improve its efficiency in delivering quality public services. This demands institutional capacity, especially in areas of regulation, service delivery, and social spending'.
4. See Ul Haque and Khan (1998) or Butkiewicz and Yanikkaya (2005) for a more detailed survey of the main results and shortcomings of that literature.
5. Ul Haque and Khan (1998) and Dicks-Mireaux et al. (2000) claim that the more recent studies using the GEE methodology are more relevant for our purposes than the former counterfactual studies; Butkiewicz and Yanikkaya (2005) do however insist on the poor evaluation that is made of the underlying model and assumptions.
6. See Easterly et al. (1997), Ul Haque and Khan (1998), Bird (2001) or Butkiewicz and Yanikkaya (2005).

7. See Quah (1998) and Temple (1999) for a survey of the way these variables explain growth in empiric models; see Sala-i-Martin (1997) and Sala-i-Martin et al. (2004) for their degree of robustness in growth regressions.
8. Empirical studies traditionally measure financial integration by a proxy for government restrictions on capital flows like the IMFrestriction measure, by a measure of actual international capital flows or by the average ratio of broad money to GDP.
9. See Edison et al. (2004) for a more complete survey of methods and results.
10. Rodriguez and Rodrik (2001) show in a crucial survey that some of the proxies used to measure openness are cautious, and those estimations are often biased by endogeneity problems.
11. By then, an institutional variable is often introduced in growth regressions. See Quah (1998) and Temple (1999) for a survey.
12. See Svensson (2003).
13. See Conway (1994), Killick (1995), Mussa and Savastano (2000) Easterly (2005).
14. This will in some cases explain a shift between the consensus policy instruments and the selected variables.
15. The sources of all these data are World Bank (2003) and Gwartney et al. (2003). They are detailed in Appendix 7.A.
16. While Williamson (1990) 'believes that there are circumstances in which carefully targeted subsidies can be a useful instrument', the IFI program aims at lowering the government's role.
17. As we do not refer to any particular exchange rate regime to reach this particular objective, ER applies for Williamson's Consensus as for IFIs one.
18. Williamson (1990) however is 'not persuaded that public service is always inferior to private acquisitiveness as a motivating force. Under certain circumstances, such as where marginal costs are less than average costs (for example, in public transport) or in the presence of environmental spillovers too complex to be easily compensated by regulation (for example, in the case of water supply), [he] continue[s] to believe public ownership to be preferable to private enterprise. But this view is not typical of Washington.'
19. Essentially, PCA maximizes the correlation between the original variables to form new variables that are mutually orthogonal, or uncorrelated. It is a special case of factor analysis which transforms the original set of inter-correlated variables into a new set of an equal number of independent uncorrelated variables or principal components (PCs) that are linear combinations of the original variables. The principal components are ordered in such a way that the first PC explains most of the variance in the data, and each subsequent one accounts for the largest proportion of variability that has not been accounted for by its predecessors. Although the number of PCs equals the number of independent original variables, most of the variation in the data set can generally be explained by the first few PCs, which can be used to represent the original observations.
20. The few data gaps (about 3 percent) are filled by substituting means based on values for neighboring or economically similar countries.
21. This method would imply that the Consensus implementation positively influences growth because the most dynamic countries during the 1980–2000 period have a higher average WCI for the year 2000 than the least dynamic ones. However, the first group could have not applied any Consensus measures during this period, whereas the second could have been in complete agreement with it.
22. Our sample is then reduced to 63 countries for which ΔWCI can be computed. For a detailed discussion on ΔWCI computation and comments, see Berr and Combarnous (2005).
23. In our 63-country sample, only nine have never received structural adjustment loans nor faced the Paris Club until 2000, namely Barbados, Botswana, Colombia, Fiji, the Islamic Republic of Iran, Malaysia, Paraguay, Singapore and the Syrian Arab Republic.

24. Knight et al. (1992) and Dinopoulos and Thompson (1999) follow that way of proceeding. Temple and Johnson (1998) also use this method in order to introduce a social capacity variable in the MRW basic regression.
25. We follow Anderson and Hsiao's procedure (Anderson and Hsiao, 1981) to account for unobserved country-specific effects by using the first-differences of all the term of the equation (7.3) with time-specific effects controlled for by time-period dummies.
26. Or the elimination of the problem of residuals autocorrelation associated with the panel framework.
27. Sample size is limited by the availability of data. Observed countries are reported in Appendix 7.B, data measures and sources are reported in Appendix 7.C and summary statistics for data in Appendix 7.D.
28. This is not a surprising result as changes in human capital measured by school enrolments 'appear to explain little of the variation in changes of output' (Temple, 1999, p.139); see also Temple (1999) for a review of the shortfalls of school enrollment rates to proxy educational stocks or flows.
29. Let 'high initial WCI' be 1 for countries with WCI value in 1980 higher than the sixty-sixth percentile level and 0 otherwise.
30. The only exclusion is the constant term which is not statistically significant any more in models (3) and (4).
31. This threshold corresponds to the value that solves $dx/dy = 0$ (with y for higher growth probability and x for ΔWCI).
32. The t-test for equality of means for all the constitutive variables of ΔWCI between the two sub-groups of countries is significant at the 5 percent level for variables IR and DE.
33. Bruno and Easterly (1998) and Barro (1991) showed that inflation penalizes growth at levels higher than 15 percent, or even 40 percent; Stiglitz (1998) claims that 'below that level ... there is little evidence that inflation is costly ', and he adds that monetary policy should try to minimize or to avoid major economic contractions instead.

REFERENCES

Anderson, T.W. and C. Hsiao (1981), 'Estimation of dynamic models with error components', *Journal of the American Statistical Association*, **76**, 598–606.

Arteta, C., B. Eichengreen and C. Wyplosz (2001), 'On the growth effects of capital account liberalization', mimeo, Berkeley, CA: University of California.

Bagci, P. and W. Perraudin (1997), 'The impact of IMF programs', Global Economic Institutions Working Paper, No.24, GEI, London.

Barro, R. (1991), 'Economic growth in a cross-section of countries', *Quarterly Journal of Economics*, **56** (2), 407–43.

Barro, R. (1997), *Determinants of Economic Growth*, Cambridge, MA: MIT Press.

Barro, R. and J.-W. Lee (2003), 'IMF programs: who is chosen and what are the effects?' *Australian National University*, RSPAS working papers, Trade and Development.

Barro, R. and X. Sala-i-Martin (1995), *Economic Growth*, New York: McGraw-Hill.

Berr, E. and F. Combarnous (2005), 'Vingt ans d'application du consensus de Washington à l'épreuve des faits', *Economie Appliquée*, **58** (2), 5–44.

Bird, G. (2001), 'IMF programs: do they work? Can they be made to work better?' *World Development*, **29** (11), 1849–65.

Bird, G. and D. Rowlands (2003), 'Political economy influences within the life-cycle of IMF programs', *World Economy*, **26** (9), 1255–78.

Birdsall, N. and A. de la Torre (2001), *Washington Contentious: Economic Policies for Social Equity in Latin America*, Washington, DC: Carnegie Endowment for International Peace and Inter-American Dialogue.

Bordo, M.D. and A.J. Schwartz (2000), 'Measuring real economic effects of bailouts: historical perspectives on how countries in financial distress have fared with and without bailouts', *Carnegie-Rochester Conference Series on Public Policy*, **53**, 81–167.

Bordo, M.D. and B. Eichengreen (2002), 'Crises now and then: what lessons from the last era of financial globalization?' NBER Working Paper no. 8716, Cambridge, MA: National Bureau of Economic Research.

Bresser-Pereira, L.C. and C. Varela (2004), 'The second Washington consensus and Latin America's quasi-stagnation', *Journal of Post Keynesian Economics*, **27** (2), 231–50.

Bruno, M. and W. Easterly (1998), 'Inflation crises and long-run growth', *Journal of Monetary Economics*, **41** (1), 3–26.

Burnside, C. and D. Dollar (2000), 'Aid, policies, and growth', *American Economic Review*, **90** (4), 847–68.

Butkiewicz, J. and H. Yanikkaya (2005), 'The effects of IMF and World Bank lending on long-run economic growth: an empirical analysis', *World Development*, **33** (3), 371–91.

Caselli, F., G. Esquivel and F. Lefort (1996), 'Reopening the convergence debate: a new look at cross-country growth empirics', *Journal of Economic Growth*, **1** (3), 363–89.

Conway, P. (1994), 'IMF lending programs: participation and impact', *Journal of Development Economics*, **45**, 365–91.

Davidson, P. (2004), 'A Post Keynesian view of the Washington consensus and how to improve it', *Journal of Post Keynesian Economics*, **27** (2), 207–30.

De Gregorio, J. (1992), 'Economic growth in Latin America', *Journal of Development Economics*, **39** (1), 59–84.

Dicks-Mireaux, L., M. Mecagni and S. Schadler (2000), 'Evaluating the effect of IMF lending in low-income countries', *Journal of Development Economics*, **61**, 495–526.

Dinopoulos, E. and P. Thompson (1999), 'Reassessing the empirical validity of the human-capital augmented neo-classical growth model', *Journal of Evolutionary Economics*, **9** (1), 135–54.

Dollar, D. and J. Svensson (1998), 'What explain the success or failure of structural adjustment programs', *Economic Journal*, **110** (October), 894–917.

Easterly, W. (1993), 'How much do distortions affect growth?' *Journal of Monetary Economics*, **32** (2), 187–212.

Easterly, W. (2001), 'The lost decades: explaining developing countries: stagnation in spite of policy reform 1980–1998', *Journal of Economic Growth*, **6** (2), 135–57.

Easterly, W. (2003), 'The effect of World Bank and IMF programs on poverty', in Dooley, M. and J. Frankel (eds), *Managing Currency Crises in Emerging Markets*, NBER Conference Report, Chicago, IL: University of Chicago Press.

Easterly, W. (2005), 'What did structural adjustment adjust? The association of policies and growth with repeated IMF and World Bank adjustment loans', *Journal of Development Economics*, **76** (1), 1–22.

Easterly, W., N. Loayza and P. Montiel (1997), 'Has Latin America's post-reform growth been disappointing?' *Journal of International Economics*, **43**, 287–311.

Edison, H., M. Klein, L. Ricci and T.T. Slok (2004), 'Capital account liberalization and economic performance: survey and synthesis', IMF Staff Papers, **51** (2), 220–56.

Edison, H., R. Levine, L. Ricci and T. Slok (2002), 'International financial integration and economic growth', *Journal of International Money and Finance*, **21**, 749–76.

Edwards, S. (2001), 'Capital mobility and economic performance: are emerging economies different?' NBER Working Paper 8076, Cambridge, MA: National Bureau of Economic Research.

Fernandez-Arias, E. and P. Montiel (2001), 'Reform and growth in Latin America: all pain, no gain?' IMF Staff Papers, **48** (3), 522—46.

Fischer, S. (1993), 'The role of macroeconomic factors in growth', *Journal of Monetary Economics*, **32** (3), 485–511.

Fischer, S. (1997), 'Applied economics in action: IMF programs', *American Economic Review*, **87** (2), 23—7.

Gnos, C. and L.-P. Rochon (2004), 'What is next for the Washington consensus? The fifteenth anniversary, 1989–2004', *Journal of Post Keynesian Economics*, **27** (2), 187–93.

Goldstein, M. and P. Montiel (1986), 'Evaluating stabilization programs with multi-country data: some methological pitfalls', IMF Staff Papers, **33** (2), 304–44.

Gore, C. (2000), 'The rise and fall of the Washington Consensus as a paradigm for developing countries', *World Development*, **28** (5), 789–804.

Gwartney, J., R. Lawson and N. Emerick (2003), 'Economic freedom of the world: 2003 Annual Report', Vancouver: Fraser Institute.

Ul Haque, N. and M. Khan (1998), 'Do IMF-supported programs work? A survey of the cross-country empirical evidence', IMF Working Paper 98/169, Washington, DC: International Monetary Fund.

Hutchinson, M.M. (2001), 'A cure worse than the disease? Currency crises and the output costs of IMF-supported stabilization programs', NBER Working Paper 8305, Cambridge, MA: National Bureau of Economic Research.

Khan, M.S. (1990), 'The macroeconomic effects of fund-supported adjustment programs', IMF Staff Papers **37**, 195–231.

Killick, T. (1995), *IMF Programs in Developing Countries: Design and Impact*, London and New York: Routledge.

Killick, T., R. Gunatilaka and A. Marr (1998), *Aid and The Political Economy of Policy Change*, London and New York: Routledge.

King, R.G. and R. Levine (1993), 'Finance and growth: Schumpeter might be right', *Quarterly Journal of Economics*, **108** (3), 717–37.

Klein, M. (2003), 'Capital account openness and the variety of growth experience', NBER Working Paper 9500, Cambridge, MA: National Bureau of Economic Research.

Klein, M. and G. Olivei (1999), 'Capital account liberalization, financial depth and economic growth', NBER Working Paper 7384, Cambridge, MA: National Bureau of Economic Research.
Knight, M., N. Loayza and D. Villanueva (1992), 'Testing the neo-classical theory of economic growth: a panel data approach', IMF Working Papers, Washington, DC, December.
Knight, M. and J.A. Santaella (1997), 'Economic determinants of IMF financial arrangements', *Journal of Development Economics*, **54** (2), 405–36.
Krueger, A. (2003), 'IMF stabilization programs', in Feldstein, M. (ed.), *Economic and Financial Crises in Emerging Market Economies*, NBER conference series, Chicago, IL: University of Chicago Press.
Kuczynski, P. and J. Williamson (eds) (2003), *After the Washington Consensus: Restarting Growth and Reform in Latin America*, Washington, DC: Institute for International Economics.
Levine, R., N. Loayza and T. Beck (2000), 'Financial intermediation and growth: causality and causes', *Journal of Monetary Economics*, **46** (1), 31–77.
Levine, R. and D. Renelt (1992), 'A sensitivity analysis of cross-country growth regressions', *American Economic Review*, **82** (4), 942–63.
Lora, E. (2001), 'Structural reforms in Latin America: what has been reformed and how to measure it', Washington, DC: Inter-American Development Bank Working Paper 466.
Mankiw, N.G., D. Romer and D.N. Weil (1992), 'A contribution to the empirics of economic growth', *Quarterly Journal of Economics*, **107** (2), 407–37.
Manuel, T. (2003), 'Africa: finding the right path', *Finance and Development*, **40** (3), 18–20.
Mercer-Blackman, V. and A. Unigovskaya (2004), 'Compliance with IMF program indicators and growth in transition economies', *Emerging Markets Finance and Trade*, **40** (3), 55–83.
Milanovic, B. (2003), 'The two faces of globalization: against globalization as we know it', *World Development*, **31**(4), 667–83.
Moreno-Brid, J.C., E. Pérez Caldentey and P. Ruiz-Napoles (2004), 'The Washington consensus: a Latin American perspective fifteen years later', *Journal of Post Keynesian Economics*, **27** (2), 345–65.
Mussa, M. (1997), 'IMF surveillance', *American Economic Review*, **87**, 28–31.
Mussa, M. and M. Savastano (2000), 'The IMF approach to economic stabilization', *NBER Macroeconomics Annual 1999*, Cambridge, MA and London: MIT Press.
Przeworski, A. and J.R. Vreeland (2000), 'The effect of IMF programs on economic growth', *Journal of Development Economics*, **62**, 385–421.
Quah, D. (1998), 'The new empirics of economic growth', NBER Working Paper Series, 6422, Cambridge, MA: National Bureau of Economic Research.
Rodriguez, F. and D. Rodrik (2001), 'Trade policy and economic growth: a skeptic's guide to the cross-national literature', in Bernanke, B. and K.S. Rogoff (eds), *NBER Macroeconomics Annual 2000*, Cambridge, MA: MIT Press.

Rodrik, D. (1996), 'Why is there multilateral lending?' in Bruno, M. and B. Pleskovic (eds), *Annual World Bank Conference on Development Economics, 1995*, Washington, World Bank, 167–93.
Rodrik, D. (1998a), 'Why do more open economies have bigger governments?' *Journal of Political Economy*, **106** (5), 997–1032.
Rodrik, D. (1998b), 'Who needs capital-account convertibility?' in Fischer S., R.N. Cooper, R. Dornbusch, P.M. Garber, C. Massad, J.J. Polak, D. Rodrik, and S.S. Tarapore, (eds), *Should the IMF Pursue Capital Account Convertibility? Princeton Essays in International Finance*, No. 207, May, International Economics Section, Departement of Economics, Princeton University, New Jersey.
Rodrik, D. (2003), 'Growth strategies', Harvard University, mimeo.
Rodrik, D. (2004), 'Rethinking growth policies in the developing world: Luca d'Agliano Lecture in Development', Turin, October 8.
Sala-i-Martin, X. (1997), 'I just ran two million regressions', *American Economic Review*, **87** (2), 178–83.
Sala-i-Martin, X., G. Doppelhofer and R. Miller (2004), 'Determinants of long-term growth: a Bayesian averaging of classical estimates (BACE) approach', *American Economic Review*, **94** (4), 813–35.
Schadler, S., F. Rozwadowski, S. Tiwari and D. Robinson (1993), 'Economic adjustment in low-income countries experience under the enhanced structural adjustment facility', IMF Occasional Paper, 106, Washington, DC: International Monetary Fund.
Stiglitz, J. (1998), 'More instruments and broader goals: moving toward the post-Washington Consensus', the 1998 WIDER Annual Lecture, Helsinki, Finland, 7 January, http://www.globalpolicy.org/socecon/bwi-wto/stig.htm.
Stiglitz, J. (1999), 'The World Bank at the millenium', *Economic Journal*, **109** (459), 577–97.
Stiglitz, J. (2000), 'Capital market liberalization, economic growth, and instability', *World Development*, **28** (6), 1075–86.
Stiglitz, J. (2002), *Globalization and its Discontents*, New York: Norton.
Summers, R., A. Heston and B. Aten (2002), 'Penn world tables version 6.1', Center for International Comparisons, University of Pennsylvania.
Svensson, J. (2003), 'Why conditional aid does not work and what can be done about it?', *Journal of Development Economics*, **70** (2), 381–402.
Taylor, L. (1983), *Structuralist Macroeconomics: Applicable Models for the Third World*, New York: Basic Books.
Taylor, L. (1988), *Varieties of Stabilization Experience. Towards Sensible Macroeconomics in the Third World*, WIDER Studies in Development Economics, Oxford: Clarendon Press.
Temple, J. (1999), 'The new growth evidence', *Journal of Economic Literature*, **37**, March, 112–56.
Temple, J. and P.A. Johnson (1998), 'Social capability and economic growth', *Quarterly Journal of Economics*, **113** (3), August, 965–90.

Williamson, J. (1990), 'What Washington means by policy reform', in Williamson, J. (ed.), *Latin America Adjustment: How Much Has Happened?*, Washington, DC: Institute for International Economics.
Williamson, J. (2000), 'What should the World Bank think about the Washington Consensus?' *World Bank Research Observer*, **15** (2), 251–64.
Williamson, J. (2004a), 'The strange history of the Washington consensus', *Journal of Post Keynesian Economics*, **27** (2), 195–206.
Williamson, J. (2004b), 'The Washington Consensus as policy prescription for development', Practioners of Development Lecture, Washington, DC, 13 January.
World Bank (1997), *World Development Report*, Washington, DC: Oxford University Press.
World Bank (1998), 'Assessing Aid: What Works, What Doesn't, And Why', World Bank Policy Research Report, Oxford University Press.
World Bank (2003), 'World Development Indicators CD-ROM', World Bank Group, Washington, DC.
Yanikkaya, H. (2003), 'Trade openness and economic growth: a cross-country empirical investigation', *Journal of Development Economics*, **72** (1), 57–89.
Zaki, M.Y. (2001), 'IMF-supported stabilization programs and their critics: evidence from the recent experience of Egypt', *World Development*, **29** (11), 1867–83.

8. The political economy of global economic disgovernance

Luiz Carlos Bresser-Pereira

INTRODUCTION

Global governance is an expression which became popular in the 1990s to convey the idea that, in the world arena, nation-states have lost autonomy and relevance insofar as a multitude of other players – multilateral institutions, organizations of civil society, global social movements, multinational enterprises – have an increasing role to play. Roseneau (1990, 1997) was probably the first theoretician to discuss fully – and at a sophisticated academic level – this theme, which today has accumulated a large bibliography. The general idea was that globalization was causing the nation-states to lose relevance, while a large number of other global actors, beginning with international financial institutions, passing by non-profit organizations constituting a global civil society, and ending in the multinational business enterprises, were creating a network that effectively governed the world. In other words, the world was changing from international to global. I am not going to discuss here this idea which I understand to be moderately based on reality and strongly charged with ideology. There is no doubt that since World War II mankind is gradually building an international political system under the umbrella of the United Nations, that should not be confused with this fuzzy governance concept; it is also true that some kind of global civil society is emerging; but the idea that nation-states lost relevance because they became more interdependent is a way through which developed countries try to check the competition coming from cheap-labor middle-income countries rather than a reality. In fact, greater interdependence among nation-states makes them more directly competitive in the global arenas, and thus,more strategic, not less.

On its turn, economic global governance is the transposition of the concept for the world-level economic problems that nation-states face today. Since the major actors are by far the nation-states, we should speak of international economic governance rather than global economic governance. Independently however of the word that we use – international or global – what we see today is that world economic governance is precarious. First, because insofar as their respective nation-states are involved in intense international competition, the respective national governments are not able to cooperate effectively and coordinate actions, thus avoiding major crises; second, because a fundamentalist belief in a self-regulating market prevents the necessary actions; third, because the differences of powers and levels of development among nation-states remain substantial, opening room for hegemonic patterns;[1] fourth, because old and new forms of economic populism – particularly exchange rate populism – plague poor and rich countries' economic policies.[2] The first two causes make global economic governance ineffective insofar as it is unable to coordinate actions; the latter two make the system unjust and unstable, tending to balance-of-payments crises.

In this contribution to this edited volume, my central question is to know whether international economic governance really holds in the world today, or whether 'disgovernance' is a better word to express present reality. Global governance per se is non-existent, since only nation-states and the formal international organizations play relevant roles, but is international economic governance a fact or is 'disgovernance' a word that better depicts what is happening? Do we see coordinated macroeconomic policies around the world, or at least among the rich countries, or is what we see today deep imbalances, a looming crisis and an uncertain future? If this is so: why? Which are the immediate and particularly the structural and institutional causes? In order to answer these questions, I will focus my attention on the exchange rate and on the current account. My argument in this chapter is that the world does not really count with economic global governance. We rather have global disgovernance, given the recurrent crises in the developing countries, and the huge current account deficit in the United States. Their direct causes are obviously poor macroeconomic policies on the part of all national actors. Their more indirect causes, however, lie in economic populism, or more specifically, in exchange rate populism, and in the recommendation to adopt the strategy of growth with foreign savings that rich countries have being giving to middle-income ones. Economic populism is not surprising in developing countries, where societies are poorly organized, and elites are often corrupt. It is surprising, however, in the case of the US. Yet, I will suggest some reasons why fiscal and exchange rate populism is today a real problem to this country. In the second section, I will make a brief survey of the previous attempts to create an international economic governance; in the third section, I will discuss the 'emerging markets' crises of the 1970s and particularly of the 1990s, and relate them with the strategy of growth with foreign savings; in the fourth, I will discuss the current account imbalance in the US and look for its indirect causes to exchange rate populism, and the political and social retrocession that this country has been experiencing since World War II, probably as a consequence of the emergence of an aggressive individualism, which rejects the notion of the public and deprives it of the unique moral and political criteria adopted by modern secular societies.

SHORT UPDATE

In a relatively recent past, world economy counted with a governance system. It was clearly an international governance system, not a global one. It was created in 1944, in the Bretton Woods Conference. Its well-known objective was to set an economic governance system based on fixed exchange rates, where the IMF would play the role of chief financial controller and bank of last resource. We may say that the system was fragile and incomplete; that its main shortcoming was the prevalence of the US approach to the problem over the proposal made by Keynes. The fact, however, is that we witnessed its demise in 1971, when the dollar floated. Since then, country after country, with the exception of some Asian economies, liberalized in several degrees their international flows and engaged in some sort of exchange rate floating.

With the floating of national currencies and the great increase in capital flows, the central Bretton Woods institution, the International Monetary Fund (IMF), lost relevance as a lender of last resource, and ended up being just a watchdog for the Washington authorities in relation to developing countries. It lost relevance and credibility not only because its reserves were small in comparison with the debts that certain countries were able to achieve in the international financial market, but also because it proved to be an increasingly mistaken policy, in relation to developing countries, to grow with foreign savings, that is, with current account deficits. This strategy appeared for the first time in the 1970s, responding to the possibility and need of recycling the large international reserves accumulated by the oil-producing countries after the 1973 first oil shock. In the end of that decade, a second oil shock, coupled with inflation in the US and a huge increase in the international interest rates, led a large number of developing countries – the ones heavily indebted[3] – to default: a default which was not decided by them, but by the creditor banks that, one by one, suspended the rollover of the debts. This crisis, besides involving enormous costs for the developing countries (they are still today paying the price of this crisis with decreased rates of growth), represented a threat to the large international banks, and so a risk to the developed economies. Given the threat, their finance ministers, led by the US Treasury, and having as agents the IMF and the World Bank, demonstrated an outstanding capacity of coordination. They gave full support to their banks, and imposed on the highly indebted countries not only necessary fiscal and exchange rate adjustments but also practically the full payment of the debt.[4] The 1985 Baker Plan is usually presented as an example of this coordination, but actually it started before this, when the debt crisis broke down, and was informal rather than formal.

The formal coordination of the world economy was, first, assumed by the G-5 and later by the G-7 – informal institutional devices putting together the finance ministers of the rich countries. They had some successes in coordinating the world economy in the 1980s, when they had to face two major financial problems: the developing countries' debt crisis, and the overvaluation of the dollar. These two problems were new: since the 1930s the world economy had not faced similar challenges. The latter problem was successfully tackled in 1985, with the Plaza Agreement, and involved a coordinated action by the major central banks. Such coordination was relative, but it was sufficient to cause the desired depreciation of dollar, and the elimination of the US current account deficit. The great winner with this agreement was the US, which equilibrated its current account, rescued the dollar, and assured the continuance of its role as the world reserve currency, without incurring a rise in inflation; the major loser was Japan – the country that had based its growth on a relatively devaluated exchange rate. The coordination of macroeconomic policies continued with the Louvre Accord in 1986, but the agreed reference indicators soon collapsed.

It is difficult to deny the success of the Plaza Agreement. Not only because it was effective in achieving the stated objectives, but also for a question of correspondence: if countries are supposed to make macroeconomic policy, there is no reason why the world should not. Yet, immediately after the agreements, the classical argument that the devaluation of the dollar would take place anyway was presented: market forces would correct the situation (Feldstein, 1988, pp. 1, 5; Frenkel and Rockett, 1988). Feldstein was strong in his opposition to exchange rate and, more broadly, macroeconomic policy cooperation: 'I believe that the pursuit of exchange rate goals is likely to be both futile and economically damaging.' Why? Because, given the difficulties in putting together different nation-states, 'the attempt to pursue coordination in a wide range of macroeconomic policies is likely to result in disagreements and disappointments', and given the assumption that the dollar would anyway continue to decline 'because the future trade deficit implied by the dollar's current level would be too large to finance otherwise', the agreements would be meaningless anyway.

The obvious difficulties involved in international coordination coupled with these critiques probably explain the demise of international macroeconomic policy coordination in the 1990s. A third explanation, however, is less well known: the theoretical support for large current account deficits in the developing countries. If since the early 1990s the US Treasury, through the IMF and the World Bank, was advising these countries to engage in a growth cum foreign savings strategy and opening of the capital accounts, it made little sense to think in coordinate exchange rates: at least the exchange rate of the developing countries which accepted that strategy would necessarily get out of balance (here understood a balanced exchange rate just as the one that assures a current account around zero): they would have to be overvalued for the duration of the strategy.[5] This in fact happened and, not surprisingly, that decade was marked by huge financial crises. Now, in the first half of the 2000s, another major imbalance threatens international finances: the dollar has again appreciated dangerously in relation particularly to East and South-East Asian currencies, and the American current account deficit is achieving new records. Given these facts, it is understandable that one can doubt the existence of global economic governance. Instead, what they suggest is global economic 'disgovernance', or a major global economic imbalance. If this is so, what are the data that support such unbalance? What are its causes? And what are the tendencies from now on?

THE 1990S CRISES AND THE STRATEGY OF GROWTH WITH FOREIGN SAVINGS

I will start with the balance-of-payments crises that hit middle-income developing economies in the 1990s and early 2000s. They began with the Mexico 1994 crisis; followed by the Asian crisis in 1997, the Russian in early 1998, the Brazilian in late 1998 and finally the Argentinean in 2002. In this way, these economies, which had just experienced the major 1980s debt crises, were again facing similar problems. The failure of the international regime established in 1971, and the incapacity of the IMF to face it, became evident. Yet, while in the case of the abandonment of the Bretton Woods fixed rates one can argue that it was inevitable – that the exchange rate regime in a world so integrated commercially and financially would not be either fixed, as Keynesians would like, or floating, as neoclassical economists dream, but managed, as they actually are (Bresser-Pereira, 2004) – in the case of the IMF the failure was evident: this organization actually contributed actively to the 1990s crises.

Although they were loosely called financial crises, they were specifically balance-of-payments crises, because they involved the suspension by the creditors of the rollover of debts.[6] They were directly related to heavy foreign indebtedness and/or with large current account deficits, increasing loss of credit and credibility, and, as a trigger point, the suspension by foreign creditors of the refinancing of their international debts – public or private. Yet, as the countries also faced fiscal deficits, the current conventional wisdom at the IMF and the World Bank attributes the balance-of-payments crises to fiscal unbalance. This was a convenient approach because it reaffirmed the belief that all problems originated in the public sector, and coupled with the argument of the twin deficits, because it permitted that international and local authorities did not concern themselves with the increasing current account deficits. On the contrary, they were definitely not concerned, insofar as since the early 1990s, while the Brady Plan was straightening out the debt crisis, a new wave of loans for what were now called 'emerging markets' was taking place, and Washington came to what I called 'the Second Washington Consensus': the consensus that legitimated the opening of the financial accounts and the growth cum foreign savings strategy.[7]

In the case of the Asian crisis, however, this kind of explanation was soon revealed to lack empirical support: while these countries showed reasonably balanced fiscal accounts, foreign indebtedness and large current account deficits were again the main causes. As Stiglitz (2002, p. 99) remarks: 'the countries in East Asia had no need for additional capital, given their high savings rate, but still capital account liberalization was pushed on these countries in the late 1980s and early 1990s. I believe that capital account liberalization was the single most important factor leading to the crisis'. To this it is necessary to add the fact that banks financed speculative and irresponsible real estate investments – a specifically financial aspect of the crises. As in the case of the Latin America crisis, the trigger point was the suspension of international credit, thus configuring a typical balance-of-payments crisis. Tables 8.1 and 8.2 summarize the current account deficits of the countries just before the crisis. They also show the current account surpluses just after the crisis – surpluses that show that these countries learned the lesson fast.

Table 8.1 Asian crisis: current account balances 1995–99 (billions of US dollars)

	1995	*1996*	*1997*	*1998*	*1999*
Indonesia	-6.4	-7.7	-4.9	+4.1	+5.8
Korea	-8.7	-23.2	-8.4	+40.4	+24.5
Malaysia	-8.6	-4.5	-5.9	+9.5	+12.6
Philippines	-2.0	-4.0	-4.4	+1.5	+7.2
Thailand	-13.5	-14.7	-3.0	+14.2	+12.4

Source: World Development Indicators Database.

As a background note prepared, just after the crisis, by the UNCTAD Secretariat (1998, p. 1) asserts:

> Although different influences have been at play in different countries in the region, a common feature is that the crisis has its origin in the private sector and has taken the form of a major market failure. One can describe it either as excessive borrowing abroad by the private sector, or as excessive lending by international financial markets. In any case, as pointed out by Alan Greenspan, Chairman of the US Federal Reserve Board, it is clear that more investment monies flowed into these economies than could be profitably employed at modest risk.

In all cases, the crises had behind the conventional economics strategy of growth with foreign savings, that is, with current account deficits, which caused the overvaluation of the local currencies, and easily developed into balance-of-payments crises. If the current account deficits had been kept rigorously under control, avoiding the increase of the debt–export ratio, the crises could have been avoided, but the relative appreciation of the local currencies (in relation to an 'equilibrium level' where the current account is zero) and the resulting substitution of foreign for domestic savings would still prevail, causing long-term burdens in terms of resource outflows in the form of interest and dividends which were not proportional to the 'net' investment originated from the foreign savings.

Table 8.2 Asian crisis: current account balances 1995–99 (% of exports)

	1995	*1996*	*1997*	*1998*	*1999*
Indonesia	-12.10	-13.56	-7.75	+7.48	+10.39
Korea	-5.89	-15.12	-5.09	+25.60	+14.25
Malaysia	-10.31	-4.89	-6.32	+11.39	+13.13
Philippines	-7.46	-11.94	-10.89	+4.05	+18.46
Thailand	-19.20	-20.59	-4.14	+21.55	+17.37

Source: World Development Indicators Database.

Thus, I am suggesting that the IMF played an active role in stimulating foreign indebtedness and in not criticizing current account deficits. This is particularly true in the cases of the Mexican 1994, Brazilian 1998 and Argentinean 2002 crises. Contradictorily and pathetically, the IMF – which was well known for its 'orthodox', 'tough', demanding policies (and often criticized for that reason) – showed a surprising lenience in the case of the current account deficits: it actually supported exchange rate populism. The explanation behind this is its allegiance to the US sponsorship of the strategy of growth with foreign savings.[8] It was this strategy that, since the 1970s, replaced the law of comparative advantage in neutralizing possible competition originated in developing countries, or in other words, in 'kicking away the ladder' that they were using to grow. In the 1970s, with the emergence of the first NICs (newly industrialized countries), the rich world understood that its anti-protectionist strategy had become exhausted (now they needed protection), and concluded that the law of comparative advantage had now little use for them. Given the new conditions, they gradually realized that the growth cum foreign savings strategy, coupled with the opening of capital accounts and the protection of property rights, could play the role of checking the threat represented by the middle-income developing economies. Countries were advised to incur current account deficits and finance them with foreign borrowing or with foreign direct investment. Growth was transformed into a competition among developing countries to obtain more credibility and more foreign savings. Yet, as foreign loans or investments implied evaluation of the exchange rate and the increase in consumption, there was a massive substitution of foreign for domestic savings, and little or no growth in the rates of capital accumulation and in the gross domestic product (GDP) growth rates. Foreign debt, however, increased and eventually explained the balance-of-payments crises in the 1990s.

This explanation for the 1990s crises, based on current account deficits and high foreign indebtedness, is different from the conventional 'fiscal deficit explanation' and from its derivatives. Alves et al. (2004) listed the conventional models explaining exchange rate or balance-of-payments crises, all based on the hypotheses of 'efficient markets' and on disequilibria in the public sector. The first generation models explain the crises directly with the fiscal deficits; the second generation models add the games that economic authorities are engaged in when they face crisis and have to decide whether they will maintain the exchange rate fix or float it; the third generation models include the argument classically adopted by Keynesian economics: the unregulated and speculative character of financial institutions. The foreign indebtedness explanation for the 1990s crises is also different from the post-Keynesian, or the Regulation School explanation, which emphasizes the uncertainty and fragility of financial markets, and rejects the hypothesis of efficient markets.[9] They are correct in rejecting the efficient markets hypothesis, and in emphasizing the speculative character of financial markets. These are well-known characteristics. Yet, in most cases, financial fragility and speculation will not lead to balance-of-payments crises if the country has an effective policy of limiting current account deficits and foreign indebtedness: not only public but also private indebtedness. In other words, if a country has sound fundamentals (particularly a moderate foreign debt and small or negative current account deficits, a moderate public debt and small budget deficits) it is unlikely that it will get into a balance-of-payments crisis. There are some famous cases of countries having sound fundamentals and falling in crisis, but they are obviously exceptions. Usually the crises involve fundamentals. They may have a fiscal origin, but since the 1970s they have been strongly related to foreign indebtedness – a foreign indebtedness perversely stimulated by the Washington authorities and the New York financial markets. Although historical experience shows that developed countries developed principally by using domestic savings, developing countries are encouraged to walk on the edge of the abyss of high foreign indebtedness, which would be their 'natural' condition, but the wise counselors do not fail to recommend them to be careful and not fall. Worse, in this game, is that there is no advantage in walking on the edge of the abyss. Even if the country controls its current account deficits and its total indebtedness, and is not caught into crises, its growth performance will be impaired by that fact that the capital inflows evaluate the domestic currency, cause an increase in real wages and in domestic consumption, and the substitution of foreign for domestic savings.[10]

THE US CURRENT ACCOUNT

After the 1997 and 1998 crises, the American Treasury and the IMF probably changed some of their more radical views on the subject, but conserved their main assumptions and goals. On the other hand, no governance or institutional solution was presented to this problem at the international level. In its report, the Meltzer Commission (1999), which was created by the US Congress to study the problem, suggested that the IMF should act as a lender of last resort. The countries meeting certain *ex ante* conditions for solvency would be eligible for automatic financing, no additional conditionalities or negotiations being required. Yet, as the, United Nations Conference on Trade and Development (UNCTAD) 2001 *World Trade Report* (p. 72) pointed out:

> without discretion to create its own liquidity, the Fund would have to rely on major industrial countries to secure the funds needed for such operations. In such circumstances it is highly questionable whether it would really be able to act as an impartial lender of last resort, analogous to a national central bank, since its decisions and resources would depend on the consent of its major shareholders, who are typically creditors.

That was all. The idea of restructuring the architecture of global economic governance was discarded.

Like the Asian countries, the Latin Americans also partially learned the lesson, and, as we can see in Tables 8.3 and 8.4, they stopped to incur in huge current account deficits. All the signals, however, are that the US did not. Contradictorily, if not pathetically, the country that so adamantly persuaded developing countries to engage in the growth cum foreign savings strategy – a strategy that did not consult the recipient countries' national interest – made itself prisoner of such a disastrous proposal. While the Asian and the Latin American countries were recovering from their crises, the United States has been caught by huge budget deficits and extremely high current account deficits. These deficits are absolute records, and are transforming the United States, the richest and most powerful nation-state in the world, into a 'debtor nation'. According to Cline (2005, p. 1), who wrote a book with that title, 'The [current account] deficit is larger than at any other time in the 135 years for which data are available'. The data that he presents show that after a period between 1869 and 1914 that was characterized by deficits being compensated by surpluses, the United States economy experienced a long period of current account surpluses that run up to the early 1980s. From this moment on, we have a first major fall between 1982 and 1987, current account deficits reaching 3.4 percent of GDP, a recovery up to 1992, and, since then an increasing deficit which reached 6 percent of GDP in 2004, and today is around 7 percent of GDP. As Tables 8.3 and 8.4 show, in 2004 the US$665.9 billion current account deficit represented 58 percent of exports.

This is definitely a serious problem. Some authors insist on disregarding the problem, with the argument that despite having become a debtor country, the spread of returns between those earned by US residents on their investments abroad and the average yield of foreign investments in the United States is large.[11] This fact plus the revaluation effects of the 2002–03 depreciation have been neutralizing the financial costs of the negative net international position, but it does not essentially change the picture. If we understand that in the present imbalance of the American economy there is a stock and a flow aspect – the foreign debt and the current account deficit – this argument really reduces the weight of the net debt, but does not reduces the fact that the current account is highly in deficit despite the higher return on US foreign investments. There is another argument, which is mostly shared by governors of the Federal Reserve Bank.[12] According to this argument, which is more explicit and more arrogant in its disregard for the foreign account deficits, the deficit is not the US's fault, but the fault of the countries that have depreciated currencies. As *The Economist* reported (28 April 2005): 'lately almost all the governors of America's Federal Reserve have made speeches on the country's current-account deficit, now 6.3 percent of GDP and rising. Several have sounded remarkably relaxed. Yes, they say, the gap's big, but it's not America's fault; most likely, it will be closed without too much trouble.' Thus, adjustment will have to be proceeded by others, not by the US.

The United States will probably remain the great economic and political power for many years, but it will be a declining power insofar as the dollar will tend increasingly to lose its position as an international reserve, probably to the euro. As James Galbraith (2004), wrote:

> For decades, the Western World tolerated the 'exorbitant privilege' of a dollar-reserve economy because the United States was the indispensable power, providing reliable security against communism and insurrection without intolerable violence or oppression, thus conditions under which many countries on this side of the Iron Curtain grew and prospered. Those rationales evaporated 15 years ago, and the 'Global War on Terror' is not a persuasive replacement. Thus, what was once a grudging bargain with the world's stabilizing hegemon country is now widely seen as a lingering subsidy for a predator state.

The assumption that the rest of the world, particularly the Asian dynamic countries, will continue to finance the United States indefinitely, and that what we have now is just a 'new Bretton-Woods' (Dooley et al., 2003) is just not realistic. These countries will be interested in financing the United States and in increasing reserves insofar as this strategy checks the appreciation of their currencies and keeps their export-led economies growing fast.[13] But there are limits for such strategy – limits on the part of these countries, which are seeing the fragility of the American economy, limits on the part of the United States. They are seeing that the debt situation of the country is deteriorating, and that no actions are being taking to correct such trend. As Jarret remarks (2005, p. 14): 'baseline projections of what would happen to the external accounts in the coming years absent any change in the dollar vary significantly, but show a rapid widening of the deficit'. Thus, it is becoming increasingly clear that the total 'transition costs' in postponing adjustment are steadily increasing. If the decision to adjust is taken at an early stage, net transition costs will probably be high, but, as a trade-off, the economy will return sooner to stability and growth: total transition costs will be smaller. To try to postpone adjustment indefinitely will normally end up in a major crisis which will impose it.[14]

THE STRUCTURAL AND POLITICAL ECONOMY CAUSES BEHIND

I will not discuss the prospects of this major current account deficit. The literature on the subject is already extensive, authors dividing themselves between pessimists who believe in a 'hard landing', and optimists predicting a 'soft landing'. On this subject, it should only be remembered that there is an important difference between the 1985 and the present imbalance. At that time, the supremacy of the dollar was not being questioned, today it is. Additionally, at that time the United States was a net creditor internationally, today it is a net debtor:

from a US$298 billion net positive position in 1983, it went to a US$2430 billion negative net position in 2003 (Nonnenberg, 2005). Also I will not discuss the remedies for the crises. Although the United States government (Congress and Treasury) insists on attributing the problem to an 'artificially depreciated' Chinese currency, the fact is that the Chinese surplus explains only a small part of the United States deficit. Actually, the required American macroeconomic adjustment will involve fiscal adjustment plus the dollar depreciation. Just fiscal adjustment will probably not be enough: when the Clinton administration reached equilibrium in the fiscal account, the current account was still showing a deficit.

Table 8.3 Current account balance 1999–2004 by regions (billions of US dollars)

	1999	*2000*	*2001*	*2002*	*2003*	*2004*
USA	-296.8	-413.4	-385.7	-473.9	-530.7	-665.9
European Union[1]	+21.0	+5.3	+18.9	+62.7	+97.5	+88.5[4]
Latin America[2]	-57.0	-58.4	-53.4	-21.1	-3.5	+4.2[5]
Dynamic Asian[3]	+236.1	+241.1	+186.9	+234.2	+295.6	+386.4[4]
Oil exporters [4]	+15.9	+66.7	+45.8	+48.2	+77.2	+118.6
Other countries	+88.0	+165.0	+188.8	+154.3	+67.2	+71.5

Notes: 1. European 15 plus Switzerland.
2. Excludes Venezuela.
3. Japan, China, India, Korea, Indonesia, Thailand, Malaysia, Singapore, Philippines and Vietnam, and Russia.
4. Venezuela, Norway, Kuwait and Saudi Arabia.
5. Estimates.

Sources: World Development Indicators Database and www.cepal.org.

What I will do is to ask the political economy behind. In the case of the United States, the direct causes of the current account deficit are implied in the remedies: fiscal profligacy and an overvalued dollar. As regards the rest of the world, the explanation is China's relatively depreciated currency, and the other Asian dynamic countries' still more depreciated currencies (since China has a large trade surplus with the United States, but a deficit with its neighbours).

Table 8.4 Current account balance 1999–2004 by regions (% of exports)

	1999	*2000*	*2001*	*2002*	*2003*	*2004*
USA	-30.72	-38.60	-38.31	-48.56	-52.00	-58.05
European Union	+0.72	+0.18	+0.63	+1.97	+2.58	+2.08[4]
Latin America	-17.77	-15.63	-14.69	-5.77	-0.88	+0.87[4]
Dynamic Asian	+16.58	+14.20	+11.93	+13.80	+14.67	+15.70[4]
Oil exporters	+10.30	+30.88	+23.36	+24.00	+31.81	+37.72

Notes: See Table 3.
Sources: World Development Indicators Database and www.cepal.org

Yet, a new and major factor in explaining the increase of the current account deficit in 2005 (which was running at around US$800 billion) was the sharp increase in oil prices. According to IMF estimates, that year the current account surplus of the oil producers could reach US$400 billion against US$200 billion two years before.[15] Only Saudi Arabia was expected to have an average surplus of US$100 billion, corresponding to 32 percent of its GDP, against China's surplus of just 6 percent of GDP.[16]

In a conference on the political economy of global governance, the relevant causes of looming crisis are the ones behind these direct causes. In relation to this, the central question is why the United States, that was facing relatively devalued Asian currencies for several years, and that is now confronting a major oil shock, was not able to act in time to avoid the build-up of such a huge foreign account imbalance. My argument is that there are two causes internal to the country which, combined, become particularly powerful. The first cause is rather a structural than a political economy cause. In a reference to the 'curse of natural resources', which particularly plague the oil-producing countries, I will call this cause the 'curse of having a currency as an international reserve'. Usually this is viewed not as a curse but as a blessing. A country that possesses such a valuable currency, first, is able to borrow in its own currency; second, it can borrow at a very low cost. This is certainly true, but as a trade-off, the incentive to consume too much, to save too little, and to borrow irresponsibly is strong. Not only because the costs involved in foreign borrowing are small, but also because the prestige of the national currency will push it up, will help to appreciate it. If the economic authorities are not vigilant, actively promoting investment instead of consumption, and actively managing the national currency, the tendency will be toward increasing foreign indebtedness. Given, however, the market fundamentalism that has dominated the United States administrations since the 1980s, such vigilance and management are improbable.

Combined with this structural cause there is a strictly political economy cause: 'exchange rate populism'. In developing countries this is a well-known practice which was first detected by a distinguished Argentinean economist, Canitrot (1975).[17] Can it be applied to a developed country like the United States – a country that, through the IMF, has been consistently criticizing fiscal populism? My answer is yes, for two reasons. First, because fiscal populism is a well-discussed phenomenon, but exchange rate populism is not. Although the concept of exchange rate populism is already present in Canitrot's classical paper, this paper is poorly known in the North. Additionally, the expression 'exchange rate populism' is new: it was probably used for the first time in 2002.[18] If fiscal populism is the state apparatus to expend more than it gets, exchange rate populism is the nation-state to expend more than it gets. Second, because Americans resist the idea that economic populism can be applied to their government. Yet, since the end of World War II, United States is experiencing a worrying political retrocession which makes it prone to both kinds of populism. In relation to exchange rate populism, the objective evidence is that the large current account deficits in the 1980s and the 2000s were associated to two populist administrations: the Reagan and the George W. Bush administrations. Such administrations were not the fruits of hazard, however. While the United States continues to grow in economic and technical terms, the political and social retrenchment is becoming increasingly evident. Increasing income concentration is the combined outcome of the technology of information revolution which reduced the demand for unskilled labor while increasing the demand for skilled and managerial labor, of the imports of industrial goods from cheap-labor developing countries, and of the immigration coming from the South.[19] The existence of a large number of citizens excluded from the benefits of economic growth recalls developing countries like Brazil. For that reason, the pejorative expression 'Brazilianization' is increasingly applied to the United States. It is also applied to Europe, but the situation there is less disquieting: income is substantially less concentrated, social rights are more universally guaranteed, and elections depend less on money.

The fact is that, in the aftermath of World War II, the United States was the example of democracy for the world, and President Roosevelt, with the New Deal, had put the United States ahead of all other countries in the protection of the poor. Today, this is over. Why? To answer this question is still more difficult, but probably a large part is related to the aggressive individualism which has taken hold of the American society since the war. For some time, in the 1960s, not only the utopian, but principally the republican values that were behind the Founding Fathers of the American republic, seemed to hold. But already at that time an individualist and neoliberal (or ultra-liberal, the opposite of what Americans call 'liberal') ideological wave was taking hold of hearts and minds. Sophisticated economists and philosophers like Buchanan, Olson, Friedman and Nozick, proposing 'public choice', 'the impossibility of collective action in large organizations', the 'freedom to choose' or 'the minimum state', were not just defending market fundamentalism, but preaching radical individualism and denying the existence and relevance of the public interest as an effective motivation for public action. This was a serious thing. When they were rejecting the public interest, they were automatically rejecting democratic politics which can only survive when politicians and public officials have as one of their motivating forces the fight for the public interest. Only based on considerations of the public interest were politicians able to lead the liberal social contract of the nineteenth century which limited the abuses of the authoritarian state, and the democratic contract of the twentieth century which established some limits to robber barons' capitalism. The moral consequences of this denial for secular capitalist societies like ours are catastrophic. In the religious societies of the past, salvation and revelation offered moral criteria to subjects. In modern secular societies, however, when the public interest or the common good is discarded from political life, citizens immediately cease to have a public and moral criterion to follow. The only things that are valued are private interests, and the only rule to follow is the one of the market: to compete while simultaneously searching for monopolistic advantages. In this framework, public and social life is reduced to the market. The brute forces of capitalism – injustice, greed, corruption and disregard for the natural environment – take hold of everything. This danger has been present since capitalism became dominant in Great Britain, and since then men and women have been trying to keep it under control using as a tool the republican concept of public interest. In the seventeenth century, within the realm of the absolute state, a new and noble activity was rising, politics – republican and democratic politics – whose role would be to limit the excesses either of the absolute state or of the greedy market. The political history of the liberal state of the nineteenth century, and of the democratic state of the twentieth century, is the history of the endeavor of republican individuals fighting to curb the absolutism of the state and the excesses of the market. In the second part of the twentieth century, however, such republican convictions grew weaker and weaker in the United States, which allowed for all types of individualist if not cynical behaviors and theories. The disorganizing and demoralizing consequences of this type of individualism are powerful, and probably help to explain the political and social retrocession in the United States, and the fact that governments are again resorting to populist practices without being punished in the elections.

THE LOGIC BEHIND GLOBALIZATION

Summing up, the huge current account deficit of the United States and the current account deficits of the middle-income developing countries in the 1970s and again in the 1990s have exchange rate populism behind them. But, in the times of globalization, the later ones respond also to a strategy of domination: the growth cum foreign savings strategy. While, within the United States, economic populism is just a demand of society that self-interested politicians supply, in the case of developing countries' current account deficits and balance-of-payments crises, beside self-interested and populist local politicians, we have another cause: a hegemonic power giving counsel, making recommendations and imposing conditionalities through international financial institutions.[20] Yet, such an imperial strategy has involved a non-predicted boomerang effect. Since the Bretton Woods agreements, the United States believed that it could exert, almost alone, the leadership of the international financial system. After the dollar floated, and the agreements were buried, the United States continued to believe that it would be able to keep its control of the system untouched. The market – the supposed self-regulating market – would facilitate the job. Thus, the United States always rejected any attempt to create a more organized and structured international financial system, where vigilance on the exchange rates could be exerted. Instead, their different administrations preferred to assume, first, that the United States itself, with its sound macroeconomic policies, would be a source of rationality; second, that they could count on the support of the other developed countries, whose problems were similar to the ones they faced; third, that the IMF and the World Bank, with their present mandates, and duly controlled by the US Treasury, would be sufficient to keep the whole system under control – particularly the populist developing economies. But the problem that the United States and the other rich countries faced in relation to these economies was not only their 'populism' or their 'nationalism': it was also the economic threat that they represented since the instant that they began to export manufactured goods. To neutralize this threat, they proposed that these countries adopted the growth cum foreign savings strategy and opening of capital accounts, and that they accepted globalization not as a fact but as an ideology – the ideology that nation-states had become irrelevant in the 'borderless society'.

This strategy, however, had a disastrous consequence for the developing countries while it represented a threat for the rich ones. The 1980s foreign debt crisis constrained the United States to organize a quasi-cartel of creditors to defend their commercial banks. In the 1990s, when the growth cum foreign savings strategy was repeated, the first major crisis – the Mexican 1994 crisis – represented a threat to the American economy, and constrained the United States government to intervene with huge sums which the IMF did not have. As Davidson (2002, p. 200) remarks: 'the Mexican crisis spilled over into the dollar problem … the dollar was initially dragged down by the peso'. The other crises were also disastrous for the developing countries which endured them, and threatening for the rich ones. The present crisis or threat of crisis represented by the American current-account deficit and the increasing foreign debt is a consequence of exchange rate populism combined with the arrogant belief that the United States has become so powerful after the collapse of communism that it could permit itself everything.

What we really have behind the present global economic disgovernance is a combination of lax exchange rate policies, economic populism, and a mistaken strategy in relation to medium-income developing countries. This combination presents six major problems. First, the crises provoked by the growth cum foreign savings strategy, in the countries which obediently adopted it, were greater than expected: the idea was to limit their exports and increase the dollar income of the profits made by multinational enterprises in those countries, not to cause crises. Second, the dynamic Asian countries did not believe in that strategy, and profited from the opportunity to devise an opposite strategy of growth cum negative foreign savings. In this way, they were able to maintain their exchange rates relatively depreciated, and kept their export-led strategies going even if productivity gains did not warrant it. Third, the current account surplus achieved by the Asian countries made viable the maintenance of high levels of domestic consumption and increasing current deficits in the United States. Fourth, the sharp 2005 increase in oil prices and the enormous trade surpluses that the oil producers experienced accentuated the current account disequilibria. Fifth, the market efficiency assumption, the idea that markets are self-regulating, is proving once again to be just ideological. Sixth, practice did not corroborate the assumed rationality on the part of the macroeconomic policies adopted by the US Treasury and the Federal Reserve. Mr Greenspan ended his 18 years as Chairman of the Federal Reserve Bank widely acclaimed for the competence and flexibility that he employed in managing the institution – and I subscribe to such praise, particularly in relation to his management of the interest rate – but it was above his powers to prevent the policy mistakes which led to the dangerous situation which the American and the world economies are in today.

CONCLUSION

I share with many the belief that a better architecture of the international financial system is required. The United States must recover control over its budget deficit, and depreciate the dollar. The IMF must stop being governed by stockholders and start being a real multilateral organization, and must have the necessary resources to act as a real lender of last resource. Exchange rates and current account deficits must be more closely followed; their equilibrium must be seen not as depending on market forces alone, but on a combination of such forces with competent macroeconomic management. Developing countries must recover control over their capital accounts, keep control of their fiscal accounts, and limit foreign borrowing. There is no heterodoxy here. Heterodox or unusual is my attribution of the developing countries' crises to the growth cum foreign savings strategy, not the recommendation of prudence. Competent economists such as Williamson (2005) and Eichengreen (2003), for instance, are saying similar things. While the more general policies are not adopted, however, what developing countries should learn is that growth is made essentially with domestic resources – that capital is made at home, with domestic savings; that foreign savings are desirable only on special occasions, when the domestic investment opportunities, expressed in high expected profit rates, hamper the natural tendency of economic agents to increase consumption when their real income is increased; that the alternative reason for desiring foreign savings – the scarcity of the domestic savings – is the typical commonsense idea that scientific reasoning is supposed to reject. I believe that it is more realistic, at the moment, to denounce exchange rate populism and the strategy of growth with foreign savings than to place all our bets on the reform of international financial architecture. Sooner or later such reform will take place, but while it does not, the economic authorities in each nation-state, developed or developing, should remember that the exchange rate is the more strategic macroeconomic price, and that the alternative 'fix or float' is false: the only sensible policy is: 'manage it'. After all, developed countries do that: why should not developing ones?

NOTES

1. I could say 'imperialist' but I say 'hegemonic' just to distinguish classical imperialism, which implied colonies and direct economic pressures, from modern 'hegemony' or 'hegemonism', which uses ideological hegemony as a main instrument of domination. It is interesting to note that the word is used by Americans, but was first utilized by Gramsci to mean domestic ideological domination.
2. Observe that I am speaking of 'economic', not of 'political' populism. Economic populism takes place when wither the state organization or the nation-state, to expend more than it gets, incurring respectively in chronic budget deficits or in current account deficits; political populism is essentially the practice of charismatic politicians speaking directly to the people without the intermediation of political parties.
3. With exception of Colombia, which was not indebted, but had the rollover of its credit suspended.
4. I participated directly in this crisis as Finance Minister of Brazil in 1987. For an account of this experience and also of the proposal that I made at that time with the technical support of First Boston and Warburg banks, see 'A turning point in the debt crisis' (Bresser-Pereira, 1999).
5. I know that the concept of what the equilibrium exchange rate is, is a theme open to huge academic debate. Here I am just proposing a pragmatic and simple criterion to define what is a 'balanced exchange rate', assuming that this is less demanding than the 'equilibrium exchange rate' concept.
6. Financial crises *stricto senso* are banking and financial markets crises. Debt crises are also financial, but I prefer to call them balance-of-payments crises to indicate their specific nature.
7. The first consensus, defined by John Williamson, did not include the opening of the capital accounts, and strategy of growth with foreign savings. This strategy was defined by the US Treasury at the beginning of the Clinton administration (Bresser-Pereira and Varela, 2004).
8. This strategy was more formally formulated when Laurence Summers was Under-Secretary of the Treasury, in the Clinton administration. I have been working on the critique of such strategy for several years (Bresser-Pereira and Nakano, 2003; Bresser-Pereira and Varela, 2004; Bresser-Pereira and Gala, 2005), because I believe that to reject it is today as important for middle income developing countries as it was to criticize the law of comparative advantage at the beginning of their industrialization.
9. For a comprehensive exposition of the post-Keynesian view, see Davidson, (2002); for the Regulation School view, see Aglietta (2002).
10. For the formal critique of the strategy of growth with foreign savings see Bresser-Pereira and Gala, (2005).
11. See, for instance, Hausmann and Sturzenegger (2005). According to these two authors, in 2004 the net foreign income was US$30billion, a number similar to that in 1980, despite the fact that

between 1980 and 1994 the US accumulated a current account deficit of US$4500billion. We should, however, keep in mind that despite this positive US$30billion net figure, the US current account deficit in 2004 was US$665.9billion, as we can see in Table 8.3.

12. Not by Greenspan, but notably by the new President of the Federal Reserve Bank, Ben S. Bernanke (2005).
13. More recently these three authors Dooley, Folkerts-Landau and Garber (2005) came up with the claim that, contrary to the 'conventional analysis', the US current account deficit is also no cause of concern because the euro is supposed to appreciate in relation to the dollar, and, in a second phase, the euro and the dollar will appreciate relative to the renminbi, but these are just predictions. Eventually this will happen, but probably in a troubling way, not in the smooth way that the authors suppose.
14. On the concept of net and total transition costs, see Bresser-Pereira and Abud (1997).
15. The difference between this figure and the corresponding 2004 figure in Table 8.3 is the consequence of a smaller number of oil producers in this table.
16. *The Economist,* November 12 2005: 'Recycling the Petrodollars': 75–77.
17. Besides Canitrot, the classical papers on the subject are O'Donnell (1978), Diaz Alejandro (1981) and Sachs (1989). All these papers are republished in Bresser-Pereira (1991).
18. Bresser-Pereira and Nakano (2003).
19. A recent study by the Bureau of the Budget of the US Congress shows that, in the US, the incomes of Latin American immigrants working in construction, textiles, maintenance operations, catering and restaurants are 50 percent less than is paid to Americans for the same jobs. In only the last decade, the number of immigrant workers increased from 13 to 21 million. Such growth represented half of the growth of the labor force in that period. (*Valor* [*Financial Times*] 15 November 2005).
20. Americans prefer to call their country the 'benevolent hegemon', but we know well that all countries that achieve economic and military dominance tend to act in imperial ways in relation to others, that is, they tend to protect their interests at the costs of the others' interests by using their greater power. The forms under which this power is exerted change. In the past, the use of force and direct exploitation was the norm, in present days it is essentially ideological, and is conveyed through recommendations and pressures for weaker countries to adopt policies that do not consult their national interests.

REFERENCES

Aglietta, M. (2002), 'Problèmes posés par la régulation monétaire', in Jacquet, P., J. Pisany-Ferry and L. Tubiana (eds), *Gouvernance Mondiale*, Paris: La Documentation Française, 375–92.

Alves, Antonio J., Fernando Ferrari Filho and Luiz Fernando de Paula (2004), 'Crise cambial, instabilidade financeira e reforma do sistema monetário', in Filho F.F. and L. F. de Paula (eds), 369–461.

Bernanke, B.S. (2005), 'The global saving glut and the US current account deficit', Sandridge Lecture, Virginia Association of Economics, Richmond, 10 March.

Bresser-Pereira, L.C. (ed.) (1991), *Populismo Econômico*, São Paulo: Editora Nobel.

Bresser-Pereira, L.C. (2004), 'Exchange rate: fix, float, or manage it?' in Vernengo, M. (ed.), *Financial Integration or Dollarization: No Panacea*, Cheltenham, UK and Northampton, MA, USA: Edward Elgar, xiii-xix.

Bresser-Pereira, L.C. and J. Abud (1997), 'Net and total transition cost: the timing of economic reform', *World Development*, **25** (6), 905–14.
Bresser-Pereira, L. Carlos and Y. Nakano (2003), 'Economic growth with foreign savings?', *Revista de Economia Política*, **22** (2) April, 3–27.
Bresser-Pereira, L.C. and P. Gala (2005), 'Crítica do crescimento com poupança externa', Discussion paper, Foundation Getúlio Vargas, 14, October.
Bresser-Pereira, L.C. and C.A. Varela (2004), 'The second Washington Consensus and Latin America's quasi-stagnation', *Journal of Post Keynesian Economics*, **27** (2), 231–50.
Canitrot, A. (1975), 'La experiencia populista de distribución de renta', *Desarrollo Económico*, **15** (59), October, 331–51.
Cline, W.R. (2005), *The United States as a Debtor Nation,* Washington, DC: Institute for International Economics.
Cline, W.R. and S. Weintraub (eds) (1981), *Economic Stabilization in Developing Countries*, Washington, DC: Brookings Institution.
Davidson, P. (2002), *Financial Markets, Money and the Real World*, Cheltenham, UK and Northampton, MA, USA: Edward Elgar.
Diaz Alejandro, C. (1981), 'Southern Cone stabilization plans', in Cline, W.R. and S. Weintraub (eds), *Economic Stabilization in Developing Countries*, Washington, DC: Brookings Institution, 119–48.
Dooley, M., D. Folkerts-Landau and P. Garber (2003), 'An essay on the revived Bretton Woods system', NBER Working Paper 9971, Cambridge, MA. September.
Dooley, M., D. Folkerts-Landau and P. Garber (2005), 'Interest rates, exchange rates and international adjustment', NBER Working Paper 11771, November.
Eichengreen, B. (2003), *Capital Flows and Crises.* Cambridge, MA: MIT Press.
Feldstein, M.S. (1988), 'Distinguished lecture on economics in government: thinking about international economic coordination', *Journal of Economic Perspectives*, **2** (2), 3–14.
Frenkel, J.A. and K.A. Rockett (1988), 'International macroeconomic policy coordination when policy-makers do not agree on the true model', *American Economic Review*, **78**, 318–40.
Galbraith, J.K. (2004), 'Apocalypse not yet', mimeo.
Hausmann, R. and F. Sturzenegger (2005), 'Dark matter makes the US deficit disappear', *Financial Times*, 8 December.
Jacquet, P., J. Pisani-Ferry and L. Tubiana (eds) (2002), *Gouvernance Mondiale*, Paris: La Documentation Française.
Jarret, P. (2005), 'Coping with the inevitable adjustment in the US current account', Economics Department Working Paper, 467, December.
Nonnenberg, M.J.B. (2005), 'Aumento do déficit em conta corrente norte-americano e perspectivas de desvalorização do dólar. Nota técnica', *Brasília*: *Boletim de Conjuntura* (do IPEA), **68**, March, 82–4.
O'Donnell, G. (1977), 'State and alliances in Argentina, 1956–1976', in O'Donnell, G. (ed.), *Counterpoint: Selected Essays on Authoritarianism and Democratization,* Notre Dame: Indiana University Press, 3–33.
Roseneau, J.N. (1990), *Turbulence in World Politics: A Theory of Change and Continuity*, Princeton, NJ: Princeton University Press.

Roseneau, J.N. (1997), *Along the Domestic–Foreign Frontier: Exploring Governance in a Turbulent World*, Cambridge: Cambridge University Press.
Sachs, J.D. (1989), 'Social conflict and populist policies in Latin America', in Brunetta, R. and C. Dell-Arringa (eds), *Labor Relations and Economic Performance*, London: Macmillan Press.
Stiglitz, J.E. (2002), *Globalization and its Discontents*, New York: W.W. Norton.
The Economist, November 12 2005: 'Recycling the Petrodollars': 75–77.
UNCTAD (2001a), *Trade and Development Report*, Geneva: United Nations Conference on Trade and Development.
UNCTAD Secretariat (1998), 'The financial crisis in East Asia: a background note', Geneva, January.
Williamson, J. (2005), *Curbing the Boom–bust Cycle: Stabilizing Capital Flows to Emerging Markets*, Washington, DC: Institute for International Economics.

9. Tobin, globalization and capital flows

Robert W. Dimand

INTRODUCTION

Known to macroeconomists as an outspoken Old Keynesian critic of the New Classical resurgence, James Tobin won the Nobel Memorial Prize in Economic Sciences in 1981 for his contributions to monetary macroeconomics, notably portfolio balance models and the q theory of investment, work that did not emphasize open-economy macroeconomics. To the wider public who are interested in economic issues without being professional economists, however, Tobin's name brings to mind his proposal to tax quicksilver international capital flows, inspired by J.M. Keynes's plan to inhibit stock speculation by taxing securities trades. Tobin first suggested what became known as 'the Tobin tax' in passing in 1972 in a series of lectures honoring his teacher Joseph Schumpeter, lectures which Tobin chose to use to reflect on his experience on President Kennedy's Council of Economic Advisers (published as Tobin, 1974). He devoted his Eastern Economic Association presidential address to 'A proposal for monetary reform' (Tobin, 1978 [2003]). Ignored at the time of publication and long thereafter (Tobin said 'it sank like a rock'), 'A proposal for monetary reform' eventually attracted so much attention that it was reprinted in the same journal on the twenty-fifth anniversary of its original publication, his most-cited paper and the journal's most-cited paper. But his message has not necessarily been understood: Krugman (2002) holds that Tobin 'is probably best known' to the general public for two policies, the Kennedy tax cut and the Tobin tax on currency trades, 'both of which have been hijacked – his own word – by people whose political views he did not share'. The publication of *World Finance and Economic Stability: Selected Essays of James Tobin* (2003) provides a convenient opportunity to investigate his analysis of how to increase the stability of the global financial system, to evaluate his analysis tentatively in light of financial crises and developments that have occurred since he first advanced his proposal, and to compare his approach with the diversely influential views of Jagdish Bhagwati, Robert Mundell and Joseph Stiglitz.

In an interview published in *Der Spiegel* on 3 September 2001, Tobin declared, with specific reference to the French-based protest organization ATTAC (Association pour une Taxe sur les Transactions Financières pour l'Aide aux Citoyens), that (Tobin, 2003, p. 55):

> I have nothing in common with practitioners of revolution against 'globalization' ... I appreciate attention to my proposal, but much of the praise comes from the wrong side. Look, I am an economist and, like most economists, an advocate of free trade. Moreover, I support the International Monetary Fund, the World Bank and the World Trade Organization – everything that these movements are attacking. They're misusing my name.

A scholarly presentation of the ATTAC perspective is provided by Patomäki (2001), *Democratising Globalisation: The Leverage of the Tobin Tax*, which reprints Tobin (1978 [2003]) as an appendix.

Tobin was also misunderstood from the opposite side (Tobin, 2003, p. 50):

> Unfortunately, these activities [the United Nations Development Programme conference on the Tobin tax published as Huq et al. 1996] aroused the anger of Senators Dole and Helms, who apparently thought, or pretended to think, that the idea was for the UN to levy taxes on their constituents without votes of Congress.

Moreover:

> Contrary to suspicions raised by Senators Jesse Helms and Bob Dole in election year 1996, I was not advocating UN taxes. I would expect each national government to levy and collect the agreed tax by its regular procedures and to decide for itself what to do with the revenues, which might provide inducements to participate' ['An idea that gained currency but lost clarity', in Tobin 2003, 63].

Tobin (2003, p. 40) noted that President Mitterand of France, speaking favorably of the Tobin tax at the World Social Summit in Copenhagen in 1994, also seemed to think of it primarily as a source of revenue for worthy multilateral purposes.

In his Fred Hirsch Memorial Lecture, 'On the efficiency of the financial system', Tobin (1984 [1987], p. 8) remarked that:

> Keynes's pessimism on the long-term rationality of securities markets led him to the view that the liquidity these markets provide is a mixed blessing. 'The spectacle ... has

> sometimes moved me towards the conclusion that to make the purchase of an investment permanent and indissoluble, like marriage (sic!) except by reason of death or other great cause, might be a useful remedy. …' But he concluded that illiquidity would be the worse evil, because it would push savers towards hoarding of money…. Anyway, he advocated as a halfway measure a 'substantial … transfer tax …, with a view of mitigating the predominance of speculation over enterprise in the United States' [Keynes 1936, p. 160]. For similar reasons, I have advocated an international transfer tax on transactions across currencies.

Tobin was skeptical of the macro-efficiency of financial markets, and was impressed by the findings of his younger Yale colleague Robert Shiller (collected in Shiller, 1989, 2000) that stock prices fluctuate more than is justified by changes in underlying fundamental, a result comparable to Krugman's claim that exchange rates were excessively volatile in the 1980s (Krugman, 1989). Tobin feared that bubbles and excess volatility in financial markets could have 'real economic consequences devastating for particular sectors and whole economies' (Eichengreen et al. 1995, p. 164). As an Old Keynesian proponent of aggregate demand management for macroeconomic stabilization, shaped by the experience of the Great Depression, Tobin was especially concerned lest volatile portfolio capital flows and currency speculation constrain domestic stabilization policies, just as the gold standard had constrained domestic policies during the Depression. Such portfolio capital flows had become larger and more volatile because:

> Obstacles to international capital movements have been reduced, in the Third World as well as the First. (I must say however, that my own bank is slow and expensive when confronted with a check or wire transfer in a foreign currency. I assume that recent MBAs at Goldman Sachs are spared these annoyances.) (Tobin, 2003, p. 4)

Tobin (1978 [2003], p. 154) identified the basic problem of the international monetary system as that:

> Goods and labor move, in response to international price signals, much more sluggishly than fluid funds. Prices in goods and labor markets move much more sluggishly, in response to excess supply or demand, than the prices of financial assets, including exchange rates. These facts of life are essentially the same whether exchange rates are floating or fixed.

Consequently, Tobin (1978 [2003], p. 154) saw only:

two ways to go. One is toward a common currency, common monetary and fiscal policy, and economic integration. The other is toward greater financial segmentation between nations or currency areas, permitting their central banks and governments greater autonomy in policies tailored to their specific economic institutions and objectives. The first direction, however appealing, is clearly not a viable option in the foreseeable future, i.e., the twentieth century. I therefore regretfully recommend the second, and my proposal is to throw some sand in the wheels of our excessively efficient international money markets.

Notice that this clear statement differs in two ways from the representation of the Tobin tax proposal by many both of its proponents and opponents: the goal is to reduce the international mobility of liquid funds, with no objection to free trade in goods, and the use to which the resulting tax revenues might be put is entirely incidental to Tobin's intention. Tobin was a free trader, and the Tobin tax is not a scheme to raise revenue. Also notice Tobin's depiction of the 'two ways to go': Mundell (1973a, 1973b [2003]) took the other path, advocating a European currency a century after the experiment of the Latin Monetary Union and after Walter Bagehot's proposal for a joint Anglo–American–German currency to parallel, and eventually merge with, the Latin Monetary Union (Dimand and Dore, 2000).

According to Tobin (1978 [2003], p. 524), financial markets are 'incredibly efficient' in

a mechanical sense: transactions costs are low, communications are speedy, prices are instantaneously kept in line all over the world, credit enables participants to take large long or short positions at will or whim. Whether the market is 'efficient' in the deeper economic-informational sense is very dubious. ... As a technical matter, we know that a rational expectations equilibrium in markets of this kind is a saddle point. That is, there is only a singular path that leads from disequilibrium to equilibrium. If the markets are not on that path, or if they don't jump to it from wherever they are, they can follow any of a number of paths that lead away from equilibrium – paths along which, nonetheless, expectations are on average fulfilled. Such deviant paths are innocuous in markets – as for rare coins, precious metals, baseball cards, Swiss francs – which are sideshows to the real economic circus. But they are far from innocuous in foreign exchange markets whose prices are of major economic consequence.

The list of markets analogous in importance to that for baseball cards teased gold bugs and the 'gnomes of Zurich'.

As such, Tobin

was naturally disappointed by the proposal's summary rejection. Usually, those of my professional colleagues who took any notice of it at all rejected it on the same general

> grounds that incline economists to dismiss out of hand any interferences with market competition, including, of course, tariffs and other barriers to international trade in goods and services. They seemed to presume that the same reasoning extends to trade in financial assets. Those who did make specific objections said the tax would damage the liquidity of currency markets. They said it would move the world's currency markets to tax-free jurisdictions, like Indonesia or the Cayman islands. They said it wouldn't keep exchange rates from fluctuating; it wouldn't save overvalued currencies from speculative attacks and devaluations. And they said those things as if I had overlooked them. Most disappointing and surprising, critics seemed to miss what I regarded as the essential property of the transactions tax – the beauty part – that this simple, one-parameter tax would automatically penalize short-horizon round trips, while negligibly affecting the incentives for commodity trade and long-term capital investments. (Tobin, 2000, p. 40, from his prologue to Haq et al. 1996)

A few recent commentators, notably Davidson (1997), deny the 'beauty part' of Tobin's proposal, arguing that the Tobin tax would impose a severe burden on commodity trade and long-term investment without being large enough to impede speculative flows (so that direct controls on capital flows are needed, rather than a small tax), but most (including other post-Keynesians such as Arestis and Sawyer, 1997) agree that a heavier (but not necessarily sufficiently heavy) burden would fall on speculative short-term flows of funds. As Tobin (2000, p. 40) pointed out:

> A 0.2 per cent tax on a round trip to another currency costs 48 per cent a year if transacted every business day, 10 per cent if every week, 2.4 per cent if every month. But it is a trivial charge on commodity trade or long-term foreign investment.

Such a tax would not be nearly large enough to prevent a speculative attack on a overvalued fixed exchange rate in such exceptional circumstances as when the Bank of England provided speculators with a 'one-way bet' in September 1992 (heads the speculators win, tails they break even), but would work by diminishing the pool of speculative funds by reducing the overall profitability of currency speculation.

Davidson's criticism had a non-post-Keynesian predecessor: Dornbusch (1988, p. 256) sympathized with the goal of the Tobin tax, but wrote that:

> It might be argued that it is too late for stopping the flow of international capital, that throwing sand in the wheels is no longer sufficient. But why stop there and not use rocks? An operational way of doing this is to combine the stability of inflation and real activity that comes from fixed rates with a dual exchange rate system for capital account transactions. If capital markets are irrational and primarily speculative it might be as well to detach them altogether from an influence on real activity. Rather than use

scarce macropolicy tools to adapt the real sector to the idiosyncrasy of financial markets, a separate exchange rate would detach the capital account and deprive it from distorting influences on trade and inflation.

However, in a United Nations Conference on Trade and Development (UNCTAD) paper in 1997, Dornbusch was more enthusiastic about the Tobin tax (quoted by McQuaig, 1998, pp. 167–8):

> A financial transactions tax is no panacea, just as gun control would not stop all murder; poison and knives would make a comeback ... A financial transactions tax will not stop speculation altogether. But it certainly will help lengthen the horizon and focus the mind of capital markets on enterprise and investment rather than trading ... True, some trading will move offshore. But the risk is easily exaggerated, and in any event it can be checked ... The G-7 has not done anything useful for years. Why not surprise the world with a genuine innovation? ... [A] financial transactions tax can tame capital flows ... [making] the world capital market safe for development finance.

While Tobin (1974, 1978 [2003]) attracted little discussion beyond 'dismissive footnotes', the dramatic increase in the volume of foreign exchange trading, the speculative attacks that drove Britain and Sweden from the European Monetary System in September 1992, the Mexican crisis of 1994, the Brazilian and East Asian crises of 1997–98, and the Russian crisis of 1999 created a more attentive audience for Eichengreen et al. (1995). Haq et al. (1996), Michalos (1997), Griffith-Jones (1998), Griffith-Jones et al. (2000) and Dasgupta et al. (2001), among others, gave sympathetic consideration to the Tobin tax and other possible measures to reduce the volatility of global capital flows, while Hammond (1997) provides an example of the indignant response of the financial institutions on whose transactions such a tax would be levied (with Hubbard, later chair of the Council of Economic Advisers under the second President Bush, among its contributors).

BHAGWATI: SURPRISINGLY CLOSE TO TOBIN ON CAPITAL FLOWS

Jagdish Bhagwati of Columbia University is an exceptionally eloquent defender of free trade and scourge of protectionism (Bhagwati, 1988, 1998, 2000, 2004). Unlike Tobin, Mundell and Stiglitz, Bhagwati has not yet won the Nobel Memorial Prize, but correction of this oversight is widely expected. Many of

Bhagwati's articles on neoclassical trade theory (treated as an application of general equilibrium analysis), and his influential graduate textbook in the field, are co-authored by Srinivisan, Tobin's Yale colleague and friend. Bhagwati highlights the benefits to all parties of outsourcing jobs to developing countries, and strenuously denies that the theoretical possibilities of gains from strategic trade policy weaken the practical and empirical case for free trade. On the back cover of Bhagwati (2000), Sylvia Ostry warns, correctly, 'Beware anti-globalizers! Your most formidable opponent speaks out with his customary eloquence, wit, and incisive reasoning.' One might naturally suppose that Bhagwati and Tobin would have opposing views about controls on global capital flows, just as one might expect Bhagwati, as the author of *In Defense of Globalization* (2004), to have looked approvingly on the proposed Multilateral Agreement on Investment (MAI) and Free Trade Agreement of the Americas (FTAA). But people are more complex than 22nd sound bites: Tobin, acclaimed by opponents of globalization such as ATTAC in France, and Bhagwati, defender of globalization, presented strikingly similar analyses. As Bhagwati (2000, p. 13) told a National Bureau of Economic Research (NBER) conference on capital controls (by videotape): 'But somehow, the public expects that if you are for one sort of globalization, you must logically be for another: that free trade, free DFI, free capital flows, free immigration, free love, free ... whatever should go together! Well, they are wrong.' Thus Bhagwati (2000, p. 313) opposed the MAI because it was 'conceived as a set of rights of corporations, instead of systematically including their obligations. The latter would also require that notions such as the "stakeholder" obligations of corporations to the communities they operate in should also be laid down by the agreement.' Bhagwati (1998, Chapters 25–30; 2000, Chapter 27) insists that 'free trade agreements' such as the FTAA are really trade-diverting 'preferential trading agreements', an unconscious echo of Adam Smith's critique of the Methuen Treaty on the exchange of Portuguese wine for English cloth.

Responding to the East Asian financial crisis in 'The capital myth: the difference between trade in widgets and dollars' in *Foreign Affairs* in 1998 (reprinted as Chapter 1 of Bhagwati, 2000), Bhagwati insisted that 'the claims of enormous benefits from free capital mobility are not persuasive' and that unregulated flows of portfolio capital could destabilize developing economies. He followed this by telling an NBER conference on capital controls 'Why free capital mobility may be hazardous to your health' (Bhagwati, 2000, Chapter 2) and writing in the *Wall Street Journal* on 'Free trade, yes; free capital flows, maybe' (reprinted in Bhagwati, 2000, Chapter 3). Writing in 1998, Bhagwati

(2000, p. 17) not only deplored International Monetary Fund (IMF) pressure for capital account liberalization, but also argued:

> the IMF can, and indeed did in the current Asian crisis, get its conditionality badly wrong as well. I am persuaded by Sachs and Radelet's arguments, and by a recent brilliant essay by Max Corden, that the IMF should not have gone in for deflationary policy but should have instead undertaken a Keynesian-style reflationary policy to offset the initial and induced effect of the capital outflow.

This position was in accord with Stiglitz (2002) and with Tobin's Old Keynesianism: in July 1998, Tobin published 'Tighten belt? No, spend cash' in the *Straits Times* (reprinted in Tobin, 2003).

Bhagwati (2000, p, xvii) remarks that:

> The subsequent writings in late 1998 on capital flow controls by Paul Krugman (in *Fortune* and elsewhere) and by Joe Stiglitz (from the World Bank) supported the position that I had taken. Over time, Barry Eichengreen, IMF's adviser on the subject, also appears to have had a change of heart on the matter.

Eichengreen was a co-author of Eichengreen et al. (1995), the article that revived the Tobin tax as an approach to capital controls, and wrote the conclusion to Haq et al. (1996), as well as co-authoring the volume's opening chapter with Wyplosz, so Bhagwati's claim that his 1998 article converted Eichengreen from opposition to capital flow controls may be discounted. Bhagwati's cautious support for capital controls did not extend to considering whether the Tobin tax should be part of such controls (Tobin's name is absent from the indexes of Bhagwati, 1998 and 2000, just as Bhagwati's name is absent from the index of Stiglitz (2002) and appears only once in the index of Stiglitz, 2003, in connection with intellectual property rights, not capital flows or conditionality). Nonetheless, he shares with Tobin (and, as he notes, Krugman, 1998, Eichengreen, 1999 and Stiglitz, 2002) an insistence on a fundamental asymmetry between the case for free movement of goods and foreign direct investment and the case for free movement of portfolio investment. Cooper (1998) also warned that, given imperfect information, free capital flows would lead to excessively risky behavior and to large, costly crises. Tobin stood not with the anti-globalization movement (except as regards portfolio capital flows), but with a group of leading mainstream economists at major US universities who debunk protectionist fallacies, both long-standing and new, about trade in goods (see Bhagwati, 1988 and Krugman, 1997) but recognize the destabilizing potential of unregulated portfolio flows. What distinguished Tobin

(1974, 1978 [2003], 2003) from Bhagwati, Cooper, Dornbusch or Krugman on the regulation of portfolio capital flows, apart from the specifics of the form of intervention he proposed, was that he raised the issue two decades earlier.

Why did the dominant 'Washington Consensus' diverge so sharply on capital account liberalization from the views of such prominent economic theorists? Bhagwati (2000, p. xvii), as befits the founding editor of *Economics and Politics* and a pioneering student of Directly Unproductive (DUP) rent-seeking lobbying, reports that his essay on 'The capital myth'

> also introduced into the public domain and into the political-economy literature the nonconspiratorial concept of the 'Wall Street–Treasury complex' with which I, in the spirit of Dwight Eisenhower's military-industrial complex and Wright Mills's concept of the 'power elite,'sought to explain how powerful lobbying 'interests' on Wall Street, working within a network of like-minded people moving back and forth between Washington and Wall Street, had combined with a growing shift to markets imprudently extended to capital flows to push the developing countries into a hasty embrace of capital account convertibility without adequate safeguards.

No feature of Stiglitz (2002) caused more offense, notably to the reviewer in *The Economist* (8 June 2002), than the suggestion that Stanley Fischer's move from the IMF to a Citigroup vice-chairmanship resulted from like-minded networking with former Treasury Secretary Robert Rubin, chairman of the executive committee of Citigroup's board. The Washington Consensus or Wall Street–Treasury complex does not welcome dissent – see McQuaig (1998, Chapter 5) and Schmidt (1997) on the reaction of Canada's Department of Finance to an internal working paper that was so indelicate as to conclude that a Tobin tax would be feasible (resulting in Schmidt's abrupt departure from the Finance Department in Ottawa to an aid agency in Hanoi).

STIGLITZ AND TOBIN AGAINST THE WASHINGTON CONSENSUS

As Chair of President Clinton's Council of Economic Advisers, then as Chief Economist of the World Bank, and after his return to Columbia, Joseph Stiglitz spoke out against the Washington Consensus (Rubin and Summers at the Treasury, Greenspan at the Federal Reserve, Fischer at the IMF) which urged capital account liberalization upon developing countries and used the conditionality of IMF lending to promote contractionary policies in response to financial crises (see Fischer, 2003; Rubin and Weisberg, 2003). The Mexican crisis of 1994, the successive Brazilian, East Asian and Russian financial crises from 1997 to 1999, and the Turkish and Argentine crises of 2001 served both Stiglitz and Tobin as object lessons of the disruptive dangers of hasty capital account liberalization. As both a neoclassical microeconomic theorist (sharing the 2001 Nobel Memorial Prize for research on the economics of asymmetric information) and a New Keynesian macroeconomist, Stiglitz shares both Tobin's technical insight into how markets work and his conviction that there is a role for aggregate demand management to stabilize output and employment.

When Tobin gave the keynote address on 'Financial globalization: can national currencies survive?' to the Annual World Bank Conference on Development Economics in 1998, he protested: 'Given my lack of experience and expertise in the World Bank's world, I am unqualified to speak at this conference. But my old friend and onetime colleague Joseph Stiglitz insisted that I do so anyway' (Tobin, 2003, p. 22). That Stiglitz would insist on Tobin giving the keynote address is not surprising: Tobin, a Nobel laureate and fellow Keynesian, sympathetic to capital controls and critical of the IMF response to the East Asian crisis, was a prestigious ally. What is surprising is how gingerly Stiglitz avoids invoking any such alliance in his subsequent best-selling books. Tobin's name does not appear in *The Roaring Nineties* (Stiglitz, 2003), Stiglitz's history of a decade of financial crises and turbulent capital flows, and of his battles against the Washington Consensus, nor in *Joseph Stiglitz and the World Bank: The Rebel Within* (Chang, 2001), a collection of nine of Stiglitz's speeches. Tobin's only appearance in *Globalization and Its Discontents* (Stiglitz, 2002, pp. 265–6) is buried in the twelfth endnote to the final chapter, a note which teases Lawrence Summers for having, in his pre-Treasury days, written 'an article that could be interpreted as supporting the principles underlying the tax' (Summers and Summers, 1989). In that note, Stiglitz takes care to draw attention to Stiglitz (1989) on 'significant implementation problems, especially in a world in which the tax is not imposed universally and in which derivatives and other complicated financial instruments have become prevalent'. Granted that Stiglitz had reservations about the Tobin tax as the appropriate mechanism for controlling capital flows, why doesn't he express any acknowledgement that he and Tobin held the same views on why capital flows needed to be controlled and on the folly of the IMF's advice to developing countries?

The answer is, I think, not the same as the explanation of why Bhagwati does not discuss the closeness of his views to those of Tobin. Bhagwati independently discovered in 1998 the asymmetry between the case for free trade and the case for free capital mobility. Apparently oblivious to any previous expressions of that asymmetry, he interpreted the subsequent writings of Eichengreen, Krugman and Stiglitz as evidence that he had converted them in 1998, notwithstanding, for instance, Eichengreen's participation in Eichengreen et al. (1995) and in Haq et al. (1996). Stiglitz, in contrast, has long been attentive to the Tobin tax proposal (Stiglitz, 1989) and had made a point of choosing Tobin as keynote speaker for the 1998 World Bank conference. From the point of view of influencing public opinion and public policy in the United States, the problem is that the Tobin tax contains the dread, demonized word 'tax'. Capital account liberalization in developing countries may be opposed, IMF orthodoxy about the appropriate response to a financial crisis may be reversed, but a tax cannot be proposed. While an adviser to the Dukakis campaign in 1988, Lawrence Summers wrote in the *New Republic* on 'A few good taxes' including the Tobin tax, a non-technical presentation of views expressed in Summers and Summers (1989). Despite formidable later contenders, that article may still rank as the outstanding example of Summers's political tactlessness, and provided a convenient stick with which Republicans could beat the Dukakis campaign.

MUNDELL: THE OTHER PATH

James Tobin (1978 [2003]) saw two paths for international monetary reform: a global currency or throwing sand into a too-well-greased monetary mechanism (a metaphor first used in his Janeway lectures). Speculative attacks on exchange rates among national currencies could be avoided either by some form of capital control (such as a tax on currency transactions) or by eliminating the exchange rates by abolishing the national currencies. If there are no exchange rates, speculators cannot speculate on how they might change. Just as Tobin and Mundell differed on whether the success of the Kennedy tax cut was a Keynesian demand stimulus or a triumph for supply-side economics, Mundell (1973a, 1973b [2003]) differed from Tobin on international monetary reform by taking the first path, offering a plan for a European currency, expanding on his 'Plan for a world currency' presented to the Joint Economic Committee of Congress in September 1968. Such a currency now exists (see Mundell, 2000; and Mundell and Clesse, 2000 for Mundell's perspective on the creation of the euro). The key to Mundell's divergence from Tobin on international monetary reform is a feature of the Mundell–Fleming open-economy IS–LM model of the 1960s: the assumption of perfect capital mobility (perfect substitution between foreign and domestic assets, hence a horizontal BP curve). Mundell accepted perfect capital mobility as given, whereas Tobin sought to circumvent it by the imposition of a small tax on currency trades. McKinnon (2000) notes that, ironically, critics of the European Monetary Union (EMU) such as Eichengreen (1997) base their argument on Mundell (1961 [1968]), which delineated the optimum currency area as one in which economic shocks are symmetric so that the same policy response is appropriate throughout the currency area. Mundell (1973a) argued that having a common currency across countries would allow for better risk-pooling and portfolio diversification to mitigate asymmetric shocks, but in 2005 the Northern League, part of Italy's governing coalition, was demanding Italian withdrawal from the European Monetary Union (EMU) because of such asymmetric shocks (*Financial Post*, 21 June 2005).

CONCLUSION

James Tobin doubted the efficiency of financial markets in any but a mechanical sense, and proposed a tax on foreign exchange transactions to help insulate domestic real economies from currency speculation. His proposal stemmed from his more general view that financial markets, moving along one or another of a multitude of unstable paths, perhaps with expectations being fulfilled on average, have real effects on sluggishly adjusting markets for goods and labour. Although the Tobin tax has been taken up by opponents of globalization such as ATTAC, he was no opponent of free movement of goods and of long-term foreign direct investment. Rather he insisted on the asymmetry between the case for free capital mobility and the case for free trade in goods, a view shared by Jagdish Bhagwati and the late Rudiger Dornbusch, critics of free capital mobility who are widely misunderstood as defenders of all forms of globalization. Like Joseph Stiglitz, Tobin sharply criticized the IMF and the US Treasury for applying pressure on developing countries to liberalize their capital accounts and, when faced by financial crisis, to resort to demand contraction, although (perhaps because his name is associated with a tax) Tobin is little mentioned in Stiglitz's books for the general public. Mende and Menkhoff (2003) agree that 'Tobin's skepticism against the fundamental evaluation efficiency of FX markets corresponds well with the failure of relevant modeling efforts', but offer evidence from microstructure that the tax rates now generally mentioned (typically 0.02 percent on an interbank transaction, half on each bank, or one-fiftieth of the rate mentioned in Tobin, 1974) are too low to affect short-term speculation (see Song and Zhang, 2005 on how a securities transaction tax like the Tobin tax has both a volatility-reducing effect through discouraging trading by destabilizing speculators and a volatility-increasing effect as reduced liquidity results in thin markets). However, Tobin's central message on international monetary reform was not whether this rate or that rate was appropriate: it was the need to insulate domestic real economies from the excess volatility of international currency markets. Taking perfect or near-perfect capital mobility as given, Robert Mundell has taken the alternate path to resolving the same perceived problem: eliminate the international capital markets, and their excess volatility, by submerging multiple national currencies in a single international currency, at the cost of denying national monetary authorities the power to respond asymmetrically to asymmetric shocks. Tobin's message about the need to preserve this power, and about the multiple unstable paths that currency markets can follow, retains its importance.

In closing, let me raise the possibility of implementing the perhaps utopian Tobin tax by linking it to another possibly utopian scheme: Edgar L. Feige (now retired from the University of Wisconsin) has, since 1989, advocated replacing the personal and corporate income tax by an Automated Payment Transaction Tax of perhaps 0.6 percent or less, with no deductions or income tax returns, no compliance costs, diminished incentive to evade expensively such a small tax, and none of the perverse incentives of income taxes (Feige, 2000; Akst, 2003). After Feige advanced his plan at a Buenos Aires conference in 1989, several developing countries (including Argentina and Brazil) experimented with it as a supplement to all existing taxes, which missed Feige's point: his proposed tax was to replace distorting taxes, and was intended for developed countries where most payments are made electronically, notably those flowing through the three US-based clearing systems Fedwire, CHIPS and SWIFT. Implement Feige's tax (with or without a slightly higher tax on transactions involving more than one currency), and the Tobin tax is implemented, retaining what Tobin termed 'the beauty part' of his proposal, the escalating effective tax rates on rapid-turnover currency speculation.

REFERENCES

Akst, D. (2003), 'Dreaming out loud: one little tax', *New York Times*, 2 February.

Arestis, P. and M. Sawyer (1997), 'How many cheers for the Tobin transactions tax?' *Cambridge Journal of Economics*, **21** (6), 753–68.

Bhagwati, J. (1988), *Protectionism*, Cambridge, MA: MIT Press.

Bhagwati, J. (1998), *A Stream of Windows: Unsettling Reflections on Trade, Immigration, and Democracy*, Cambridge, MA: MIT Press.
Bhagwati, J. (2000), *The Wind of the Hundred Days: How Washington Mismanaged Globalization*, Cambridge, MA: MIT Press.
Bhagwati, J. (2004), *In Defense of Globalization*, New York: Oxford University Press.
Chang, H.J. (2001), *Joseph Stiglitz and the World Bank: The Rebel Within*, London: Anthem Press.
Cooper, R.N. (1998), *Should Capital Account Convertibility be a World Objective?* Princeton, NJ: Princeton Essays in International Finance, No. 207.
Dasgupta, D.M. Uzan and D. Wilson (2001), *Capital Flows Without Crisis? Reconciling Capital Mobility and Economic Stability*, London and New York: Routledge.
Davidson, P. (1997), 'Are grains of sand in the wheels of international finance sufficient to do the job when boulders are often required?' *Economic Journal*, **107** (May), 671–86.
Dimand, R.W. and M.H.I. Dore (2000), 'Keynes's casino capitalism, Bagehot's international currency, and the Tobin tax: historical notes on preventing currency fires', *Journal of Post Keynesian Economics*, **22** (4), 515–28.
Dornbusch, R. (1988), *Exchange Rates and Inflation*, Cambridge, MA: MIT Press.
Eichengreen, B. (1997), *European Monetary Unification: Theory, Practice, and Analysis*, Cambridge, MA: MIT Press.
Eichengreen, B. (1999), 'Capital controls: capital idea or capital folly?' *Policy Options*, July/August, Institute for Research on Public Policy, Canada, 47–52.
Eichengreen, B., J. Tobin and C. Wyplosz (1995), 'Two cases for sand in the wheels of international finance', *Economic Journal*, **105** (January), 162–72.
Feige, E.L. (2000), 'Taxation for the 21st century: the automated payment transaction (APT) tax', *Economic Policy: A European Forum*, **31** (October), 473–503.
Fischer, S. (2003), *IMF Essays from a Time of Crisis*, Cambridge, MA: MIT Press.
Griffith-Jones, S. (1998), *Global Capital Flows: Should They Be Regulated?* (with a foreword by James Tobin), New York: St Martin's Press, and London: Macmillan.
Griffith-Jones, S., M.F. Montes and A. Nasution (eds) (2000), *Short-Term Capital Flows and Economic Crises*, Oxford: Oxford University Press.
Hammond, S. (ed.) (1997), *Securities Transaction Taxes: False Hopes and Unintended Consequences*, Chicago, IL: Irwin Professional Publishers.
Haq, M. ul, I. Kaul and I. Grunberg (eds) (1996), *The Tobin Tax: Coping with Financial Instability* (with a prologue by James Tobin), Oxford: Oxford University Press.
Keynes, J.M. (1936), *The General Theory of Employment, Interest and Money*, London: Macmillan.
Krugman, P. (1989), *Exchange Rate Instability*, Cambridge, MA: MIT Press.
Krugman, P. (1997), *Pop Internationalism*, Cambridge, MA: MIT Press.
Krugman, P. (1998), 'Saving Asia: it's time to get radical', *Fortune*, 7 September.
Krugman, P. (2002), 'Missing James Tobin', *New York Times*, 12 March.
McKinnon, R. (2000), 'Mundell, the Euro, and optimum currency areas', in Courchene, T.T. (ed.), *Money, Markets, and Mobility: Celebrating the Ideas of Robert A. Mundell, Nobel Laureate in Economic Sciences*, Kingston, ON: John Deutsch Institute and Institute for Research on Public Policy in collaboration with McGill-Queen's University Press.

McQuaig, L. (1998), *The Cult of Impotence: Selling the Myth of Powerlessness in the Global Economy*, Toronto: Penguin Books Canada.
Mende, A. and L. Menkhoff (2003), 'Tobin tax effects seen from the foreign exchange market's microstructure', *International Finance*, **6** (2), 227–47.
Michalos, A.C. (1997), *Good Taxes: The Case for Taxing Foreign Currency Exchange and Other Financial Transactions*, Toronto: Dundurn Press.
Mundell, R. (1961), 'The theory of optimum currency areas', *American Economic Review*, **51**, 657–65. Reprinted in Mundell, R.A. (1968), *International Economics*, New York: Macmillan.
Mundell, R. (1973a), 'Uncommon arguments for common currencies', in Johnson, H.G. and A.K. Swoboda (eds), *The Economics of Common Currencies*, London: George Allen & Unwin and Cambridge, MA: Harvard University Press, 114–32.
Mundell, R.A. (1973b), 'A plan for a European currency', in Johnson, H.G. and A.K. Swoboda (eds), *The Economics of Common Currencies*, London: George Allen & Unwin, 143–72. Reprinted in Courchene, T.J. (ed.) (2000), *Money, Markets, and Mobility: Celebrating the Ideas of Robert A. Mundell, Nobel Laureate in Economic Sciences*, Kingston, ON: John Deutsch Institute and Institute for Research in Public Policy in collaboration with McGill-Queen's University Press.
Mundell, R.A. (2000), 'A reconsideration of the twentieth century', *American Economic Review*, **90** (3), June, 327–40 (with erratum, **90** (5), 1535).
Mundell, R.A. and A. Clesse (eds) (2000), *The Euro as a Stabilizer in the International Economic System*, Dordrecht, Netherlands: Kluwer Academic Publishers.
Patomäki, H. (2001), *Democratising Globalisation: The Leverage of the Tobin Tax*, London: Zed Books.
Rubin, R. and J. Weisberg (2003), *In an Uncertain World*, New York: Random House.
Schmidt, R. (1997), *A Feasible Foreign Exchange Transactions Tax*, Ottawa: North–South Institute.
Shiller, R.J. (1989), *Market Volatility*, Cambridge, MA: MIT Press.
Shiller, R.J. (2000), *Irrational Exuberance*, Princeton, NJ: Princeton University Press.
Song, F.M. and J. Zhang (2005), 'Securities transaction tax and market volatility'. *Economic Journal*, **115** (October), 1103–20.
Stiglitz, J.E. (1989), 'Using tax policy to curb speculative short-term trading', *Journal of Financial Services Research*, **3** (2–3), 101–15.
Stiglitz, J.E. (2002), *Globalization and Its Discontents*, New York: W.W. Norton.
Stiglitz, J.E. (2003), *The Roaring Nineties: A New History of the World's Most Prosperous Decade*, New York: W.W. Norton.
Summers, L.H. and V.P. Summers (1989), 'When financial markets work too well: a cautious case for a securities transactions tax', *Journal of Financial Services Research*, **3** (2–3), 163–88.
Tobin, J. (1974), *The New Economics One Decade Older: The Elliot Janeway Lectures in Honor of Joseph Schumpeter*, Princeton, NJ: Princeton University Press.
Tobin, J. (1978), 'A proposal for international monetary reform', *Eastern Economic Journal*, **4** (3–4), 153–59. Reprinted in 2003, *Eastern Economic Journal*, **29** (4), 519–26.

Tobin, J. (1984), 'The efficiency of the financial system', *Lloyds Bank Review*, **153** (July), 1–15. Reprinted in Tobin, J. (1987), *Policies for Prosperity: Essays in a Keynesian Mode*, Cambridge, MA: MIT Press.

Tobin, J. (2003), *World Finance and Economic Stability: Selected Essays of James Tobin*, (with a foreword by Janet Yellen), Cheltenham, UK and Northampton, MA, USA: Edward Elgar Publishing.

10. The impact of FDI on capital formation: the case of Mexico

Claudia Maya

INTRODUCTION

For more than 30 years, mainstream economics has made the claim that financial liberalization promotes higher levels of domestic saving, which translates into higher levels of investment and growth through efficient capital allocation. When domestic saving is not sufficient, a need arises for foreign saving in the form of direct and indirect investment. Under the aforementioned approach, efficiency is understood as the deregulation and liberalization of trade and the financial system in a market-oriented economy. This position has been reflected in the International Monetary Fund and World Bank policies applied to the developing world. The debt crises in the early 1980s in Latin America and the increasing international liquidity in the mid-1980s generated international changes, forcing developing countries to adopt free-market policies. The Mexican economy is no exception.

Since the late 1970s, Mexico has undergone a process of radical economic reforms that have involved the promotion of market mechanisms in economic activities and the reduction of direct and indirect state involvement in the economy. A liberalization process has taken place in trade and financial services in order to attract foreign investment. This process has reversed the economic conditions of the previous import substitution industrialization (ISI) growth model. ISI was characterized by strong government participation, a protected economy and lack of foreign investment, as well as a high rate of growth and capital accumulation, and low unemployment rates. In this model, the fixed capital formation variable was emphasized for the key role it played in creating and expanding capacities, incorporating technology and raising productivity, all fundamental factors in macroeconomic development.

The objective of this chapter is to study whether a positive impact of foreign direct investment (FDI) exists in terms of capital accumulation and growth in Mexico. This work is organized into five sections. Section 10.2 provides a brief review of related literature. Section 10.3 describes the role and process of FDI in Mexico during the last two decades. An analysis of banking sector privatization is developed in section 10.4, followed by the analysis of mergers and acquisitions in the banking sector. Finally, section 10.5 presents the conclusions.

LITERATURE REVIEW

Much of the theoretical work on the impact of FDI in developing economies has been done in the neoclassic tradition. Research carried out by the International Monetary Fund (IMF) and World Bank staff argues for a positive relationship between FDI and capital formation (Calderon, Loayza and Serven, 2004; Alfaro and Chanda, 2003). Authors like Carkovic and Levine (2005), and Krkoska (2001) affirm that FDI encourages technology transfers that accelerate economic growth and capital formation. Nevertheless, there is no general consensus concerning the positive impact of FDI and capital flow in economic growth due to the fact that important economic interactions have been omitted or ignored.

Several researchers have provided strong evidence of the null or even negative impact of FDI on growth as a result of the financial liberalization process (Ghose, 2004; Vidal, 2000). Other non-conventional authors have found that the flow of FDI has been unstable over the years and has been directed primarily to developed economies rather than to developing countries. In the latter cases, FDI was channeled into financing current account deficits and international reserves accumulation rather than financing industry and capital formation (Razmi, 2005; Bresser-Pereira, 2004). Lipsey (2000) found that even if FDI is a possible source of financing for a country's capital formation, it is not crucial since it plays a non-primary role. FDI does not essentially transfer capital from one country to another; it shifts ownership of certain productive assets from firms in one country to firms in another country without necessarily changing the capital positions of those countries.

Agosin and Meyer (2002) point out that the effect of FDI on domestic investment is by no means always favorable. These authors show that, especially in Latin America, in the last two decades, FDI has effectively crowded out domestic investment by orienting economic policy toward liberalization of the financial sector.

In the case of Mexico, not many empirical works that assess the impact of FDI and capital flows have been written. The amount of information available on sector performance of capital formation in the economy is minimal.[1] Most of the literature is based primarily on historical events and data comparisons that clearly demonstrate that the effects of FDI on capital accumulation and economic growth are not positive, and the havoc resulting from the liberalization process (Correa, 1992, 1998; Vidal, 2001).

GENERAL BACKGROUND

The industrialization process in Mexico started in the second half of the 1940s with the import substitution industrialization (ISI) development model. This strategy allowed Mexico to develop an important industrial platform where the domestic industrial sector was the engine of economic growth which in turn encouraged large public investment in infrastructure and in the health, education, energy and telecommunication sectors. A distinctive aspect of the ISI model was observable high capital formation and GDP rates in the absence of trade and financial liberalization, and an extremely low presence of foreign investment (see Table 10.1).

Table 10.1 Mexican manufacture growth rate and capital formation

Period	Manufacture	Fixed capital formation growth rate	
	GDP	Public	Private
1950–55	6.3	-1.4	13.9
1955–60	7.7	7.2	6.1
1960–65	8.9	10.6	7.1
1965–70	8.4	8.4	11.8
1970–75	5.8	12.5	5.3
1975–80	6.9	8.7	7.4
1980–85	1.3	-8.4	-2.5

Source: Estadisticas Historicas, INEGI.

During the implementation of the ISI strategy (1940–80), Mexico reached its highest rates of growth. Manufacturing GDP also increased, aided primarily by strong public deficits. The trend was curtailed, however, when structural adjustment policies began to be implemented after the debt crisis of 1982, promoting state downsizing and elimination of the public deficit.

According to Correa (1992), four periods are identified in which the GDP variable behaves differently. The first period corresponds to the stabilization of the economy before the peso devaluation of 1976. During the second period (1977 to 1982) the external debt of the public sector played an important role in financing the state participation in the economy just before the crisis of this external debt.[2] After the 1982 crisis the GDP rate dropped dramatically as well as fixed capital formation rate (see Table 10.1 and Figure 10.1).

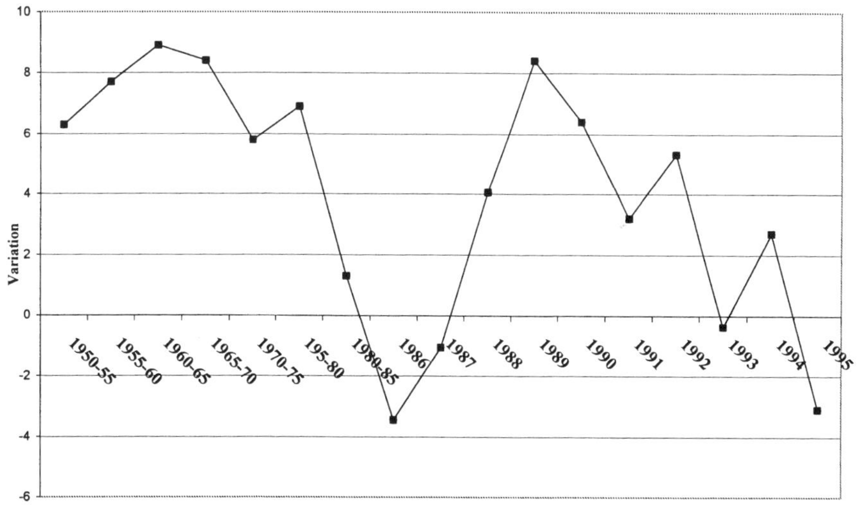

Source: Calculations are based on the 'Estadisticas Historicas', INEGI.

Figure 10.1 Mexican manufacture GDP 1950–95

The third period is known as the 'Lost Decade'. FDI displaced public investment, state enterprises were sold to private companies, and thereafter the privatization process was mostly accomplished by transnational corporations (Vidal, 2000). Big Mexico's recession in the mid-1980s promoted the implementation of different types of economic policies toward a more flexible approach to FDI. By 1988, the privatization process involved the concession of the steel industry and state monopoly of telephone services, highways and ports with the aim of reactivating the investment process by means of extensive foreign participation. These had a positive impact on investment decisions, especially in sectors dominated by transnational companies; however, restructuring of productive apparatus during these years led to a drastic decline in investment in small-scale enterprises, to the point of eliminating them from the market (Mattar and Moreno-Brid, 2002, p. 11).

During the fourth period (1995 to the present) development was expected to be financed by FDI and private capital flows. The economy had been exposed to the international environment, and the commercial and financial relation between Mexico and the USA increased. Privatization was expected to promote growth. Private investment was anticipated stimulate the economy, especially foreign resources derived from the North American Free Trade Agreement (NAFTA) since 1994. The process of FDI on the export sector has been notable in specific branches of the economy such as maquiladoras, the automobile industry and the computer sector. During the financial crisis of 1994, Mexico suffered a serious devaluation of its currency leading to the worst recession in the last 60 years, effectively stemming the flow of international capital into the country. Upon recovery from this crisis at the end of 1996, the investment process restarted. Public investment decreased dramatically in the mid-1980s from 10 percent of total investment directed to industry, to less than 1 percent in the mid-1990s.

Mexican GDP dropped dramatically in 1982, 1987 and 1995 (see Figure 10.2) correlating with financial crises perpetuated by financial liberalization (Correa, 1998). With the change to the development model called 'Modelo Neoliberal', Mexico did not recover the growth rates it had under the ISI model. This brief review of the industrial process of Mexico has shown the inconsistencies of investment behavior in the implementation of liberalization reforms modifying GDP trend and capital formation since free-market-oriented policies were implemented.

ANALYSIS OF FDI IN MEXICO

Increased international liquidity in the mid-1980s generated a deregulation process in most developing countries, and brought about the emergence of new debt financial instruments (Correa, 1998; Mantey, 1999). This led to new strategies for economic growth contrary to the protectionist policies designed to reinforce domestic markets by the means of import substitution, as seen in the Mexican case during the 1960s and 1970s.

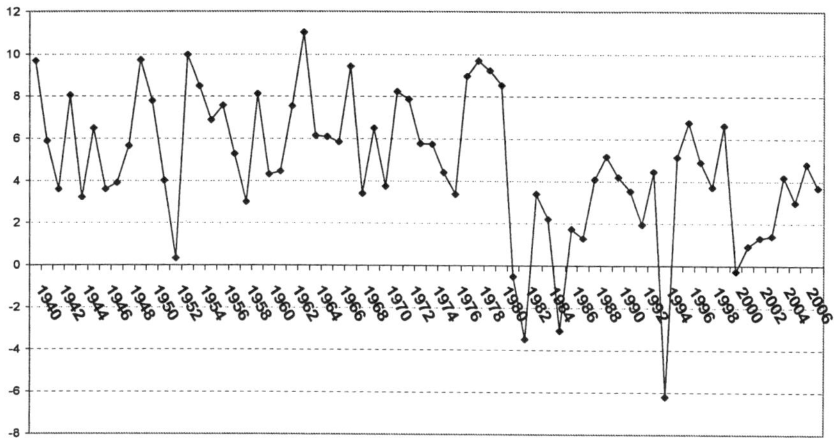

Source: INEGI.

Figure 10.2 Mexican GDP annual variation 1940–2007

The financial liberalization theoretical framework presupposes saving before spending. An increase in savings should provide financial institutions with resources available to lend for investment projects. Indeed, liberalization of the capital account and financial sector supposedly generates an increase in domestic and foreign saving which translates into a larger amount of investment, capital formation, employment and growth (MaKinnon, 1973). On the other hand, a flexible exchange rate regimen is assumed in order to balance the movement of capital flow. To maintain this regimen, restrictive monetary policy via domestic credit contraction (and high interest rates) is encouraged to avoid instability in the monetary base. High interest rates should generate higher levels of saving (both domestic and foreign) directed to productive investment, increased capital formation, and domestic productivity, which in turn would generate an increase in competitiveness in international trade. Increased productivity would help fight inflation by correcting price assignment, promoting an increase in export volume, full employment and growth. These benefits are based on the flexible exchange rate regime and free capital movements.

Another pivotal condition is required: non-public deficits. In the Neoclassical approach, government spending generates a crowding-out effect since the government has to compete for a fixed pool of savings to finance its spending, which raises interest rates and limits the access to credit for all private agents seeking funds. A fall in a government's credit demand should decrease money supply and, as a consequence, eliminate inflation and stabilize prices. Justification for the reduction of government participation in the economy is that market forces promote efficiency and clarity in agents' decision-making. This reinforces the country's monetary policy credibility which then attracts FDI and portfolio inflow. In a deregulated economy, however, the short-run interest rate depends on international interest rates, exchange rate fluctuations and future expectations. Combined, these obstruct monetary policy coordination.

The Orthodox approach holds that saving (S) is primarily a function of interest rate (r), so through r, at an aggregate level $S = I$ (Saving = Investment). If S increases, I should also increase. Saving drives investment and investment becomes a dependent variable of saving. In this case, an increase in private and public saving will have a positive effect on investment or capital formation and promote economic growth.

From a Keynesian perspective, investment drives saving, and public expenditure generates income which translates into investment and consumption. When public saving increases, the government must cut public expenditure, especially social spending such as for infrastructure, education and health. On the other hand, an increase of public saving means reduced consumption and aggregate demand, reduced sales, profits and incentives to invest, all resulting in a decrease in capital accumulation and employment.

The Orthodox approach claims that the openness of the economy to foreign investment (also called foreign saving) should generate an increase in domestic saving, since FDI would reactivate the industrial process and economic growth. Such did not occur in the Mexican case. Figure 10.3 demonstrates that even with the large inflows of FDI, private domestic saving declined as a consequence of contraction of aggregate income due to the liberalization process and government spending reduction.

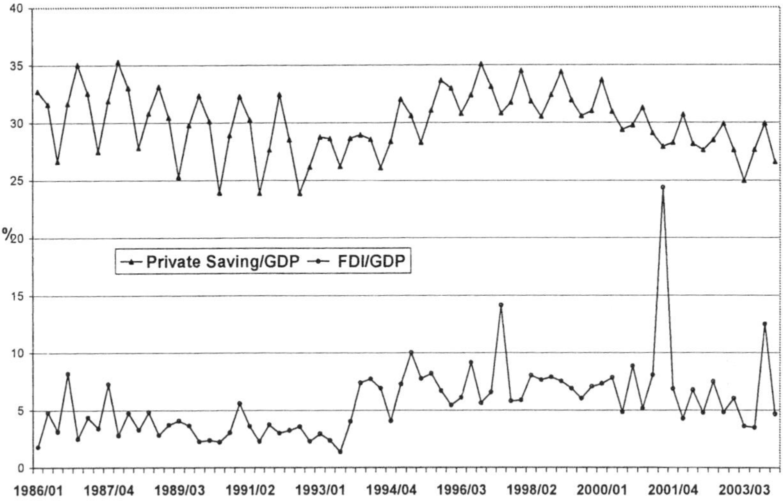

Source: Data from Banxico.gob.mx.

Figure 10.3 Effect of FDI on private saving 1986–2004

In the case of Mexico, FDI generated no impact on either capital formation or on economic growth. All the efforts and sacrifices made in the past two decades to liberalize the Mexican economy for the purpose of attracting large amounts of FDI to complement domestic investment have been in vain. As shown in Figure 10.4, with the total liberalization of financial services in NAFTA agreements after 1994, the participation of FDI in the GDP increased but fixed capital formation was not affected.

In many developing countries, FDI has come to represent a major proportion of total investment and exports. The main consequence of FDI, however has been not financing capital formation. Some authors have argued that FDI does not act primarily as a way of transferring capital from one country to another because the underlying issue is shifting ownership of particular productive assets from firms in one country to firms in another country, without necessarily changing the capital position of either or both countries (Lipsy, 2002, p. 13). In most cases, foreign direct investment may act like portfolio investment in the sense that FDI invested in mergers and acquisitions can easily be transferred from one country to another or from one industry to another (Lipsey, 2002; Kregel, 1996) without contributing to capital formation.

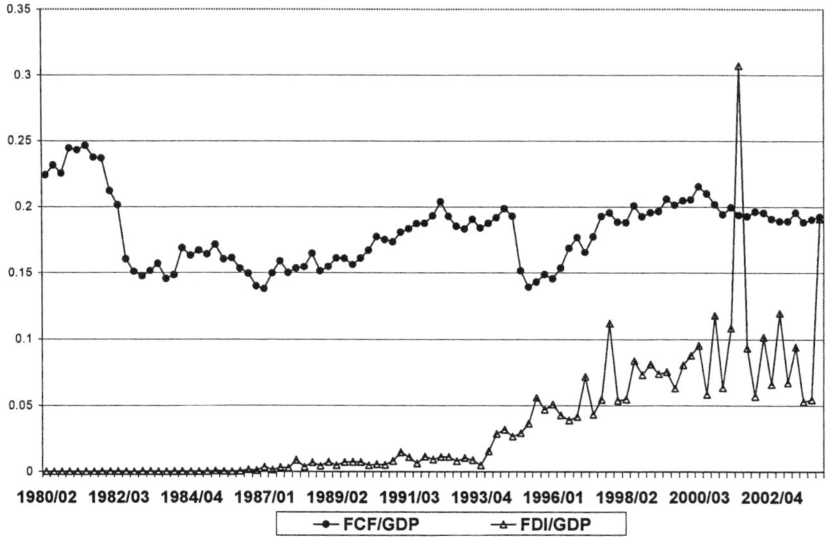

Source: Banxico.gob.mx.

Figure 10.4 FDI and FCF as a percentage of GDP

In the Mexican case, privatization, cross-border, mergers and acquisitions sales constituted the greatest portion of FDI during the 1990s and early 2000s. The privatization process contributed another important inflow of FDI without improving fixed capital formation (FCF) (see Figure 10.5).

Razmi (2005, p. 2) demonstrates that FDI flows have been directed more to developed economies than developing countries. FDI channeled toward developing countries has predominantly financed their current account deficits and reserves accumulation. In Mexico's case, the large influx of foreign direct investment was accompanied by a dramatic increase of public and private external debt since these FDI inflows do create repayment obligations (Kregel, 1996, pp. 57–8).

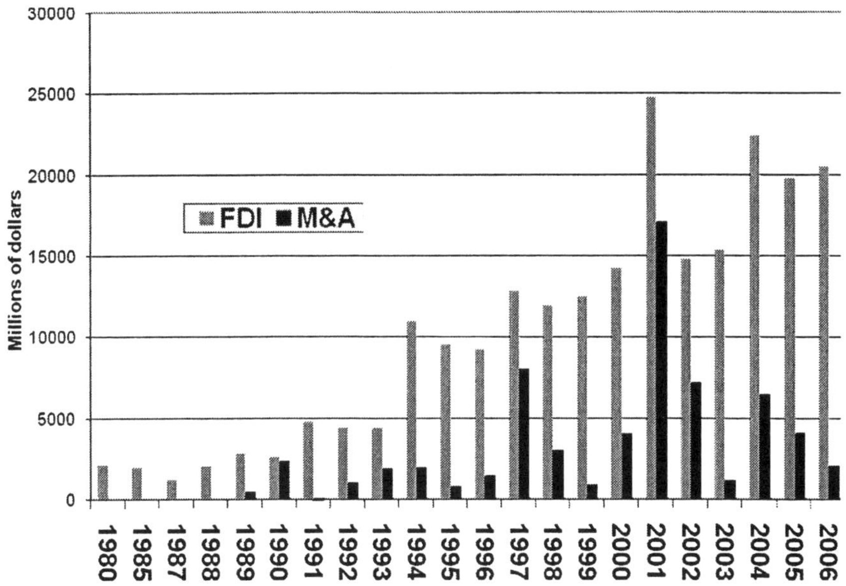

Source: Constructed with data of UNCTAD and IMF.

Figure 10.5 FDI and cross-border M&A sales in Mexico

FOREIGN INVESTMENT IN THE MEXICAN BANKING SECTOR

The goal of the liberalization reforms of the 1990s was to convert the private sector into the cornerstone of economic growth. The purpose was to enable markets to operate efficiently to attract FDI into the deregulated economy, inducing the privatization of public enterprises. Simultaneously, the Mexican financial system suffered violent transformation as a result of the bank nationalization in 1982, and a devastating financial crisis in 1995. This financial crisis triggered the banking consolidation and concentration process as well as the complete acquisition of Mexican banks by foreign banks.

The NAFTA agreement enabled extensive foreign participation and facilitated the entrance and establishment of new bank branches in 1994 (prior to this year, foreign participation in the banking sector was prohibited). With the financial crisis in 1995, many domestic banks were strongly compromised and sold to foreign investors. By the end of 1998, foreign investors controlled less than 20 percent of the bank system assets; by the end of 2001 they had more than 80 percent (see Figure 10.6).

Although the process of acquisition of domestic banks and the foreign penetration in the local market was present in most Latin America countries, the case of Mexico has been the most dramatic. As a result of the concentration and consolidation process of assets held by foreign banks, decisions of credit and financing in the bank sector became monopolistic, thereby increasing the fragility in the whole system (Gnos and Rochon, 2004). Decisions in the market structure are administered by few participants. For example, according to Comision Nacinal Bancaria y de Valores, in 2007, Citibank-Banamex, BBVA-Bancomer, Banorte, and Scotianbank controlled 85 percent of banking activity, including credits, loans, and deposits. From a total of 39 financial institutions operating in Mexico, only six concentrate 82.3 percent of total assets.

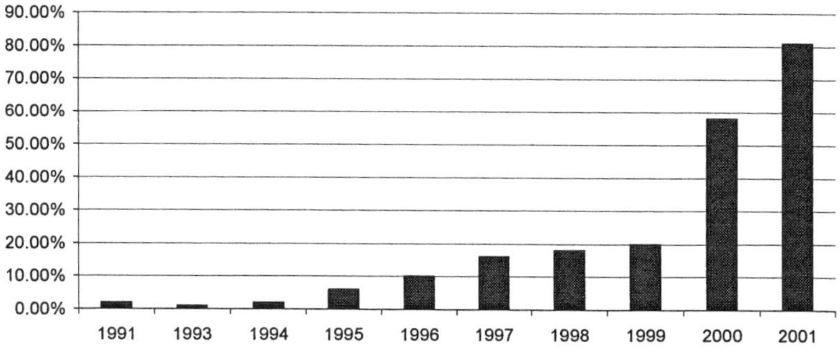

Source: *CNBV, Boletin Estadistico de Banca Multiple, Mexico.*

Figure 10.6 Foreign assets share in the Mexican banking system

The process of FDI inflow in the banking sector led to major layoffs process. Foreign investment directed to the acquisition of existing domestic banks did not create new capital assets, but rather utilized already existing infrastructure. Foreign banks did not develop or expand credit to finance investment projects in the amount expected. On the other hand, high concentration in the industry resulted in an inefficient banking system, credit rationing, and costly access to credit and loans that restrict economic activity.

CONCLUSION

FDI has had no positive impact in fixed capital formation, nor has it encouraged domestic investment and economic growth. FDI does not primarily transfer capital from one country to another because the underlying issue is shifting ownership by mean of mergers and acquisitions.

In the Mexican case, financial liberalization and state reduction contributed to promote financial crisis and the decrease of GDP and capital formation. The process of FDI discouraged domestic saving and prevented government from running a deficit. As a consequence, public expenditure shrank as did growth and employment. The Mexican banking sector was seriously affected by the liberalization process. Foreign investors acquired more than 80 percent of Mexican banks, monopolizing the provision of credit and of investment decisions.

Financial liberalization induced excessively high real interest rates to allow the necessary real investment in order to raise aggregate demand and to attain full employment. Capital mobility has reduced domestic policy autonomy. For this reason, some regulations are necessary to allow monetary policy be effective and promote growth and full employment in economies like Mexico. Foreign investment cannot replace public spending or private productive domestic investment to promote capital accumulation and growth.

NOTES

1. The available data on capital formation tend to be highly aggregated.
2. Regarding this topic, Correa (1992) and Girón (1996) have written extensively.

REFERENCES

Agosin, M. and R. Mayer (2002), 'Foreign investment in developing countries: does it crow in domestic investment?' UNCTAD/OSG/DP/146, New York: UNCTAD United Nations.

Alfaro, L. and A. Chanda (2003), 'FDI spillovers, financial markets, and economic development', WP/03/186, Washington, DC: International Monetary Fund.
Banco de Mexico, www.banxico.gob.mx.
Bresser-Pereira, L. (2004), 'Brazil's quasi-stagnation and the growth cum foreign savings strategy', *International Journal of Political Economy*, **32** (4), 76–102.
Calderon, C., N. Loayza and L. Serven (2004), 'Greenfield foreign investment and mergers and acquisitions: feedback and macroeconomic effects', World Bank Policy Research Working Papers 3192, Washington, DC: World Bank.
Carkovic, M. and R. Levine (2005), 'Does foreign investment accelerate economic growth?' in Moran, T.H., E.M. Graham and M. Blomstrom (eds), *Does Foreign Investment Promote Development?* Washington, DC: Institute for International Economics.
Comisión Nacional Bancaria y de Valores, www.cnbv.gob.mx.
Correa, E. (1992), *Los Mercados Financieros y las Crisis en América Latina*, Mexico City: Instituto de Investigaciones Económicas UNAM Press.
Correa, E. (1998), *Crisis y Desregulacion Financiera*, Mexico City: Siglo XXI Press.
Ghose, A.K. (2004), 'Capital inflows and investment in developing countries', Employment Strategic Department, Employment Strategic Papers 2004/11.
Girón, A (1996), *Cincuenta Años de Deuda Externa*, Mexico City: Instituto de Investigaciones Económicas UNAM Press.
Gnos, C. and L.-P. Rochon (2004), 'Washington consensus and multinational banking in Latin America', *Journal of Post Keynesian Economics*, Winter, **27** (2), 315–30.
INEGI, www.inegi.gob.mx.
Kregel, J. (1996), 'Some risk and implications of financial globalization for national policy autonomy', New York: UNCTAD.
Krkoska, L. (2001), 'Foreign direct investment financing of capital formation in central and eastern Europe', London: European Bank for Reconstruction and Development Working Papers.
Lipsey, R. (2002), 'Interpreting developed countries foreign direct investment', New York: National Bureau of Economic Research, NBER WP7810.
Makino, R. (1973), *Money and Capital in Economic Development*, Washington, DC: Brookings Institute.
Mantey, G. (1999), 'Desorden monetario internacional, riesgo sistémico y escasez de financiamiento para el desarrollo', in Correa, E., A. Girón and I. Martinez (eds), *Globalidad, Crisis y Reforma Monetaria*, Mexico City: Instituto de Investigaciones Económicas UNAM Press.
Máttar, J. and J. Moreno-Brid (2002), 'Foreign investment in Mexico after the economic reform', Series Estudios y Perspectivas, Mexico City: ECLAC United Nations.
Razmi, A. (2005), 'FDI, external accounts, and income distribution in developing countries: a structural investigation', WP 2005-03, Amherst, MA: University of Massachusetts Amherst.
SHCP, www.shcp.gob.mx.
UNCTAD, World Investment Report, www.unctad.org/wir
Vidal, G. (2000), *Grandes Empresas, Economía y Poder*, Mexico: Plaza y Valdes Press.
Vidal, G. (2001), *Privatizaciones Fusiones y Adquisiciones*, Mexico: Universidad Autónoma Metropolitana Press.

11. Financial liberalization, economic growth and rents

Domenica Tropeano

INTRODUCTION

The rationale behind liberalization policies in general has been to get rid of distortions due to prices, which were different from those which would prevail under competitive conditions. These distortions in turn would encourage the so-called rent-seeking activities by interest groups. In some cases, these rent-seeking activities might reduce welfare (see Krueger, 1972; Tullock, 1982; Bhagwati, 1982). The idea should apply to all markets, though most studies refer to impediments to free trade via tariffs and quotas, and resulting lobbying activities. The abolition of such distortions should improve welfare and, according to some, through their direct effect on investment, favour growth and development. Further, it has been argued that development depends not only on real factors but also on the institutional environment. According to this view, both competitive markets and democracy would contribute to economic development. If conservative interest groups, which enjoyed rents from distortions, had lost their power because of liberalizations, development would become more likely (see Bhagwati, 2002). The results of empirical studies on liberalization in developing countries, however, do not offer much support for such optimistic views. The general objective of this chapter is to discuss the issue of rents in relation to financial liberalization and growth.

In the second section, we update and critically review the current debate on rents in financial markets, particularly in the banking sector. The main bulk of the existing literature, with some exceptions, believes that the abolition of rents will foster investment and productivity growth (or simply productivity growth), which should lead to higher output growth.

In the third section, we discuss the effects of financial liberalization on income distribution. The work on income distribution and growth concludes that an increase in inequality has a negative impact on growth. The empirical work on financial liberalization and growth suggests that financial liberalization may increase growth, while it worsens income distribution. Case studies of countries that have implemented liberalization show that investment is not an important source of growth of output; the most important contributions to output growth come out of consumption and public expenditure. The main observed changes in the functional distribution of income show an increase in the share of rental income over the shares of wages and profits.

In the fourth section, we examine two case studies, South Korea and Turkey. We argue that trade liberalization affects profits in different ways in those two countries. The reaction to these changes may depend also on the corporate governance regime. All this may explain the differences in investment patterns after liberalization. These differences notwithstanding, the most powerful interest groups seem to retain their power after liberalization in both countries and increase their share of national income. This share includes different sources of income like profits and rents.

In the last section, we imagine how the objectives of interest groups may evolve after liberalization. As we have already seen, changes in the balance of power towards more productive classes do not seem to happen. In particular, those elites which were gaining in the past from trade restrictions may easily switch to other rent-seeking activities. This time, however, they have to enter the financial sector, where the new gains are concentrated. They may purchase financial institutions or stakes in financial businesses. Post-liberalization interest rates and prices of financial activities are so high that they generate those gains.

HOW SHOULD RENTS ARISING FROM IMPERFECT COMPETITION OR PROTECTION IN FINANCIAL MARKETS BE CONSIDERED?

By sweeping out rents previously present in repressed or closed financial markets, financial liberalization should increase consumers' wealth, improve the allocation of resources and achieve general economic efficiency. It should also contribute, jointly with liberalization measures in other sectors – namely trade – to wipe out many potential sources of rents and let flourish more profit-oriented businesses. That the abolition of rents on its own could improve efficiency is generally agreed, although there is some discussion that this increase in efficiency may be useful to foster growth unless there is a strong link between efficiency and productivity and investment or technological improvement. The old literature on the subject stemming from McKinnon's work stresses the financial deepening effect of liberalization rather than the efficiency argument. The new literature points more to the efficiency argument and both the improvement in allocative efficiency due to the freeing of rates, and in productive efficiency of banks due to the increase in competition.

Recently, Hellman et al. (1997, 1998) have offered a contrasting view, arguing that rents may be good to foster financial deepening; moreover a moderate degree of financial restraint, that is, a deviation of imposed rates of interest from their competitive equilibrium values, would support banks through its positive effect on bank's capital. Financial restraint is different from financial repression, for under the latter, high inflation created by the government transfers wealth from the households to the government, which in turn is the object of rent-seeking activities among various interest groups. The policy objective of financial restraint instead is to create rent opportunities within the private sector for financial intermediaries (see Aoki et al. 1997). Financial restraint would thus increase rather than decrease the mobilization of savings. Though the authors do not deal with growth, it could be reasonably argued that in this case the favourable effect of financial deepening on growth would be achieved in exactly the opposite way by retaining some degree of financial repression or restraint, as long as inflation remains low. The position defended by Hellman et al. departs from the basic proposition, implicit in almost all reform packages by international financial institutions, that allocative efficiency attained through free competition and flexible prices is always the best way to promote growth.

The basic model is the same as that of McKinnon's, although the beneficial effects are derived from the better position of banks. The rents in this case have a positive rather than negative effect since they allow banks to accumulate capital and to expand their supply. Accordingly, the gains to banks would be bigger than the losses to depositors (see Hellman et al. 1998, pp. 264–5), though the whole reasoning rests on the tacit assumption that depositors do not want to build up capital, otherwise the usual general equilibrium assumption that gains must equal losses in the economy as a whole must hold. They assume there is a unique bank in the system, capitalized with \$10 equity and \$90 deposits. In a free-market equilibrium without risk aversion both earn 5 percent. If, instead, the government imposes a ceiling of 3 percent on the yield of deposits what happens is that depositors suffer a loss of 2 percent whereas the bank see the return on equity dramatically increase to 23 percent. The franchise value of the bank, that is the capitalized value of the return on equity, has dramatically increased. This is the reason why banks lose any interest in gambling, entering high-yield and high-risk investment, having a capital to lose. Though the argument may be right in telling that some government intervention in the free market may make the banking system safer than it would otherwise have been, it is quite strange that the loss suffered by depositors is less than the gain obtained by the bank. The authors make a numerical example reported in Table 11.1.

Table 11.1 Franchise value of a bank

	Free market			Financial restraint		
	Amount invested	Gross return	Rate of return	Amount invested	Gross return	Rate of return
Assets	\$100	\$105	5%	\$100	\$105	5%
Deposits	\$90	\$94.5	5%	\$90	\$92.7	3%
Equity	\$10	\$10.5	5%	\$10	\$12.3	23%
Franchise value of equity	\$0.5/(5%) = \$10			\$2.3/(5%) =\$46		

Source: Hellman et al. (1998), p. 265.

What the authors do not consider is that the depositors' loss is calculated just as a one-period flow whereas the gains to the banks is calculated as the franchise value, the capitalized value of the return on equity, which is a stock. If depositors would like to build capital by redepositing and adding to the initial deposit the yield obtained at the end of the first period, their loss would be as great as the gain to the bank. Moreover, if they were market investments with a yield of 5 percent, depositors, under the no-risk-aversion assumption, would switch to other investments. What is plausible, certainly, is that the loss suffered by the depositors may enhance welfare through the positive effect that the franchise value of banks has on their business strategy; however, the assertion that gains to the bank are bigger than the losses to the depositors stems from a numerical example, in which different standards are used to measure gains and losses. A consistent conclusion from this argument is that in some cases allocative efficiency may not foster growth.

The direct link between efficiency and growth, beyond the effect of financial deepening on gross domestic product (GDP) growth through the investment channel, has been stressed by many – old and new – studies (see McKinnon, 1973; Levine, 2001; Demirgüc-Kunt and Levine, 1996). McKinnon claimed to show that financial liberalization, by abolishing rents in the banking sector arising from financial repression, could boost savings and consequently the accumulation of capital. Recently it has been questioned that the accumulation of physical capital really matters for economic growth. Economists who plead for financial liberalization have replied that the latter is useful, even if the transmission channel does not pass through capital accumulation, insofar as it increases economic efficiency and total factor productivity (see Levine, 2001).

Several econometric studies have shown that liberalization both in the banking sector and in the stock exchange after the opening of the capital account leads to major efficiency, which in the banking sector means lower profits and lower overhead costs as well (Demirgüc-Kunt and Levine, 1996), and in the stock exchange an increase in various variables among which the most important one appears to be stock market liquidity. Stock market liquidity may increase efficiency because it allows the sale of shares of ongoing investment without incurring heavy losses. This in turn would foster participation in the stock exchange and new business creation. Though there is nothing against this argument it is difficult that, even in a very liquid market, investments may be profitably sold if the corporate governance is such that shares are held in a web of reciprocal stakes in the corporate sector only and are not sold unless an agreement to change strategy has been reached in advance.

Financial liberalization would thus act through two channels: the direct effects on economic growth, which are stressed by econometric studies of the relation between financial deepening and GDP, and the indirect effects on output through the efficiency channel, that is, the increase in productivity caused by the lowering of profits and the abolition of unproductive rents.

The argument by Hellman et al. (1997, 1998) is that raising interest on bank deposits will lower profit margins for the banks and induce them to expand their activities by investing in risky high-yield assets. Thus, in the end, the message is that depositors should be sacrificed to enhance economic welfare. Levine (2001), on the contrary, asserts that the liberalization policy of raising interest rates and opening the sector to more competition both internal and external, say from foreign banks, lowers previously registered profits, stemming from the imposition of a low rate on deposits. This increases the efficiency of the whole economy. Since, in most recent studies, growth appears to be related more to productivity increases than to capital accumulation, Levine (2001) claims that by making the banking sector more productive the beneficial effects will spill over to the whole economy. He studies the effects of liberalization on the banking sector of 80 countries between 1988–95, where the effects of liberalization policies are measured by the number of foreign banks. He shows, using ordinary least squares (OLS) regressions, that the entry of foreign banks increases efficiency, which means lower bank pre-tax profits over total assets and decreased costs measured as overhead costs over total assets, which include personnel expenses and other non interest costs. The independent variables are instead foreign bank share, the number of foreign banks to the total number of banks, over total assets and the number of foreign banks. It is shown that the foreign bank share decreases pre-tax profits by 0.027 percent and foreign entry by 0.028 percent. Overhead costs decrease respectively by 0.034 and 0.015. It could be argued that domestic banks facing a decrease in their profit margins due to the increase in competition decide to improve their management and organization and obtain an improvement in productivity. The improvement in productivity obtained by cutting costs should normally lead to an increase in profits, other things being equal, but in this case profits fall. Levine does not justify this conclusion but argues that profits must fall because of the increase in competition.

A further consideration, which is not drawn by the author himself, is that the improvement in productivity is not sufficient to offset the loss in market power, the decline in the mark-up. It is then assumed that this increase in productivity will foster growth. No econometric exercise is carried out to prove this assertion. The case in point is South Korea where the whole reasoning should, according to these studies, apply. In this particular case it is not very clear how the link between lower banks' profits and increase in efficiency should be interpreted. If the efficiency is just the efficiency of the banking sector, then its weight on the gross domestic product is very low so it is unlikely that it will boost growth. If instead it is meant that the improved performance of the banking sector will increase growth by its effects on the firms via lower debt costs, it is hardly conceivable that this has indeed happened in this country. First, banks were increasingly losing market share against non-bank financial institutions and moreover their share of loans to non-financial firms decreased (see Tropeano, 2001 on this point). Non-financial firms were either tapping international capital markets or resorting to securitized loans sold by non-bank financial institutions at high interest rates. The decrease in profits made banks enter new activities, which were riskier than lending to domestic firms.

The argument by Hellman et al. (1998) that imposing ceilings on rates on deposits increases the bank welfare more than it decreases consumers' welfare is based on an ad hoc way of measuring gains and losses. Imposing ceilings on rates damages consumers and favors banks. This point, however, is not clearly made by Hellman et al. (1997, 1998), who write that banks make gains without telling the reader who loses. The point is which regime is more favourable to growth. Hellman et al. (1997, 1998) think it is the first under certain circumstances (no high inflation). Levine (2001) claims that the increase in productivity of the banking sector following the increase in competition will be sufficient to boost growth.

In the following section we will try to link this discussion with the debate on income distribution and growth. There are studies that link growth to more equitable income distribution (see Barro, 1999; Alesina and Rodrik, 1994). According to the hypothesis where banking productivity fosters growth, the distribution of income should change in two ways. The direct effect of relaxing controls and regulation is an increase in interest, so the reflection in output will be an increase in the share of interest income, other things being equal. However, if the main effect of this productivity increase is to boost growth, then the incomes from production, wages and profits should increase too. The result on the distribution of income could depend upon the initial increase in the share of rents at fixed output and the change in income distribution caused by the output growth. We should therefore observe an increase in the rate of growth of output accompanied by more equality in income distribution and a relative increase of the wages and profits shares with respect to rental income. This would in turn be consistent with the thesis that growth is positively affected by equality in income distribution.

THE POLITICAL ECONOMY LITERATURE ON LIBERALIZATION AND GROWTH AND THE ROLE OF INCOME DISTRIBUTION

A third and indirect effect of liberalization is stressed in the so-called 'political economy' literature where growth is positively linked to democracy. The abolition of unproductive rents, consequence of a process of liberalization within a reform programme which includes both trade and financial liberalization measures, leads to a change in the balance of power in the countries concerned, with a shift in income distribution from unproductive elites profiting passively from protectionist measures in the real and in the financial sector to workers and potential entrepreneurs benefiting from the reduction in the prices of final and intermediate goods and from the increase in the remuneration of savings (for the definition of unproductive profit-seeking activities see Bhagwati, 1982). This change in income distribution would further contribute to economic growth.

Moreover the political economy literature stresses that the erosion of rents may foster democracy, which is beneficial to growth since it hurts the lobbies who derive their political and economic power from collusion with the state and are interested in retaining their current source of wealth, rather than implementing policies to promote output growth. According to this the liberalization process would cause a shift in income distribution away from rents, which may be extracted from different markets, and towards incomes more related to productive activities such as wages and profits. There is however the presumption that since financial liberalization is often accompanied by stock market booms and the owners of stocks are often the richest, often closely connected to the government, they could benefit more from liberalization thanks to better access to information (see Bhagwati, 1996).

A recent paper by Das and Mohapatra (2003) shows that the income distribution in a sample of 11 countries[1] that have undertaken liberalization in the capital account and in the stock exchange changes in the four years following the implementation of these measures, with a net increase in the share of the richest quintile and with a net decrease in the share of middle incomes, which are identified with the second, third and fourth quintiles. The poorest, that is the last quintile, do not experience any change in their relative share of income. Since the middle classes, the bourgeoisie, are particularly important in industrialization processes – because they are more endowed with knowledge and skills and more inclined to start entrepreneurial initiatives – this would not support the last thesis on the beneficial effect of liberalization deriving from the supposed increase in non-rent-oriented incomes and entrepreneurial classes. These new rents may take the form of capital gains from observed, large increases in stock market prices, which often do not bear any relation to better performances from listed firms. Rents in the banking sector and in the market for state debt may increase because of a positive differential between the domestic interest rate and the world interest rate, due to imperfect capital markets. The increase in the share of the highest quintile would support the hypothesis that the richest before liberalization become richer after this has happened. This means that those who were favoured by the previously used protectionist measures are still more favoured by the new liberalized environment. How could this be reconciled with the literature on interest groups and the canonical representation of unproductive industrial lobbies as opposed to liberalization measures?

Das and Mohapatra (2003) argue that the improvement in the relative share distribution of the highest quintile is linked to their holdings of shares and to the stock market booms that usually follow liberalization. In many emerging countries shares are held most exclusively by the highest classes. The lowest quintiles may be damaged by exclusion from the credit market due to market imperfections and credit rationing. The stock market boom is accompanied, according to many studies, by an increase in investment triggered by the increase in profitability due to the lower cost of capital (see Henry, 2000), and by the increase in retained earnings. One could argue from these findings that firms, given the increase in profitability due to the lower cost of capital, do not distribute higher dividends but instead reinvest them. This process would also be accelerated by the fall in the share of loans in total financing of the corporate sector.

If the link from liberalization to growth passes through capital accumulation or better yet through productivity increases, it must increase investment or at least investment in research. From the country studies in Taylor (2001), the most common source of growth in income in liberalizing countries does not appear to be either investment or exports but quite surprisingly consumption and public expenditure. Among the countries examined in Taylor (2001),[2] the only countries where investment led to an increased contribution to output growth are India and Korea. In the latter country, however, the increase in investment rates after liberalization has been accompanied by declining profitability. Thus the explanation that links financial liberalization to a decrease in the cost of capital and improved profitability cannot be accepted.

The increase in public expenditure helps to explain why the income share of the lowest quintile does not decrease. The increase in consumption may be reconciled with a change in income distribution from profits to rents, the propensity to consume from rents usually being higher than that from other types of income. If the rise in income is to be imputed to consumption because of the wealth effect of rising stock prices and rising yields of financial assets with multiplier effects on non-traded sector goods production, the thesis that liberalization is beneficial to growth because it increases efficiency and thereby total factor productivity appears misleading since those sectors interested in the expansion are by far the less productive ones. The increase in output which is registered among the main achievements of the liberalization strategy has to be considered jointly with the simultaneous increase in public and private debt. The deterioration in public finances, the increase in income notwithstanding, occurs often because of the qualitative changes in the structure of the employment and the distribution of income. The relative decrease in the middle incomes means that most incomes subject to taxation disappear, whereas the increase in the upper quintile due to capital income often does not contribute much to tax revenues because of tax evasion or elusion. The increase in the share of the non-traded sector share on gross domestic product means that most jobs are informal ones. The remunerations of these informal jobs are not taxed.

INVESTMENT DECISIONS UNDER BOTH TRADE AND FINANCIAL LIBERALIZATION

In this section, we consider that both trade and financial liberalization affect investment decisions. The sequence in which those liberalizations are carried out matters too. Investment decisions, however, depend also on the corporate governance regime ruling in each country. Thus, liberalization measures may affect investment in different ways.[3] We will examine two cases, South Korea and Turkey, which indeed show different patterns of investment after liberalizations.

Two possible scenarios are investigated, one in which trade liberalization, realized in many countries which at the same time pursue export growth strategies, depresses the price of products exported and thus profits, and the other in which financial liberalization raises the gains from investing in financial assets or in risky segments of the financial intermediation. If both events occur at the same time we can distinguish three cases. The differential between the rate of interest and the rate of profit may induce substitution between real and financial capital according to the neoclassical view; in this case the high real rate of interest would crowd out real investment. Nothing changes, rather if entrepreneurs are depicted as committed to pursuing the objective of growth in the market share in any case, even if this means not exploiting investments with higher yields. An increase in both real and financial investment may happen instead if they can profit from the increase in the financial resources and expand in both markets by raising more debt, thus decreasing the price of shares. This would not of course apply to a managerial economy, in which managers maximize the price of shares being subject to takeover threats. This case may apply to what happened in South Korea.

Trade liberalization has been implemented before financial liberalization but due either to non-tariff barriers to trade or to other impediments has not depressed profits of old industrial groups, which continue to enjoy the same rent as before with an unchanged mark-up or even an increased one, due to the repression of wage costs. The question to be asked then is how the old industrial groups will use these rents in a liberalized financial environment. If the rate of profit, though entailing a rent from insufficient de facto trade liberalization, is structurally low due for example to a lack of technical change and improvements in productivity, the profits and borrowed money may be invested in the flourishing financial markets or be used to finance a higher level of consumption, often oriented towards imported goods. This second case may apply to Turkey. In the latter case neither capital accumulation nor productivity increased, whereas consumption, yields of financial instruments, imports and external debt did.

TWO EXAMPLES: SOUTH KOREA AND TURKEY

South Korea and Turkey represent two cases in point since, though both of them present the same pattern of income distribution which is common to many liberalized countries, with an improvement in the first quintile and a worsening in the middle quintiles, the behaviour of different types of income according to the source is different. In South Korea the profit share is continuously falling and the wage share is rising jointly with the interest income share. In Turkey instead the profit share is rising or remaining constant, the wage share is decreasing in the first phase after liberalization and increasing in the second phase, and the interest income share is rising the whole time. Surprisingly enough, the contribution of investment to the growth of output is high in South Korea and low in Turkey.

In South Korea the business sector reacted to the fall in profits and the increase in rents by increasing investment but also debt, used both to finance investment and to increase financial assets and portfolio investment. Both balance sheets and national accounts data show this marked increase in the assets and liabilities of the business sector (see Tropeano, 2001, 2008b). In particular the financial liberalization by creating new bank and non-bank accounts with higher real yields than before favoured the accumulation of financial capital. The balance sheet data for the first four big chaebol show that the increase in the flow of debt was used to finance the acquisition of current assets (particularly bank assets), the construction of new plant (tangible assets) and investment assets (among which participations in affiliated companies is the most important item).[4] This expansion of all assets was financed by raising debt, often in international capital markets. Since the debt ratio was already high this meant an increase in it and a fall in the value of the shares. Since the managers of the big groups were not worried about the value of their shares they did not care about. The crisis hit them not only for the part of debt denominated in foreign currency but also for the fall in the value of participations due to the collapse of the whole regional market. We can therefore argue that the fall in the profit rate set in motion, given the larger availability of credit due to the opening of the capital account, a process of expansion of the productive activity to prevent competitors from enlarging their market share but also an expansion of the acquisition of portfolio assets and bank assets whose proportions were never experienced in the past (while very high investment rates had already occurred at the beginning of the 1990s).[5] While the literature on the financial crisis has considered the moral hazard argument as the only possible explanation of such behaviour, the attempt to win an ongoing competition in an overcrowded market with falling prices and to profit from high real yield both on bank assets and on shares abroad could be, in my opinion, a more plausible explanation. The problem of debt was exacerbated by the low inflation of the 1990s whereas in the past an escape from debt problems has always been a moderate degree of inflation and government support.

The Turkish Case

The Turkish case is an example of both trade and financial liberalization in which the share of profits does not decrease with respect to the preceding period, although the share of interest income clearly increases. The high mark-up over costs shows that the trade liberalization notwithstanding, national firms enjoyed some preferential treatment in the domestic market. In this case the opening did not directly depress profits. In the first phase 1989–94 (before the first financial crisis) the wage share was declining and there was a depreciation of the currency which should help the policy oriented towards promoting exports. All this notwithstanding, the investment in the manufacturing sector declined instead of increasing. In the second phase 1994–2000 the investment was driven mainly by internal demand whose growth was related to the growth in real wages though the inflation was high. High inflation, increasing need for funds to finance the public debt and capital inflows drove the real interest rates very high and contributed to high interest income share over the national product (see Boratav et al. 2001;

Boratav and Yeldan, 2002). The informalization of labour and the tax evasion of capital income meant an increasing need for funds to finance public expenditure, particularly the part used to pay interest on public debt. In this case the change in the distribution of income stressed by Das and Mohapatra (2003) may be interpreted in the following way. The industrial lobbies never lost their power, thus retaining an oligopolistic position in the domestic market while at the same time profiting from the high real interest rates. In the second phase before the second financial crisis, the exchange rate appreciated due to the continuing inflow of capital and the export performance worsened. The new financial crisis in 2001, accompanied by a heavy depreciation of the currency, and a fall in output and real wages, ended this phase. The crisis was triggered by the successful strategy of disinflation and lower short-term interest rates on public debt which eventually destroyed the big part of the economy based on the high real interest rates and caused capital outflows. This sounds a bit strange if compared with the emphasis put on fundamentals by exchange rate theories as determinants of investors' expectations.

DO OLD LOBBIES INCREASE OR LOSE THEIR POWER AFTER FINANCIAL LIBERALIZATION?

This short look at what happened in two particular cases, Turkey and South Korea, in the distribution of income and wealth after both trade and financial liberalizations may help us to answer the question asked in the first section: how should rents arising in the financial sector be considered from the viewpoint of social welfare?

We have seen in the first section that quite different views on the rents in the financial sector are present in the literature. There is a strand of literature stemming with McKinnon which sees in these rents and in the insufficient financial deepening the main burden of financial repression. Liberalizations should then work exactly in such a way as to wipe out those rents, increase deposits and increase the efficiency of the whole productive system. This insight by McKinnon is shared by many other economists working on the nexus between finance and growth. Among them some recent work by Levine stresses the positive effects of the declining or disappearing rents in the financial sector as the main engine of growth, in contrast with the preceding view that linked growth to financial liberalization through financial deepening, and increase in saving, and in capital accumulation. Stiglitz argues in the opposite way, though carefully distinguishing between financial repression and financial restraint. Others like Caprio et al. (2001a) argue on the one hand that financial liberalization is essential for growth; on the other hand they deny both that rents in the financial sector or even in the goods sector have in fact decreased after liberalization and that financial liberalization increases saving and real investment, as would be consistent with the story told by McKinnon. Their theoretical position is therefore not very clear unless their proposal is to implement liberalization only if adequate institutional structures are already available, for example anti-trust law and other legislative tools. Even if this could be true for the persistence of rents, it is doubtful that, even under a different institutional structure, saving will increase unless some sort of credit rationing is reintroduced. The conclusion in Bandiera et al. (2000) is that generally financial liberalization does not increase saving, rather the opposite happens. They argue however that this should not be worrying since the financial resources for investment are available through the increased supply of credit and the return of funds previously invested abroad.

The consideration of rents and distribution in this literature is only static, since it examines just the gains or losses from the change in the price of financial assets, which is supposed to increase from the low administered price to a higher market price, which should be the equilibrium one. In reality, however, this does not happen either, as is stated in Honohan's study of the behaviour of interest rates using cross-country estimates (see Honohan, 2001). Interest rates after financial liberalization rise well above the supposed equilibrium levels. At the same time old lobbies, especially industrial or agricultural producers, do not lose their privileges, as is stated in many country studies in the same book. This may happen because of the increase in debt, both private and public. The increase in debt at higher interest rates affects the functional distribution of income, favouring especially the holders of state debt. The nexus between liberalization and rents must not be dealt in a static partial equilibrium framework, but in a dynamic framework which takes into account the changes in income and the changes in the composition of gross domestic product. What matters empirically is not the static shift in the price of financial assets and its welfare effects, but the shift in the composition of gross domestic product as to the source of income after liberalization, with the increase in the share of non-labour income in comparison to pre-liberalization periods.

The idea underlying the contributions in the book by Caprio et al. (2001) is that financial liberalization is always better than repression and should be adopted by developing countries, but with caution, only after some structural reforms are implemented and only if macroeconomic stabilization has been reached. The hidden assumption here is that that macroeconomic instability and collusive behaviour are exogenous to the liberalization process, instead of being the very results of the liberalization process itself (see Tropeano, 2003). Public debt may increase because firms' or banks' debt, piled up after liberalization, is replenished by the state or because the government revenues decrease after the deregulation process has been implemented, since most regular jobs are replaced by temporary informal jobs and the rising amount of income from interest is not taxed (see Turkey for example). Public debt may be nourished by the necessity of funding rising interest expenses. This increase in interest expenses on public debt may be due to inflationary expectations alone, but also to the power of interest groups who own most of the state debt.

The interest groups, as can be seen from these empirical studies, may not have just static objectives, for example maintaining their mark up over costs in the agricultural or industrial sector, and thus opposing trade or financial liberalizations. They may adapt themselves to the change in the environment using their influence, not necessarily through corruption, to get the better possible outcome, the liberalization notwithstanding. Industrial groups may just increase their prices as response to an increase in costs, including interest costs, while at the same time benefiting from the high interest rates as holders of the increasing stock of debt in the economy. Alternatively if they sell products only in the world market and therefore have no market power they may resist interest rate increases on their debt and obtain delays in the implementation of the liberalization measures on one hand while on the other hand profiting from the increase in the yield of some new financial activities either as their direct purchasers or through the acquisition of financial companies. They may even make pressures to obtain regulations that increase their revenue from such expansion of their core business in other sectors.[6] The rise in real interest rates to very high levels after liberalization, as documented in Honohan (2001), may be a key element in explaining the change in the objectives of interest groups who use financial liberalization just as a means to increase or at least maintain the share of national product they own. This share consists of both profits and rents. The adjustment after financial crises happens in most cases through reductions in wages rather than in profits. This interpretation may be consistent with the results of the studies on income distribution changes after liberalization. This may explain why domestic interest groups in conservative countries may agree with so-called reform packages recommended by international institutions since the realization of these reform packages does not decrease their influence and their income. The observed fact that aggregate savings usually decrease in percentage of GDP after financial liberalizations are implemented[7] should be linked not only, as is often the case in the empirical literature on the subject, to the relaxation of credit constraints for households, but also to the change in the composition of domestic product with the rise in income from interest. The higher the propensity to consume out of this income, the higher the decrease in aggregate savings, if a rising share of income comes from this source. Since most of this consumption is directed towards luxury goods, the overall propensity to import rises too.[8]

CONCLUSION

Most studies on financial liberalization have found that it affects growth positively through its effect on the availability of finance and its contribution to total factor productivity. The link between financial liberalization and growth would therefore pass through the investment or improvement in productivity link. If this thesis were correct, then it would be reasonable to expect a growth triggered by investment expenditure or expenditure in research and technology improvements, as well as from a change in the distribution of income that decreases the weight of incomes derived from rents, which should have been wiped out by the liberalization measures, and increasing the weight of incomes deriving from productive activities. Most empirical studies found that neither the first or second hypotheses are consistent with the data for most liberalizing countries.

In this chapter, it has been suggested that investment decisions after liberalization processes must take into account both the effects of the trade liberalization measures and the effects of the financial liberalization measures in the sequence in which they were implemented in different countries. The combination of different effects on the rate of profit and on the rate of interest combined with different corporate governance structures may explain the divergence in investment profiles. In any case what appears evident from the data is that in most cases the share of incomes from holding financial activities increases more the share of incomes from labour and entrepreneurial activity. A brief look at two cases, South Korea and Turkey, has helped to imagine explanations for these empirical findings, which contradict the most accepted theory on the effects of financial liberalization.

The role of interest groups in liberalization coalitions should be more carefully examined. In fact, if both trade and financial liberalization are implemented, existing strong interest groups may still retain their power by exploiting the gains from the very high real interest rates that usually follow liberalization. They may not pursue policies that help promote the growth of exports, the subsidies notwithstanding, but enjoy a better outcome than in the pre-liberalization period by holding financial assets or by expanding in the financial business. The objective of agricultural or industrial lobbies should not be considered in a static way, as merely defending existing privileges, but also in a dynamic setting. Their strategy could be to increase their power in a changed environment by using new opportunities. In this case a coalition between international financial lobbies asking for liberalization and domestic conservative lobbies linked to agriculture or non-productive industries could arise. This could also explain why in fact economic liberalization is undertaken in countries with very conservative governments.

NOTES

1. The countries considered in this work are: Brazil, India, South Korea, Rep., Malaysia, Mexico, Nigeria, Pakistan, the Philippines, Sri Lanka, Thailand and Turkey. In some of these countries the highest quintile already owns around the 50 percent of total output (Brazil, India, Mexico).
2. The chapters of Taylor (2001) consisting of country studies regard Argentina, Colombia, Cuba, India, Mexico, Russia, South Korea, Turkey, Zimbabwe. Four countries, namely India, South Korea, Mexico and Turkey, are considered by both Taylor (2001) and Das and Mohapatra (2003).
3. For the relation between different types of liberalization policies in different institutional contexts see Tropeano (2008a).
4. Most studies on the financial crisis in South Korea support the thesis that the rising debt of the business sector in the years preceding the 1997 crisis was due to the excessive investment in real capital, which should be reflected in balance sheet data the item as 'tangible assets'.
5. The accumulation of financial assets may have different reasons for large enterprises and small and medium-sized ones. For the former, it was part of an industrial strategy while for the latter it was a sort of insurance policy against the very high variability of profit rates (see Tropeano, 2008b).
6. In South Korea, the main conglomerates first expanded in the new financial intermediaries sector (buying merchant banks), then pressed for and obtained that the commercial paper discounted by these new financial institutions could be purchased by the trust accounts of commercial banks, thereby giving the merchant banks more liquidity to be promptly reinvested.
7. See, among others, Bandiera et al. (2000).
8. See the country studies in Taylor (2001).

REFERENCES

Alesina, A. and D. Rodrik (1994), 'Distributive politics and economic growth', *Quarterly Journal of Economics,* **109** (2), 465–90.

Aoki, M., K. Murdock and M. Okuno-Fujiwara (1997), 'Beyond the East-Asian miracle: introducing the market-enhancing view', in Aoki, M., H.K. Kim and M. Okuno-Fujiwara (eds), *The Role of the Government in East-Asian Economic Development: A Comparative Institutional Analysis*, Oxford: Clarendon Press, 1–37.

Bandiera, O., G. Caprio, P. Honohan and F. Schiantarelli (2000), 'Does financial reform increase or reduce savings?', *Review of Economics and Statistics*, **82** (2), 239–63.

Barro, R. (1999), 'Inequality Growth and Investment', NBER working paper 7038.

Bhagwati, J. (1982), 'Directly unproductive profit-seeking activities', *Journal of Political Economy*, **90** (5), 998–1002.

Bhagwati, J. (1996), *Political Economy and International Economics*, Cambridge, MA: MIT Press.

Bhagwati, J. (2002), 'Democracy and development: cruel dilemma or symbiotic relationship?' *Review of Development Economics*, **6** (2), 151–62.

Boratav, K. and E. Yeldan (2002), 'Financial liberalization, macroeconomic instability and patterns of distribution', April, mimeo.

Boratav, K., E. Yeldan and A.H. Kose (2001), 'Turkey: globalization, distribution and social policy 1980–1998', in Taylor, L. (ed.), *External Liberalization, Economic Performance, and Social Policy*, Oxford: Oxford University Press, 317–64.

Caprio G., J.A. Hanson and P. Honohan (2001a), 'Introduction and overview: the case for liberalizations and some drawbacks', in Caprio, G., P. Honohan and J.E. Stiglitz (eds), *Financial Liberalization: How Far, How Fast?* Cambridge: Cambridge University Press, 3–30.

Caprio, G., P. Honohan and J.E. Stiglitz (eds) (2001b), *Financial Liberalization: How Far, How Fast?*, Cambridge: Cambridge University Press.

Cho, Y.J. (2001), 'The role of poorly phased liberalizations in Korea's financial crisis', in Caprio, G., P. Honohan and J.E. Stiglitz (eds), *Financial Liberalization: How Far, How Fast?*, Cambridge: Cambridge University Press, 159–87.

Das, M. and S. Mohapatra (2003), 'Income inequality: the aftermath of stock market liberalization in emerging markets', *Journal of Empirical Finance* **10** (1–2), 217–48.

Demirgüc-Kunt, A. and R. Levine (1996), 'Stock market development and financial intermediaries: stylized facts', *World Bank Economic Review*, **19**, 291–322.

Demirgüc-Kunt, A., R. Levine and H.G. Min (1998), 'Opening to foreign banks: issues of stability, efficiency and growth', in Lee, S. (ed.), *The Implications of Globalization of World Financial Markets*, Seoul: Bank of Korea, 83–115.

Hellman, T., K. Murdock and J. Stiglitz (1997), 'Financial restraint: towards a new paradigm', in Aoki, M., H.K. Kim and M. Okuno-Fujiwara (eds), *The Role of the Government in East-Asian Economic Development: A Comparative Institutional Analysis*, Oxford: Clarendon Press, 163–207.

Hellman, T., K. Murdock and J. Stiglitz (1998), 'Financial restraint and the market enhancing view', in Hayami, Y. and M. Aoki (eds), *The Institutional Foundations of East Asian Economic Development*, London: Macmillan, 255–79.

Henry, P. (2000), 'Do stock market liberalizations cause investment booms?', *Journal of Financial Economics,* **58** (1), 301–34.

Honohan, P. (2001), 'How interest rates changed under liberalizations: a statistical review', in Caprio, G., P. Honohan and J.E. Stiglitz (eds), *Financial Liberalization: How Far, How Fast?* Cambridge: Cambridge University Press, 63–95.

Honohan, P. and J.E. Stiglitz (2001), 'Robust financial restraint', in Caprio, G., P. Honohan and J.E. Stiglitz (eds), *Financial Liberalization: How Far, How Fast?* Cambridge: Cambridge University Press, 31–59.

Krueger, A. (1972), 'The political economy of the rent seeking society', *American Economic Review*, **64**, 292–303.

Levine, R. (2001), 'International financial liberalization and economic growth', *Review of International Economics*, **9** (4), 688–702.

McKinnon, R. (1973), *Money and Capital in Economic Development*, Washington, DC: Brookings Institution.

Taylor, L. (2001), *External Liberalization, Economic Performance, and Social Policy*, Oxford: Oxford University Press.

Tollison, R. (1982), 'Rent-seeking: a survey', *Kyklos*, **35**, 575–602.

Tropeano, D. (2001), *Liberalizzazioni e Crisi Finanziarie*, Rome: Carocci editore.

Tropeano, D. (2003), 'Review of Caprio, G., P. Honohan and J.E. Stiglitz (eds), *Financial Liberalization: How Far, How Fast?' Financial History Review*, **10** (1), 109–12.

Tropeano, D. (2008a), 'Globalisation and macroeconomic policies for developing countries', in Della Posta, P., M. Uvalic and A. Verdun (eds), *Interpreting Globalization: A European Perspective*, London: Palgrave Macmillan (forthcoming).

Tropeano, D. (2008b), 'Investment financing, financial markets development and corporate governance: the case of South Korea 1980–2005', unpublished paper.

12. The Argentine Jefes program: from a post-financial crisis emergency safety net to a long-run policy promoting development

Corinne Pastoret

INTRODUCTION

While for many countries neoliberal economic policies might mean economic growth, this comes at the cost of increasing economic, political and financial fragility. When economic and financial crises occur, new safety nets are desperately needed to prevent the country from collapsing as a result of social unrest, increased poverty and historically high levels of unemployment.

This chapter draws lessons for developing countries from the Jefes y Jefas program (usually referred to as simply the Jefes program), a 'universal' public employment policy that the Argentine government implemented after the 2001 crisis to provide jobs to the poorest heads of households.

The chapter is organized as follows. The second section briefly explores the evolution of unemployment in Argentina since the end of the nineteenth century and looks at the emergence of new safety nets for the poor and the unemployed. As a matter of fact, it is the failure of neoliberal policy to promote economic stability, more equal income distribution and full employment that led to the emergence of new forms of public policy to fight unemployment and poverty.

The third section studies the effectiveness of one of these new Argentine policies, the Jefes program, through its impact on unemployment, poverty, effective demand and employability.

The fourth section argues that this kind of program ('employer of last resort' – ELR – type) is not only a successful post-crisis emergency solution, but can also be a crucial element of a long-run strategy to support economic growth, human development and full employment in developing countries. Finally, the monetary theory behind the ELR literature (Wray, 1998) and the relationships between money and economic growth will be analyzed.

THE JEFES PROGRAM: A LOGICAL RESPONSE TO THE ECONOMIC, FINANCIAL, POLITICAL AND SOCIAL FRAGILITY RESULTING FROM NEOLIBERAL POLICY

This section briefly explores the evolution of unemployment in Argentina since the beginning of the nineteenth century and looks at the emergence of new policies to protect the poor and the unemployed. Based on Polanyi's double movement, it is argued that these policies were in fact logical reactions against the social dislocation resulting from free-market policy.

The evolution of employment and protective public policy in Argentina seems to follow the logic of Polanyi's *Great Transformation.*[1] While Argentina has progressively liberalized its commodity, labor and money markets, the consequence of this transformation was a countermovement aiming at protecting society from collapsing.

Polanyi's Double Movement

According to Polanyi, the idea of a self-regulating market is an absurd utopia (Polanyi, 1957, p. 148) which, in the absence of state intervention, would destroy society. Polanyi (1957, p. 138) claims that societies put in place inevitable measures to protect themselves against 'the perils inherent in a self-regulating market system':

> For a century the dynamics of modern society was governed by a double movement: the market expanded continuously but this movement was met by a countermovement checking the expansion in definite directions. Vital though such a countermovement was for the protection of society, in the last analysis it was incompatible with the self-regulation of the market, and thus with the market system itself. (Polanyi, 1957, p. 136)

> Social history in the nineteenth century was thus the result of a double movement … While the organization of world commodity markets, world capital markets, and world currency markets under the aegis of the gold standard gave an unparalleled momentum to the mechanism of markets, a deep-seated movement sprang into being to resist the

> pernicious effects of a market-controlled economy. Society protected itself against the perils inherent in a self-regulating market system. (Polanyi, 1957, p. 138)

In his view, state intervention was more than 'the usual defensive behavior of a society faced with change; it was a reaction against a dislocation which attacked the fabric of society, and which would have destroyed the very organization of production that the market had called into being'. (Polanyi, 1957, p. 136)

> Our own interpretation of the double movement is, we find, borne out by the evidence. For if market economy was a threat to the human and natural components of the social fabric, as we insisted, what else would one expect than an urge on the part of a great variety of people to press for some sort of protection? This was what we found. (Polanyi, 1957, pp. 156–7)

State intervention and protective regulation were in fact required by a large variety of groups (Polanyi, 1957, p. 56) and they go beyond the diverging interests of social classes:

> Let us return to what we have called the double movement. It can be personified as the action of two organizing principles in society, each of them setting itself specific institutional aims, having the support of definite social forces and using its own distinctive methods. The one was the principle of economic liberalism, aiming at the establishment of a self-regulating market, relying on the support of the trading classes, and using largely *laissez-faire* and free trade as its methods; the other was the principle of social protection aiming at the conservation of man and nature as well as productive organization, relying on the varying support of those most immediately affected by the deleterious action of the market – primarily, but not exclusively, the working and the landed classes – and using protective legislation, restrictive associations, and other instruments of intervention as its methods. (Polanyi, 1957, p. 133)

Polanyi believes that state regulation naturally arises, while laissez-faire is artificially created and 'enforced by the state' (Polanyi, 1957, p. 145). Indeed, the need for state protection spontaneously arose under diverse forms, as a consequence of the destructive consequences of free trade on both the economy and society. Even trade classes asked for state regulation and restriction to implement free markets and to 'protect' them:

> The countermove against economic liberalism and laissez-faire possessed all the unmistakable characteristics of a spontaneous reaction. At innumerable disconnected points it set in without any traceable links between the interests directly affected or any ideological conformity between them. Even in the settlement of one and the same problem as in the case of workmen's compensation, solutions switched over from

> individualistic to 'collectivistic,' from liberal to antiliberal, from 'laissez-faire' to interventionist forms without any change in the economic interest, the ideological influences or political forces in play, merely as a result of the increasing realization of the nature of the problem in question. (Polanyi, 1957, p. 156)

Polanyi finally criticizes liberals for blaming inefficient state intervention ('the antiliberal conspiracy') and individuals' greed and shortsightedness, for the failures of the free market myth:

> While in our view the concept of a self-regulating market was utopian, and its progress was stopped by the realistic self-protection of society, in their view [refers to the liberals] all protectionism was a mistake due to impatience, greed, and shortsightedness, but for which the market would have resolved its difficulties. (Polanyi, 1957, p. 148)

> This, indeed, is the last remaining argument of economic liberalism today. Its apologists are repeating in endless variations that but for the policies advocated by its critics, liberalism would have delivered the goods; that not the competitive system and the self-regulating market, but interference with that system and interventions with that market are responsible for our ills. And this argument does not find support in innumerable recent infringements of economic freedom only, but also in the indubitable fact that the movement to spread the system of self-regulating markets was met in the second half of the nineteenth century by a persistent countermove obstructing the free working of such an economy. (Polanyi, 1957, p. 150)

Polanyi instead believes that what is seen by liberals as shortsightedness is in fact a natural response to protect society. It therefore does not make sense to blame the 'realistic self-protection of society' for sabotaging the benefits of a harmonious free market system.

A closer look at the economic history of Argentina indicates that the destructive consequences of the intensification of free trade were, in fact a 'threat to the human and natural components of the social fabric', thus making natural the necessity of protective measures, in particular for the poor and the unemployed since the liberal experience in the 1980s.

Economic Policy, Unemployment and Protective Measures in Argentina

Diaz Alejandro, in 'No less than one hundred years of Argentine economic history' (1988, p. 230) depicts Argentinean economic history as a pendulum oscillating between liberal and import substitution policies. The alternation of these two kinds of policy has been accompanied by specific unemployment levels and by the emergence of new forms of state regulation and intervention.

Diaz Alejandro (1988, p. 231) reports that 'mythology' makes Rosas, in 1832, the first industrializer in 'Argentina' for imposing tariffs that encouraged industrialization. This early import substitution policy was accompanied by low unemployment. However, low unemployment resulted from repressive and exploitive measures. As pointed out by Cardoso (1979, p. 49), 'the social base of his rule was the exploitation of farm labor and the incorporation of the rural marginal population into the labor force or the army. The legal instrument of repression used by the estancieros was the formation of rural militias and the placing of their sympathizers in the judicial and political apparatus in order to guarantee labor discipline on the estancia'.

A free-trade period (1860–1929) with low protection, multilateralism and limited public intervention followed, that Diaz Alejandro calls the 'belle époque'. After 1880, immigration was encouraged in order to provide a labor force for the growing agricultural sector. Immigration was a major factor making possible the success of the export-led model. Argentina had a population of 2.5 million in 1880; it received 3.2 million immigrants during 1880–1910. Diaz Alejandro (1988, p. 238) explains that domestic cheap labor coexisted with massive immigration. Instead of selecting 'skilled' migrants, Argentina made important educational efforts in order to increase their skills. From 1913–29, agriculture was extending, thus employing a large part of the labor force, estimated at 39.3 percent (according to Berlinsky, 2000, p. 9). Limited welfare measures and increased public investment were implemented at that time (1916–30) by the radical party.

A strong welfare state then emerged after the Great Depression and ISI policies were implemented. In 1947, 25.2 percent of the active population work in agriculture, 22.1 percent in manufacturing, 5.2 percent in construction, 13.3 percent in commerce, 21.3 percent in services.[2] The unemployment rate was estimated at 2.8 percent of the active population. Unemployment remained low during the ISI period. Unemployment started going up after the first liberal experience in the 1980s.[3] It then dramatically increased after the implementation of neoliberal policies.[4] A major proportion of employment was provided by services, since industry was not able to develop sufficiently in the free-market environment. Public employment policies were developed to compensate for the impact of neoliberal policy on employment; the Trabajar program (Jalan and Ravallion, 1999), introduced in 1997, was the first experience.

Economic activity and employment in Argentina deteriorated after 2000. From

October 2000 to May 2002, the unemployment rate rose from 14.7 percent to 21.5 percent. Meanwhile, gross domestic product (GDP) (at 1993 market prices) fell from 280 million pesos to 235 million pesos in 2002, then recovered to 256 million pesos in 2003.

After the 2001 crisis, a universal program called Jefes was created to provide an emergency solution to unemployment. Every head of household was assured to receive 150 pesos, provided that he worked 20 hours in the program. The unemployment rate decreased to 17.8 percent in October 2002 and remained there[5] until May 2003. The active population rate increased, from 41.8 percent (May 2002) to 42.9 percent in October 2002; in May 2003, the rate was 45.6 percent. The Jefes plan explains much of the improvement in unemployment rates; it also probably accounts for much of the increased active population.

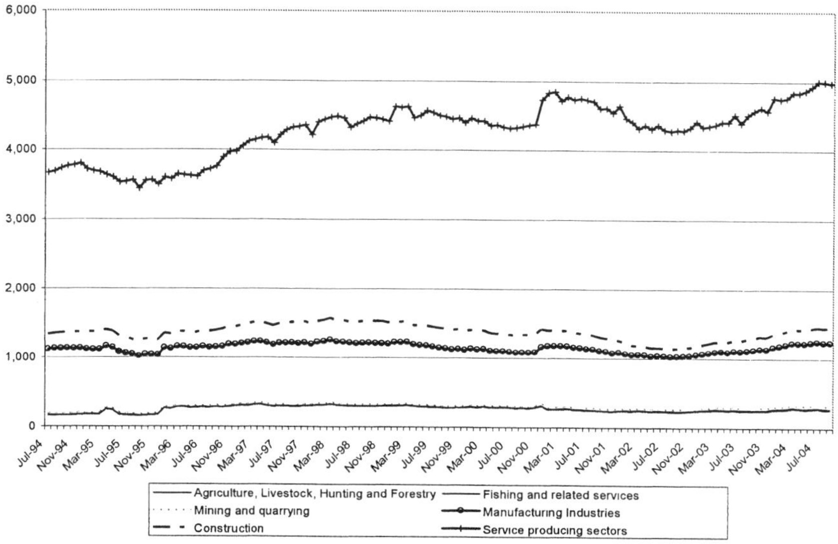

Source: INDEC.

Figure 12.1 Distribution of jobs by economic activity

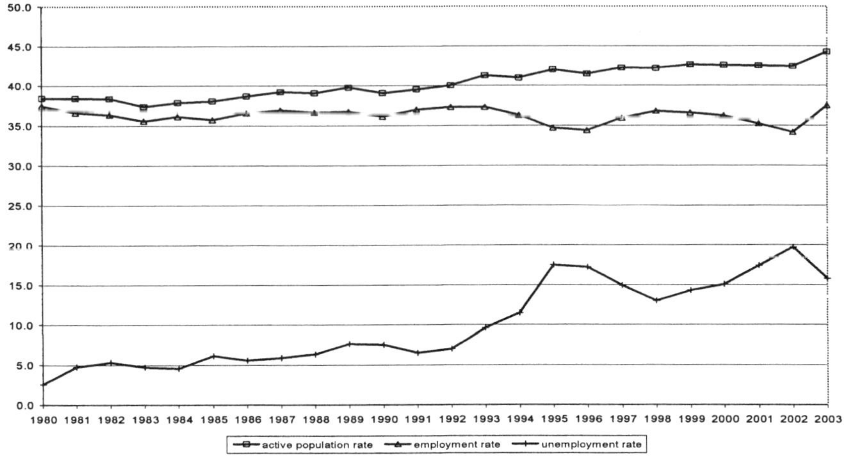

Source: INDEC.

Figure 12.2 Unemployment rates since 1980

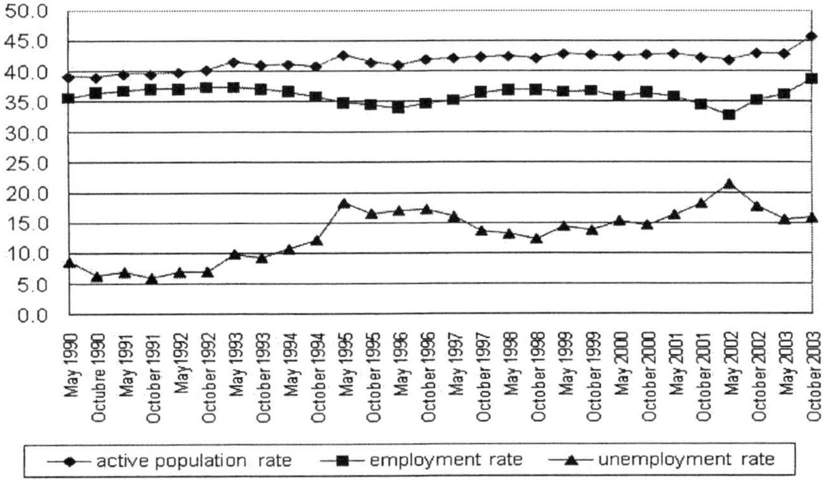

Source: INDEC.

Figure 12.3 Active population, employment and unemployment rates since 1990

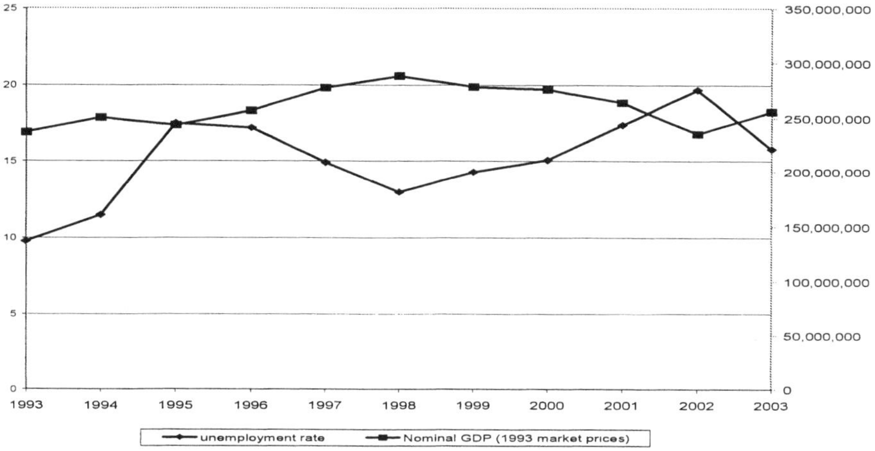

Source: INDEC.

Figure 12.4 Unemployment rate and GDP in thousands of pesos (1993 market prices)

EFFECTIVENESS OF THE JEFES PROGRAM

This section examines unemployment in Argentina after the 2001 crisis and assesses the impact of the Jefes program on unemployment, employability, effective demand and poverty from October 2002 to May 2003.

The Plan Jefes is a form of 'employer of last resort' policy which was implemented in Argentina in June 2002 to help families severely hit by the 2001 crisis. A pre-existing policy, the Trabajar program, was already in place but its scope was limited. The numbers of participants in the Jefes program increased from 1.2 million in 2002 to 1.8 million in 2003. The Argentinean government, supported by the World Bank, financed this program for an amount of US$500 million (Galasso and Ravallion, 2004, p. 2) in 2002 and US$600 million in 2003. This public employment policy consists in offering a wage to the poorest heads of household with dependents who are willing to work. Participants must have no formal sector job and work 20 hours a week in a private or a public establishment. In return, participants receive 150 pesos per month, which is below the minimum wage which was 200 pesos from 2002 through May 2003.[6] There is no time limit for program participants.

Who Are the Jefes Participants?

Descriptive statistics have been built from the October 2002 *Encuesta Permanente de Hogares* realized by the INDEC[7] twice a year.[8]

- Women: a major proportion (71.47 percent) of the Jefes participants is constituted by women whose age is on average 34.68 years; 40.44 percent of the participants are heads of households, 31.93 percent are spouses of heads of household and 63.86 percent of participants are married or co-habiting. Compared to the total population, the Jefes program attracts more women and younger individuals. These results are surprising because the Jefes is targeted toward unemployed heads of households.
- Larger households: on average, households are larger than for the rest of the population, with on average 5.65 members. Of the Jefes participants, 88.89 percent live in a house; 83.18 percent own it. The proportion of heads of households, and of their wives, in the Jefes is also more important. Of the Jefes participants, 50.85 percent have a low level of education (primary level or less), as compared to 33.52 percent for the total population.
- Very low-income households: the average Jefes household income is 423.46 pesos monthly, as compared to 769.84 pesos for the total population. The household income per capita is on average 81.55 pesos for the Jefes participants and 206.12 pesos for the total population. As a comparison, the adult equivalent indigent line is 105 pesos and the adult equivalent poverty line is 232 pesos in April 2002. Despite some limited fraud (a few rich individuals participate in the program), the Jefes program is relatively well targeted toward the poorest households. The poverty effects of the Jefes are thus maximized because state funding is directed toward the poorest households who have been very severely hit by the 2001 crisis.
- Public employees for community works: 81.68 percent of the Jefes participants work in the public sector (against 31.21 percent of the total population employed) at providing community works. Jefes participants work on average 21.75 hours a week, 1.75 hours more than the program requires, because some individuals have a second occupation.

Impact on Employment

According to the Argentine Labor Ministry, the Jefes program has a direct impact on employment because it provides a job for individuals who would otherwise be unemployed.

The unemployment rate in October 2002 (17.8 percent) would have been 5.8 points higher in the absence of the Jefes. Similarly, unemployment in May 2003 (17.8 percent) would have been 5.2 points higher.

In fact, the Labor Ministry has overestimated the impact of the Jefes in May 2003, by unrealistically considering the Jefes participants as 'otherwise unemployed'. In October 2002, a second hypothesis – more pessimistic – was also made by the government. This hypothesis considered as 'otherwise unemployed' only the Jefes participants who were actively looking for a job. It is unfortunate that this hypothesis was abandoned in the subsequent evaluation of the Jefes impact on unemployment. In fact, the Jefes program might also have attracted inactive individuals who were not (or would not be) looking for a job. Galasso and Ravallion (2004, p. 11) find that, in October 2002, 43 percent of Jefes participants were employed a year earlier, while 38 percent were inactive and 19 percent were unemployed. I reached a similar conclusion for May 2003 (see Table 12.1): 57.41 percent of the Jefes participants were in the program in October 2002, 7.41 percent came from another workfare policy, 13.76 percent were previously employed, 8.06 percent were unemployed and 13.76 percent were inactive. Contrary to Galasso and Ravallion (2004, p. 2), it is not here considered realistic to assume that many Jefes participants would otherwise have found a job, considering the low level of the Jefes' wage. Moreover, individuals previously counted as inactive might also decide to look for a job (thus becoming 'unemployed') to reduce the impact of the crisis on household income. For this reason, the estimates provided by Galasso and Ravallion of 2.8 points are too pessimistic. It remains that the positive impact of the Jefes on employment is undeniable and should be between 2.8 and 5.8 percent percent.

Impact on Poverty and Effective Demand

In 2003, the Jefes provided 150 pesos a month to 1.8 million individuals[9] (9.62 percent of the active population), which amounted to 3.24 million pesos a year. This corresponds to 0.8 percent[10] of the annual 2003 nominal GDP ($376 million) expressed in current prices. By spending their wages, these 1.8 million individuals sustain economic activity in a crisis situation. The impact on effective demand is almost complete since wages are distributed to the poorest households with a high marginal propensity to consume. Moreover, most of the Jefes wage bill is not spent on imports, whose price has become dissuasive since the crisis.[11] Jefes wages have therefore contributed to the recovery of the Argentinean economy since 2002. Since May 2002, economic recovery has been continuous.[12] Since 2002, unemployment has partly been reduced by the implementation of the Jefes program. From the second quarter 2002 to 2005, the Labor Ministry has announced that 2 million regular jobs[13] were also created.

Table 12.1 Official impact of the Jefes program on employment

		'Otherwise' considered as unemployed:	
		All Jefes participants	Jefes participants
October 2002	General rates (%)		Searching for a job
Active population	42.9	42.9	41.8
Employment	35.3	32.7	32.7
Unemployment	17.8	23.6	21.7
May 2003	General rates	Without the Jefes plan	
Active population	45.6	45.6	
Employment	37.4	35.1	
Unemployment	17.8	23	

Source: 'Mercado de trabajo: principales indicadores de los aglomerados urbanos', December 2002 and 2003, edited by the INDEC, the Economy Minister and the Argentine State.

Impact on Employability

Even if the Jefes was initially developed to provide a job in an emergency situation, it could also have generated employability effects for participants; indeed, Jefes participants are likely to acquire additional working experience, thus increasing their likelihood of finding a job. To assess the employability effects of the Jefes from October 2002 to May 2003, we are using a sample built from the October 2002 and May 2003 *Encuesta Permanente de Hogares.*[14]

Table 12.2 highlights the evolution of Jefes participants' employment status from October 2002 to May 2003.

The main results are the following: 70.57 percent of those who participated in the program in October 2002 are still in the program, 14.51 percent had found a job, and 11.91 percent had become inactive. Among these remaining Jefes participants, 48.94 percent did not look for another occupation in May 2003. As a comparison, it is also important to notice that 36.87 percent of the individuals unemployed in October 2003, who did not join the Jefes had found a job in October 2002. Similar conclusions were reached by applying Heckman's two-step procedure[15] to our sample. The participation in the Jefes program in October 2002 negatively affects the odds of finding a job in 2003: the coefficient for the variable 'participation in the Jefes in October 2002' is negative and highly significant.[16] Individuals in the population with a higher probability of finding a job are those unemployed, and then Jefes participants and finally, inactive individuals (which is not surprising). High education, relative to primary education, is a factor that positively affects the odds of finding a job in May 2003. The coefficients for the two last levels of education are positive and highly significant.

Some Lessons can be Drawn from the Absence of Employability Effect Generated by the Jefes Program

The following lessons can be drawn from the Jefes program:

- The Jefes program was not initially created to provide skills for individuals who have been unemployed for many years, but to provide a safety net for individuals who were previously employed and lost their job in the aftermath of the 2001 crisis. The work requirement was initially implemented to avoid fraud and not mainly to provide the skills immediately required by the labor market. Besides, more time was also necessary for the educational structure for Jefes participants to be better organized in order to increase the human capital of Jefes participants. Argentina is therefore not to blame for these limitations because it had to find an immediate solution and create a short-term institution to manage catastrophic unemployment.

Table 12.2 Situation in May 2003: comparison between unemployed, employed and Jefes participants in October 2002

Situation in May 2003 of the October 2002 participants	**October 2002**	**October 2002**
Total participants in October 2002	999	
Still in the Jefes program in 2003	**705**	**70.57%**
Employed in 2003	145	14.51%
Inactive in 2003	119	11.91%
Among the 705 still in the Jefes program in May 2003	**May 2003**	**May 2003**
Look for another occupation in 2003	360	51.06%
Do not look for another occupation	345	48.94%

Situation in May 2003 of the October 2002 unemployed	**May 2003**	**May 2003**
Unemployed in October 2002	2316	
Employed in 2003	854	36.87%
Jefes participants in 2003	94	4.06%
Unemployed in 2003	736	31.78%
Inactive in 2003	632	27.29%

Origins of the May 2003 Jefes participants	**October 2002**
Jefes participants in October 2002	57.41%
Other workfare program in October 2002	7.41%
Employed in October 2002	13.76%
Unemployed in October 2002	8.06%
Inactive in October 2002	13.76%

- The macroeconomic environment in 2003 was still hostile for the unemployed and individual characteristics are probably not the first to blame for unemployment. Individuals find a temporary occupation through the Jefes, in a period of very high unemployment.
- The Jefes program attracts individuals who were not previously unemployed, and most of them might not have looked for another occupation on the labor market. Individuals who were working in the informal sector with wages far below the minimum wage might have become Jefes participants.[17] The Jefes has also massively attracted formerly inactive 'housewives' who have joined the Jefes to provide an additional income to the household. For this reason, a dependency effect of the Jefes program might occur. These factors provide explanations for the low percentage (53 percent) of October 2002 Jefes participants actively looking for another occupation
- Women have also found through the Jefes program a means to be integrated into the life of their community by providing community works and this could count for part of the lack-of-employability effect. Further studies should be conducted to understand the gender dimension of the Jefes. It is somewhat unexpected that the Jefes, which was almost exclusively directed towards men as heads of households, ended up mostly attracting women. The reasons for the lack of attractiveness of the Jefes for men need to be elucidated if the Jefes aims at becoming a universal ELR program. Several answers are possible: the low level of wages that led men toward the informal market, the 'bad image' associated with community works and state subsidies or, probably, a household strategy where men and women occupy the jobs they are more likely to find in a period of crisis.
- The period under study is maybe too short to capture employability effects. Subsequent studies should be carried out in the future, in particular to extend our results. Most Jefes jobs should not be seen as permanent occupations, but as transitory ones. Subsequent studies on period of formal employment recovery (not related to an increased Jefes participation) would be necessary to study the eventual dependency of participants toward the Jefes.

As a conclusion, the Jefes did contribute to decrease poverty, to modestly sustain effective demand and to limit the increase of unemployment. The Jefes thus served its function of safety net, but failed to be a universal response to unemployment. Indeed, most male heads of households refused to participate, partly because of the low level of the Jefes wage. The implementation of the Jefes has instead generated an increased participation of women in the labor market.

These results do not negate the necessity of the Jefes in an emergency period to provide a job to the poorest households, but highlight the necessity to adapt the Jefes program to the long-run development goals of Argentina.

THE JEFES EMERGENCY PROGRAM COULD ALSO BE A CRUCIAL LONG-RUN POLICY TO MEET LONG-RUN DEVELOPMENT GOALS

Lessons can be drawn from the Argentine Jefes program in order to propose a job guarantee program for developing countries. On the basis of the Argentine experience, it is argued that this kind of program is not only a successful post-crisis emergency safety net, but that it can also be a crucial element of a long-run strategy to support economic growth, human development and full employment in developing countries.

This last section proposes to extend the ELR theory – which is traditionally designed for coping with economic fluctuations in developed countries – to developing countries. While the Jefes program does not meet all the requirements for the functioning of a theoretical ELR program, it is nevertheless a 'real-world' experience which provides useful knowledge to build a permanent job guarantee program for developing countries that Argentina could also develop in the future.

Presentation of the ELR: Macroeconomic Job Guarantee Program for Developed Countries

The ELR is presented as a universal program 'designed to offer a job to anyone who is ready, willing and able to work'; it is presented neither as slavery, nor as a form of workfare (Wray, 1998, pp. 124–5). The ELR is also considered as a tool that allows the government to influence the level of wages in the economy, and thus inflation, by setting the ELR wage: 'two primary components of the proposal: the government would (a) act as employer of last resort, and (b) exogenously set the "marginal" price of labour' (Wray, 1998, p. 124).

The ELR can have other secondary benefits by increasing effective demand, aggregate supply and efficiency in the private sector. The ELR can also have employability effects, by enhancing the education and skills of the ELR participants:

> Social spending on the unemployed prevents aggregate demand from falling excessively, but little is done to promote aggregate supply (or growth of potential output). With ELR in place, however, labour is paid for working, which can lead to production of publicly supplied goods and services, can promote efficiency of the private sector (if, for example, BPSE[18] generates productivity-enhancing public infrastructure) and reduce private sector costs (for example, by reducing crime), and can increase the education and skills of ELR workers (compared with education and skill levels of the unemployed). Thus ELR might increase aggregate supply (or potential output) and thereby place downward pressure on prices, rather than causing inflation. (Wray, 1998, p. 133)

The ELR does not aim at providing a permanent job for individuals. Participants can be laid off (Wray, 1998, p. 125) if they do not conform to the requirements of their job. More importantly, the ELR 'allows the "storage" of labour – when it is not needed by private employers (and non-ELR public employers), it can be stored in the ELR buffer stock pool' (Wray, 1998, p. 135). In other words, the ELR provides a substitute for the private sector when economic conditions are not good enough to guarantee full employment. The 'fate' of most ELR participants is to return to the private sector without losing their skills or education. It is also expected that 'those who do show up for ELR work will become more employable, and thus operate as a better "reserve army" buffer stock than do the unemployed' (Wray, 1998, p. 133).

According to Chartalists, the implementation of the ELR does not meet any financial constraint, if the state is sovereign, because the ELR wage bill is financed through money creation:

> In all modern economies, the government 'spends' by issuing fiat money, which ends up in the hands of the public as cash holdings and in the banking system as bank reserves. If a government can create at will the money that the public willingly offers goods and services (especially labour services, for our purpose here) to obtain, then the government's spending is never constrained by 'narrow financing' decisions. The government can offer to hire all unemployed workers at any price it chooses, allowing the government deficit to float as high as necessary to ensure that unemployment is eliminated'. (Wray, 1998, p. 137)

By allowing the government deficit to float, the government would 'technically' be able to finance the ELR program.

ELR and the Jefes Program

The Jefes program in Argentina only meets some of the characteristics of the theoretical ELR. Like the ELR, the Jefes aimed at being a 'universal' emergency program absorbing the unemployment that was suddenly generated by an economic crisis. Despite its large scale (2 million participants in 2003), the program was not targeting all the unemployed individuals, but only the poorest – usually low-skilled heads of households. The Jefes thus could not fully serve as a buffer stock for the private sector. Moreover, the Jefes wage was far below the minimum wage so that it could not set a downward limit to the fall of other wages, except for wages in the informal sector.

In contrast to the ELR, the Jefes was not totally financed through money creation, but mostly relied on funds from the World Bank. After the collapse of the currency board and the dismissal of neoliberal policy by Nestor Kirchner, Argentina nevertheless refused to get its sovereignty back and therefore, to create money to deficit spend. Indeed, despite Kirchner's frontal attack of the International Monetary Fund (IMF) on the debt problem, he did accept a target of 3 percent of gross domestic product (GDP) primary surplus for 2004. As a consequence, the state was financially constrained when the Jefes program was created: the program could not be made universal and not enough money was available to create the costly infrastructure that would provide workers with the training and skills that firms require. It followed that the macroeconomic impact of the Jefes was limited, compared to the expected impact of an ELR in Argentina.

Finally, the Jefes was not meant to be a permanent macroeconomic tool to promote full employment, but a temporary solution to help the poorest households. For this reason, it needs to evolve in order to encourage economic development.

Money, Production and Productive Jobs: the ELR as a Development Strategy

In Chartalist theory, money can be created endogenously to finance jobs for ELR participants. How, if the state was able to guarantee full employment, would the economy be able to meet the economic needs of the population? This illustrates the limitations of applying the ELR and functional finance (Lerner, 1943) to support economic growth in developing countries. Let us take the example of a sovereign country that creates all the money required both to employ its labor force and to purchase goods. Nothing can spontaneously guarantee and provide the right incentives for the developing economy to grow and satisfy the needs of its population. In the extreme case, full employment would be associated to poverty and underdevelopment. This is an extreme case used to show that full employment does not imply that the money created by the state always provides the amount of goods and services needed. Full employment in itself is not the magical solution. If each jobless person in developing countries was proposed community work, would this solve the unemployment and development issues in these countries?

Elsewere (see Pastoret, 2006a, p. 159), I have argued that that Chartalist and Circuit theories could be made complementary if a parallel was drawn between the monetary circuits at the firm level and at the state level. It was claimed that, in contrast to state spending on existing goods, the ELR could be associated to the formation of new products and new incomes; the value of state production would then be measured by the ELR wage bill. Community works, even if they are very useful at the community level (in particular, public kitchens) are not sufficient to provide the goods and services required by a developing country in the long run.

In other words, state money does not only have value because it is accepted for the payment of taxes. Indeed, being accepted is a condition of existence of the value of money, not the measure of its value. Furthermore, an 'effort' or work does not mean that new production is created that would give purchasing power to state money:

> Recall that we have argued that the primary determinant of the value of the currency is the 'effort' required to obtain the money that is required to pay taxes. ELR raises the 'stakes' involved because it requires that one must at least show up, ready to work, in order to obtain money; this requires greater effort than that required to obtain 'welfare'. (Wray, 1998, p. 133)

The new money created by the state, in fact, gains value because it is associated to new incomes and new production. It is somehow unfortunate that the Jefes was not also accompanied by an increase in the aggregate supply because wages were mostly spent for 'community services' purposes.

As a consequence, to become a long-run development tool for developing countries, the impact of the ELR on production has to be taken into account. Economic growth usually needs to be the main objective of developing countries, but not the only one. In fact, the ELR can go beyond the full-employment guarantee to create the kinds of jobs that best meet the long-run economic and human goals of developing countries. A distinction needs to be made between productive jobs (in the economic sense), socially useful jobs (promote social cohesion, fighting against violence and gender inequalities) and the need to increase human capital (training, education, working experience). Based on its level of economic development and its priorities, each developing country can decide the proportion of each kind of jobs to create. Finally, the ELR in developing countries should be also able to create a wide range of jobs that can also provide safety nets to more skilled and educated individuals and also integrate them as part of the development strategy of the country.

Finally, the ELR cannot provide the ultimate solution to promote economic growth and human development. Rather, the employment guarantee scheme needs to be included as part of a development strategy to promote economic growth and economic, political and social stability. For example, the ELR can also be complemented by direct government spending policy (that would promote economic growth and employment in specific economic sectors), by diverse supports to the private sector (funding research, subsidies) or by creating public firms to complement private production.

CONCLUSION

The Jefes program was a logical response to the destructive impact of free-market policy on employment and poverty in Argentina. This program was relatively successful in providing a safety net to the poorest households, who had been the most severely hit by the crisis. The Jefes successfully contributed to slow down the increase in unemployment, to decrease poverty by targeting the poorest households and to modestly sustain effective demand. The Jefes therefore played a key role to prevent the Argentine society from collapsing after the 2001 crisis.

In contrast to the ELR, the Jefes was not meant to be a universal permanent solution to guarantee full employment, since it only targeted the poorest heads of households. Now that the Argentine economy is recovering, a new employment guarantee program ('ELR' type) could be implemented as part of a wider development strategy. Its main objectives would be to support economic growth, full employment and human development in Argentina, therefore decreasing economic, political and social fragility.

Based on the specificities of Argentina, a decision will be made on the proportion of productive jobs, socially useful jobs and ELR training to be created. To be successful, this future employment guarantee program will need to be integrated as part of the overall Argentine development strategy of the country.

APPENDIX 12.A DESCRIPTIVE STATISTICS OF THE JEFES PARTICIPANTS RELATIVE TO THE POPULATION IN OCTOBER 2002 (EPH)

	October 2002	
INDIVIDUAL DEMOGRAPHICS	**Jefes participants**	**Total population**
Age	34.68	37.18
Male	28.53%	47.14%
Female	71.47%	52.86%
Head of household	40.44%	35.92%
Spouse of head of household	31.93%	24.68%
Son/daughter of head of household	20.62%	32.52%
Son/daughter in law of head	4.00%	1.57%
Marital status		
Single	23.62%	34.01%
Married (or in cohabitation)	63.86%	53.18%
Divorced	10.91%	4.78%
HOUSEHOLD CHARACTERISTICS		
Housing		
House	88.89%	84.91%
Apartment	6.41%	12.97%
Number of rooms (kitchen & bathroom not included)	2.67	3.29
Water	95.70%	98.61%
Electricity	98.20%	99.37%
Bathroom	91.29%	96.71%
Owner of the house and land	70.87%	78.81%
Owner of the house only	12.31%	4.98%
Renter	4.20%	8.13%
Free housing	10.71%	6.21%

HOUSEHOLD INCOME AND EMPLOYMENT SITUATION

Individual demographics	October 2002	
	Jefes participants	Total population
Number of members in the household	5.65	4.63
Employed	1.96	1.51
Unemployed	0.33	0.38
Inactive	3.36	2.79
Total household income	423.46	769.84
First decile (very poor) / total EPH	24.32%	7.74%
Second decile	9.41%	7.36%
Third decile	17.62%	9.61%
Fourth decile	11.51%	9.55%
Fifth decile	11.11%	9.21%
Sixth decile	7.01%	9.00%
Seventh decile	7.31%	9.94%
Eighth decile	4.40%	10.64%
Ninth decile	3.20%	11.25%
Tenth decile	0.70%	9.07%
Household income per capita	81.55	206.12
First decile (very poor) / total EPH	31.93%	12.30%
Second decile	29.03%	13.05%
Third decile	16.62%	11.59%
Fourth decile	9.61%	9.50%
Fifth decile	5.01%	9.79%
Sixth decile	2.20%	7.68%
Seventh decile	1.10%	6.96%
Eighth decile	0.80%	7.76%
Ninth decile	0.10%	6.08%
Tenth decile	0.10%	4.93%

	October 2002	
Individual demographics	**Jefes participants**	**Total population**
Income Origin		
Only wage earning work	90.89%	32.25%
Wage earning work and self-employment	4.60%	7.99%
Education		
Literacy	97.40%	98.23%
Primary school not completed	1.70%	1.27%
Primary school completed	49.15%	32.25%
High school not completed	19.42%	23.48%
High school completed	13.01%	12.37%
College not completed	3.90%	3.12%
College completed	4.30%	5.20%
Others	1.20%	1.02%
Superior	3.50%	7.20%
University	3.80%	14.09%
Individual employment		
Total hours worked	21.75	39.59
Total hours worked (main occupation)	20.95	38.31
Would like to work more hours	52.15%	35.81%
Work in the public sector	81.68%	31.21%
Work in the private sector	13.71%	67.96%
Occupation is		
Permanent	4.80%	75.26%
Temporary	34.53%	6.70%
Period unknown	60.46%	15.95%

Looking for an other occupation	52.95%	30.51%
Not looking for another occupation	46.85%	69.35%

Individual demographics	October 2002 Jefes participants	Total population
Reasons for looking for another occupation		
Insufficient income	83.93%	36.00%

NOTES

1. Polanyi here refers to the nineteenth century; however his approach can be extended to more recent periods. Current free-trade policies and state intervention are, in fact, an extension of the movement that took place in the nineteenth century.
2. Source: Diaz Alejandro and ILO, Yearbook of Labor Statistics (Diaz Alejandro, 1988, p.240).
3. Kregel (2003, p.3) blames the neoliberal view, presented as the only solution to economic development, for totally neglecting the issues of full employment and income distribution.
4. From 1976 to 1981, liberal policies were implemented, under the supervision of the International Monetary Fund (IMF). Trade and financial reforms, flexible exchange rates policy and a stabilization program were supposed to correct the distortions created by ISI policies. After 1990, the Washington Consensus policies inspired the 'new development model' for Argentina, called 'the Cavallo plan'. This Washington Consensus policy consisted in advocating liberal policies as the engine of growth. In particular, economic activities were deregulated, competition was reinforced, external trade was liberalized, financial systems were liberalized and privatized and Argentina had to open its economy to international capital. Any controls on commercial and financial operations with the dollar, or other currencies, are eliminated. Argentina also adopted a currency board in order to fight inflation.
5. The graph (p. 7) indicates official unemployment rates. In May 2003, unemployment is estimated at 15.6 percent. This more favorable result is not taken into account because the INDEC has changed the methodology of the household survey. I have used the result (17.8 percent) that is obtained by using the old methodology for the purpose of commensurability. The same correction is made for active and inactive population.
6. The minimum wage was considerably increased at the end of 2003 (350 pesos) and in 2004 (450 pesos).
7. The INDEC is the Argentinean public institute of statistics.
8. It is a household survey conducted in urban areas, which is supposed to represent 70 percent of the population. The EPH household survey has a rolling structure in the sense that one-third of the households are re-interviewed the following semester. Specific questions and also a specific survey for Jefes participants allow us to identify the participants among the population. Data on households and on persons are derived from this survey of 28 361 households (and 83 403 persons) that were surveyed in October 2002 and of 20 728 households (61 477 persons) that were surveyed in May 2003. There are 999 Jefes participants in the October 2002 sample. I have then merged the data available on persons, households and Jefes participants. The sample is

composed of 36 201 individuals who are common to the October 2002 and May 2003 surveys. Individuals younger than 14 and older than 74 years have been eliminated. The final sample is therefore composed of 25 033 individuals.

9. Jefes participants represent 9.62 percent of the active population (estimated at 17 319 million).
10. This number might slightly underestimate the wage bill associated to the Jefes, since indirect jobs have probably also been created to manage the program.
11. Since the devaluation of the peso (1 peso = $3) and the lack of foreign exchange, imports in dollars have dramatically fallen. Imports of capital goods are estimated at $1292.8 million in 2002, which is 6.5 times smaller than in 1998. Imports of consumer goods have been divided by four for during the same period. In pesos, the amount spent to finance imports decreased by 30 percent during the same period. This translates the deterioration in the terms of trade associated with the devaluation.
12. Export growth, stimulated by the devaluation of the peso, has been the first factor to generate recovery. Domestic firms were also encouraged to produce domestic products that would be substituted for imports. Industrial production accumulated 40.4 percent growth between the first quarter 2002 and February 2005 (annual rate of 12 percent). Growth has been created not only by an increased utilization of productive capacities, but also by an increase in investment (see Argentina Economic indicators, Economy Ministry, April 2005).
13. See Argentina Economic indicators, Economy Ministry, April 2005.
14. See note 9 on sampling.
15. Heckman's two-step procedure was used to evaluate the employability effect of the Jefes program. This method had been proposed by Heckman (1979) in order to correct for selectivity bias. If we simply run a regression with employment as the dependent variable and a dummy indicating the participation in the Jefes program as one of the independent variables, we may get biased estimates. Indeed, those who chose (or were chosen) to be part of the program may differ in many characteristics from those who did not. In this first step, the selection process, which is responsible for selection bias problems, is studied using the selection model. In the second step of the Heckman procedure, we are using a logit model to estimate the impact of the Jefes participation variable on an individual's chances to find a job outside the program. We integrate the selection bias control factor lambda as an additional independent variable (see Pastoret, 2004 for a detailed explanation of Heckman's procedure and of the models estimated).
16. The probability that a Jefes participant in October 2002 will be employed in May 2003 is 98.8 percent lower than the odds that someone not in the Jefes program will be employed.
17. The Jefes program probably has limited interaction with the formal labor market because it is far below the minimum wage. Nevertheless, the Jefes wage is likely to set a lower limit to the wage in the informal market.
18. BPSE: basic public sector employment corresponding to individuals willing to work at the basic wage announced by the state (see Wray, 1998, p.126 for more details on this definition).

REFERENCES

Berlinsky, J. (2000), 'International trade and commercial policy (Argentina, from the 1940s to the year 2000)', unpublished paper.

Bryson, A., R. Dorsett and S. Purdon (2002), 'The use of propensity score matching in the evaluation of active labour market policies', Working Paper No. 4, Policy Studies Institute and National Centre for Social Research, London.

Cardoso, F.H. (1979), *Dependency and Development in Latin America*, Los Angeles, CA: University of California Press.

Cavallo, D. (2003), "Productivism" versus "neoliberalism", unpublished paper.

Diaz Alejandro, C. (1988), *Trade, Development and the World Economy: Selected essays of Carlos Diaz Alejandro*, A. Velasco (ed.), Oxford and New York: Basil Blackwell.

Galasso, E. and M. Ravallion (2001), 'Assisting the transition from workfare to work: Argentina's Proempleo experiment', Working Paper, World Bank.

Galasso, E. and M. Ravallion (2004), 'Social protection in a crisis: Argentina's plan Jefes y Jefas', Working Paper, World Bank.

Heckman, J. (1979), 'Sample selection bias as a specification error', *Econometrica*, **47** (1), 153–61.

Heckman, J., H. Ichimura and P. Todd (1998), 'Matching as an econometric evaluation estimator', *Review of Economic Studies*, **65** (2), 261–94.

INDEC, Economy Ministry and the Argentine state (2002), 'Mercado de trabajo: principales indicadores de los aglomerados urbanos', December.

INDEC, Economy Ministry and the Argentine state (2003), 'Mercado de trabajo: principales indicadores de los aglomerados urbanos', December.

Jalan, J. and M. Ravallion (1999), 'Income gains to the poor from workfare: estimates for Argentina's Trabajar program', Working Paper, World Bank.

Kregel, J. (2003), 'The perils of globalization', CFEPS seminar paper No.13.

Lerner, A.P. (1943), 'Functional finance and the federal debt,' *Social Research*, **10**, 38–51.

Ministerio de Trabajo (2004), 'Impacto macroeconomico de programas deempleo directo'.

Pastoret, C. (2004), 'Employability effects of the Jefes program in Argentina', unpublished paper.

Pastoret, C. (2005), 'Will the "Buenos Aires Consensus" dethrone the "Washington Consensus"?', unpublished paper.

Pastoret, C. (2006a), 'Fiscal policy, endogenous money and government intervention: are chartalist and circuitist theories complementary?' in Gnos, C. and L.-P. Rochon, *Post-Keynesian Principles of Economic Policy*, Cheltenham, UK and Northampton, MA, USA: Edward Elgar, 151–63.

Pastoret, C. (2006b), 'Cardoso the "political opponent" vs. Cardoso "the politician": continuity or rupture?' *Revista de Economía Institucional*, **8** (15), 69–95.

Polanyi, K. (1957), *The Great Transformation: The Political and Economic Origins of our Time*, Boston, MA: Beacon Press.

Wray, L.R. (1998), *Understanding Modern Money: The Key to Full-Employment and Price Stability*, Cheltenham, UK and Northampton, MA, USA: Edward Elgar.

Wray, L.R. (2000a), 'The neo-chartalist approach to money', CFEPS Working Paper No. 10.

Wray, L.R. (2000b), 'Modern money', in Smithin, J. (ed.), *What is Money?* London and New York, Routledge, 42-66.

Wray, L.R. (2000c), 'The employer of last resort approach to full employment', *CFEPS Working Paper* No. 9.

Wray, L.R. (2003), 'Currency sovereignty and the possibility of full employment', CFEPS Working Paper No. 9.

Name index

Subject index

Titles of publications are in *italics*.

Abbreviations used in index:
ECB – European Central Bank
NCM – New Consensus macroeconomics

NEW DIRECTIONS IN MODERN ECONOMICS

Post-Keynesian Monetary Economics
New Approaches to Financial Modelling
Edited by Philip Arestis

Keynes's Principle of Effective Demand
Edward J. Amadeo

New Directions in Post-Keynesian Economics
Edited by John Pheby

Theory and Policy in Political Economy
Essays in Pricing, Distribution and Growth
Edited by Philip Arestis and Yiannis Kitromilides

Keynes's Third Alternative?
The Neo-Ricardian Keynesians and the Post Keynesians
Amitava Krishna Dutt and Edward J. Amadeo

Wages and Profits in the Capitalist Economy
The Impact of Monopolistic Power on Macroeconomic Performance in the USA and UK
Andrew Henley

Prices, Profits and Financial Structures
A Post-Keynesian Approach to Competition
Gokhan Capoglu

International Perspectives on Profitability and Accumulation
Edited by Fred Moseley and Edward N. Wolff

Mr Keynes and the Post Keynesians
Principles of Macroeconomics for a Monetary Production Economy
Fernando J. Cardim de Carvalho

The Economic Surplus in Advanced Economies
Edited by John B. Davis

Foundations of Post-Keynesian Economic Analysis
Marc Lavoie

The Post-Keynesian Approach to Economics
An Alternative Analysis of Economic Theory and Policy
Philip Arestis

Income Distribution in a Corporate Economy
Russell Rimmer

The Economics of the Profit Rate
Competition, Crises and Historical Tendencies in Capitalism
Gérard Duménil and Dominique Lévy

Corporatism and Economic Performance
A Comparative Analysis of Market Economies
Andrew Henley and Euclid Tsakalotos

Competition, Technology and Money
Classical and Post-Keynesian Perspectives
Edited by Mark A. Glick

Investment Cycles in Capitalist Economies
A Kaleckian Behavioural Contribution
Jerry Courvisanos

Does Financial Deregulation Work?
A Critique of Free Market Approaches
Bruce Coggins

Pricing Theory in Post Keynesian Economics
A Realist Approach
Paul Downward

The Economics of Intangible Investment
Elizabeth Webster

Globalization and the Erosion of National Financial Systems
Is Declining Autonomy Inevitable?
Marc Schaberg

Explaining Prices in the Global Economy
A Post-Keynesian Model
Henk-Jan Brinkman

Capitalism, Socialism, and Radical Political Economy
Essays in Honor of Howard J. Sherman
Edited by Robert Pollin

Financial Liberalisation and Intervention
A New Analysis of Credit Rationing
Santonu Basu

Why the Bubble Burst
US Stock Market Performance since 1982
Lawrance Lee Evans, Jr.

Sustainable Fiscal Policy and Economic Stability
Theory and Practice
Philippe Burger

The Rise of Unemployment in Europe
A Keynesian Approach
Engelbert Stockhammer

General Equilibrium, Capital, and Macroeconomics
A Key to Recent Controversies in Equilibrium Theory
Fabio Petri

Post-Keynesian Principles of Economic Policy
Claude Gnos and Louis-Philippe Rochon

Innovation, Evolution and Economic Change
New Ideas in the Tradition of Galbraith
Blandine Laperche, James K. Galbraith and Dimitri Uzunidis

The Economics of Keynes
A New Guide to The General Theory
Mark Hayes

Money, Distribution and Economic Policy
Alternatives to Orthodox Macroeconomics
Edited by Eckhard Hein and Achim Truger

Modern State Intervention in the Era of Globalisation
Nikolaos Karagiannis and Zagros Madjd-Sadjadi

Financialization and the US Economy
Özgür Orhangazi

Monetary Policy and Financial Stability
A Post-Keynesian Agenda
Edited by Claude Gnos and Louis-Philippe Rochon